How to Grow Anything: Make Your Trees and Shrubs Thrive

Melinda Myers

THE
GREAT
COURSES®

PUBLISHED BY:

THE GREAT COURSES
Corporate Headquarters
4840 Westfields Boulevard, Suite 500
Chantilly, Virginia 20151-2299
Phone: 1-800-832-2412
Fax: 703-378-3819
www.thegreatcourses.com

Copyright © The Teaching Company, 2014

Printed in the United States of America

This book is in copyright. All rights reserved.

Melinda Myers

Horticulturist and Certified Arborist
Nationally Syndicated Garden Host

Melinda Myers is a gardening expert, television/radio host, author, and columnist with more than 30 years of horticulture experience. She has a bachelor's degree in Horticulture from The Ohio State University and a master's degree in Horticulture from the University of Wisconsin–Madison. She is a certified arborist and serves on the board of directors for the International Society of Arboriculture.

Ms. Myers has authored or coauthored more than 20 gardening books and has written articles for such magazines as *Better Homes and Gardens* and *Fine Gardening*. She hosts the nationally syndicated "Melinda's Garden Moment" segments, which air on television and radio stations throughout the United States, and she appears regularly as a guest expert on various national and local television and radio shows.

Ms. Myers is a columnist and contributing editor for *Birds & Blooms* magazine and writes a twice-monthly "Garden Questions" column for the *Milwaukee Journal Sentinel*. She has a regular column in the nationally distributed *Gardening How-To* magazine and in *Wisconsin Gardening*, and she has been a contributing editor and columnist for *Backyard Living* magazine. Her books include *Small Space Gardening* (Can't Miss series), *Birds & Blooms' Ultimate Gardening Guide*, and *Jackson & Perkins Beautiful Roses Made Easy: Midwestern Edition*.

A dynamic presenter, Ms. Myers travels the country each year, appearing at many of the major flower-and-garden shows and home-and-garden events. She enjoys sharing her knowledge and love of gardening with fellow gardeners at these speaking engagements.

Ms. Myers hosted *The Plant Doctor* radio program for more than 20 years, as well as seven seasons of *Great Lakes Gardener* on PBS. She also hosted *YardWorks!*, a nationally syndicated yard care and garden show, for which she interviewed many celebrities right in their own gardens.

Ms. Myers's outreach efforts across various media are rooted in decades of hands-on instruction. Before launching her own business in 2006, she was a tenured Horticulture Instructor for 12 years at Milwaukee Area Technical College. Before that, she served for 10 years as an Associate Professor with tenure at the Milwaukee County University of Wisconsin Cooperative Extension. While there, she began the Master Gardener Program in Milwaukee County and worked with backyard, community, and master gardeners.

For her work, community service, and media presence, Ms. Myers has received recognition and numerous awards, including two Garden Media Awards (a Garden Globe Award for radio talent and a Quill and Trowel Award for her television work), both from the Garden Writers Association. She also has received the Garden Communicator of the Year Award from the American Nursery & Landscape Association, the Gold Leaf Award (for Arbor Day activities) from the International Society of Arboriculture, and the Perennial Plant Association Garden Media Promoter Award. In 2012, Ms. Myers was inducted into the Wisconsin Green Industry Federation's Hall of Fame. In 2013, she received the American Horticultural Society's B. Y. Morrison Communication Award for effective and inspirational communication. Her website is www.melindamyers.com.

Ms. Myers is the host of two other Great Courses, *How to Grow Anything: Your Best Garden and Landscape in 6 Lessons* and *How to Grow Anything: Container Gardening Tips and Techniques.* ■

Table of Contents

INTRODUCTION

Professor Biography...i
Course Scope..1

LESSON GUIDES

LESSON 1
A Framework for Your Landscape 3

LESSON 2
Form and Function in the Landscape...22

LESSON 3
Trees and Shrubs for Challenging Conditions.....................................41

LESSON 4
Shopping for the Best Trees and Shrubs..62

LESSON 5
Planting Your Trees and Shrubs..81

LESSON 6
Spring and Summer Care of Trees and Shrubs 99

LESSON 7
Fall and Winter Care of Trees and Shrubs 120

LESSON 8
Pruning Old and Young Trees...138

LESSON 9
Pruning Shrubs..157

LESSON 10
When Trees and Shrubs Fail to Thrive..175

Table of Contents

LESSON 11
Restoring a Landscape to Health 195

LESSON 12
Expanding Your Landscape's Framework 212

SUPPLEMENTAL MATERIAL

Plant List..232
Bibliography..243

How to Grow Anything:
Make Your Trees and Shrubs Thrive

Scope:

Beautiful landscapes distinguish the home and garden, and trees and shrubs provide the essential framework for landscapes. Think of the outdoors as a living space of its own. Landscapes define boundaries, create four-season accents, and enhance privacy while magnifying the value of your home. This course will help you increase the beauty of your surroundings, achieving immediate results with long-term benefits. Over the course of 12 lessons, the course delivers insights into the most effective ways to plant, fertilize, mulch, and prune, illustrated by hands-on demonstrations. It offers diagnostics to optimize plant health, including soil testing, and guidelines for watering and light.

Trees and shrubs are dynamic ornaments. They are also sturdy guideposts through changing seasons. Although it takes up to 15 years and sometimes longer to establish a masterpiece landscape, getting started takes only a day. In designing your framework, keeping plant health and maintenance in mind is important, along with artistry. Shade trees provide the designer's canopy; smaller trees and shrubs are the walls, dividers, and screens.

With this in mind, it is possible to create microclimates that are both practical and aesthetic. Shade plantings can lower temperatures by 15 percent—reducing energy use—while just one tree removes up to 200 pounds of carbon dioxide annually from the atmosphere. Trees also help to absorb storm water runoff, reducing demand on water-treatment facilities. Once we fashion the framework of our landscape, we can sculpt it with smaller shrubs, annuals, perennials, and other plants. For instance, espaliering, a pruning method to make trees and shrubs grow flat against a wall or fence, is one method to customize space. Aesthetic design—adding shape and color to our surroundings—also provides habitat for birds, butterflies, and other wildlife.

You will learn how to stake a young tree, prune it, untangle its roots, and transplant it. Specialized pruning creates small-scale accents and focal points that can be used to produce varieties of shades, from dappled to medium and dense. By comparison, severe pruning can trigger latent buds beneath the bark, producing weak limbs.

Plants sometimes fool us. Little plants become big faster than expected, adding to the cost and maintenance of a landscape and sometimes culminating in the need for replacements. Without proper thought to scale, ornamental plants and "dwarfs" may quickly overwhelm their surroundings. Yearly growth assessments are a great diagnostic tool because they reflect growing conditions and the response of plants. Right-sizing the plants and properly spacing them are essential considerations. Other challenges include insects and disease. Knowing your plants and their environment will help reduce damage. We'll cover blight, cankers, chlorosis, leaf scorch, leaf spots, necrosis, and "witch's brooming." You will learn to disinfect your tools between pruning cuts to avoid spreading disease into healthy tissue. In a lesson about arboreal self-defense, you will discover how to turn burlap and twine into a trap to control flying pests.

This course helps realize positive change at home and in the environment. Its lessons will heighten your gardening success, reduce maintenance, and contribute to healthier, longer-living trees and shrubs. Seeing your vision fulfilled through a masterful landscape also contributes to the well-being of mind, body, and spirit. ■

A Framework for Your Landscape
Lesson 1

They line our streets, shade our homes, and clean our air. Trees and shrubs are an integral part of our landscape, community, and natural spaces. But these stately members of our environment often go unnoticed; we don't always appreciate them on a day-to-day basis. Then one day, we think back to a time when we were young, raking and jumping in piles of leaves, harvesting fresh fruit, or climbing a favorite backyard tree. Suddenly, we realize the unique beauty of the trees and shrubs that clean our air, absorb storm water, and bring beauty to our communities, neighborhoods, and backyards.

Create the Framework

- A beautiful landscape is good for your mind, body, and spirit, not to mention the value of your home. Trees and shrubs create the framework for building that landscape and help you create outdoor living space, whether it's on acreage or on a deck, balcony, or patio.

- Trees provide the shade, protect the space, and make the ceiling for that outdoor living space, even if it's just one bench and one tree. Smaller-scale trees and shrubs can also be used as the walls or dividers to create seating areas, screen noise, and provide privacy.

- Perennial gardens were a craze at one time, and they are both beautiful and low maintenance. But if you live in a northern climate, the winters can be long, and you can grow tired of looking at all those dead plants in the landscape. Dwarf conifers—cone-bearing evergreens—improve the vista by adding a touch of green all year. Deciduous shrubs can provide colorful foliage in the summer, flowers in the spring, and some interesting fruit over winter.

- Dwarf evergreens, such as blue spruce and golden junipers, provide not only structure but also color in the garden. Cedars offer wonderful texture, and their gray-green berries create a lovely contrast with the dark green branches.

- Many breeders are now developing dwarf evergreens and shrubs, particularly for gardeners whose space is limited. When you are looking for dwarf plants for your landscape, always check the tag. Dwarf plants are not always as small as you might expect. The tag will give you the ultimate size of the plant, give or take a few inches, and it's a much more reliable guide than simply the name "dwarf."

Anticipate Changes over Time

- Look for interesting plants that will fit the available space, but make sure your trees and shrubs will fit when they reach mature size. When shrubs outgrow your space, they become problematic; you may have to prune them extensively, in which case, they may lose their natural beauty, or replace them.

- Putting trees and shrubs in a landscape can be challenging because they change over time. That young pine tree that was beautifully pyramidal becomes more open, broad, and picturesque as it ages. It's still beautiful, but it now has a different shape in the overall landscape design.

- We often think of flowers as being the beautiful part of the landscape, and trees and shrubs offer flowers, too: dogwood, magnolia, flowering fruit trees, and many more. An important consideration with flowering trees is consistency. Magnolias, for example, are spring bloomers, and they can often be damaged by a late frost. But the butterfly magnolia, with its unique yellow flower, blooms a little later and is seldom nipped by frost; therefore, it's a more reliable bloomer in northern gardens.

- Colorful foliage is another consideration. It is a beautiful addition to the landscape. A high-bush cranberry viburnum colors beautifully in the fall, and its fruit will persist over winter. Korean mountain ash is heat and humidity tolerant and produces a beautiful pink fruit. Its leaves also turn from green to amber or apricot.

- When you're selecting a plant for fruit, be aware of its potential to create problems. Anyone who has grown a ginkgo and found out that it was a female knows what this means: The fruit smells awful. Many new varieties of crabapples have been bred for small, persistent fruit because people were tired of fighting the yellow jackets that swarm around the fallen fruit in fall and of cleaning up the fruit.

Incorporate Color and Form
- Bark is often overlooked, yet beautiful bark is visible year round. Sometimes hidden by the foliage, sometimes overpowered by flowers, bark is a consistent feature.
  - Scotch pine offers beautiful orange bark. As it ages, it becomes more intense, and the green needles against it really stand out in the landscape.

  - Red twig dogwood is a favorite of many gardeners because its bright red twigs stand out against the winter sky. It brightens a landscape that's otherwise dull.

  - Paperbark maple sports orange exfoliating bark. It's a nice specimen plant; its bark adds subtle color in the growing season and really becomes the star of the show in winter.

- Because form can be powerful in landscape design, be sure to think it through.
  - Use pyramidal plants carefully. For example, a pyramidal plant, such as a cedar or spruce, on the corner of your house emphasizes the height of the house, instead of anchoring it to the ground. Group pyramidal spruce trees with large shade trees having horizontal branches to soften the impact of the spruce.

- ○ Round bushes on the ground are common shapes in the landscape. They are easy to repeat, easy to use for unity, and soothing to the eye.

- ○ You may also want to consider some vase-shaped trees, such as the elm trees that used to line many urban streets. They reach to the sky, providing a canopy—kind of a security blanket for those of us below—as well as shade.

- ○ Weeping trees anchor structures, tie plants to water or other features, and create a nice focal point.

Consider Added Value
- • Flowers, fruit, foliage, and color are critical elements of your landscape, but what about the birds and butterflies that trees and shrubs can attract? That motion and color add interest to the landscape.

- • Have you ever seen cedar waxwings clean out the berries from a cedar tree? It's an amazing experience to watch birds feeding on your landscape plants. Further, about 86 percent of birds eat insects, which means they help control the pests that attack garden plants.

- • Fragrance is another consideration. Daphne is a wonderful shrub, with **Lilacs have a lovely fragrance and may bring hummingbirds to your yard.** fragrant flowers in the spring. Carolmackie offers nice variegated foliage; it's evergreen during mild winters, even in colder climates, and it has a lovely fragrance.

- Look at texture when selecting trees and shrubs. That's one feature that definitely changes, especially with deciduous plants.
  - Fine-textured plants have narrow or smaller leaves, tiny flowers, smooth bark, and fine branches. Coarse-textured plants have big, round leaves; much bolder texture; and coarser bark.

  - Arborvitae, with its hint of evergreen, offers a nice backdrop year round, while tiger-eye sumac has lacy leaves that are yellow-green when they emerge and later turn bright green before dropping off.

- Experiment with variations on some favorite plants. For example, if you can't grow crape myrtle, ninebark is a good alternative, especially for hot, dry areas. It comes in several varieties with colorful foliage. Summer Wine and Diablo have purple leaves and pink-white flowers, while Coppertino crosses the yellow and purple leaf varieties to create copper foliage. When the leaves drop, ninebark's shreddy bark looks great against the sky.

- Select trees and shrubs for what brings you pleasure.
  - For example, juneberry produces white flowers in the spring and fruit in June. The fruit starts out pink and turns blue, just like a blueberry. The berries make great pies, and the birds love them. Watching the birds jump in, grab a berry, go off, and munch on it as another comes in is great entertainment.

  - Perhaps, with the edible craze, you may want to get something a little more edible than juneberries. You can incorporate apples, pears, citrus, and avocado to have something that is both edible and beautiful.

Design Thoughtfully
- Mixed planting beds are great for trees and shrubs and require less maintenance, because you have one large bed to mow around, rather than 20 individual plants. This method of planting is also better for the health of the plants: Because the roots are mulched, they stay cool and moist, and there's less competition from the grass.

- Elevating your trees and shrubs in a berm is a good way to deal with poorly drained soils; this approach also enhances screening of bad views and noise and gives you faster results.

- Perhaps you want to create a mini-forest. In small spaces, you may use 3 plants in a pot; larger landscapes may be able to handle 10 or 15 plants. If you have more space, consider using some of the larger blue spruce to create the feel of a forest in your backyard.

- Design your framework with health and longevity in mind, picking the right size plants. Make sure the plants you choose are not only the right height but also have the right spread. Space your plants properly so that as they grow, controlling them and keeping them all looking their best will be less work for you and better for the plants.

- Don't surround trees with grass right up to the trunk. Grass is a significant competitor for water and nutrients, especially for young trees, and it slows growth. Add a mulch bed and eliminate the grass to promote growth and reduce hand trimming.

- Unless you plan to thin your trees and shrubs regularly, plant them right from the start.
  - Use staggered rows. Staggering the rows while properly spacing the plants gives the appearance of a solid screen. As the trees in the row grow, they'll still fit in that location, giving you short-term benefits with long-term results.

  - Put the right size plants in the location, space them correctly, and fill in the voids with annuals and perennials.

Questions to Consider

1. Take a look around. What's working in your existing landscape—and what isn't?

2. List the plants you want to keep and perhaps need a little help with. Decide if they're healthy or if you can prune them back into shape and give them the care they need.

3. Form is an important landscape consideration. Do you have trees and shrubs that emphasize the height of your house rather than anchor it to the ground? Does the canopy outline the surroundings in an eye-pleasing manner? What about tree color and texture?

A Framework for Your Landscape
Lesson 1—Transcript

They line our streets, shade our homes, and clean our air. Trees and shrubs are an integral part of our landscape, community, and natural spaces. But these majestic members of our environment are often unnoticed, that is until one day, you experience the power of the trees. Now, maybe that happened for you when you were young, raking and jumping in the leaves, harvesting fresh fruit, or climbing your favorite backyard tree. Or maybe you came upon a grand old tree hundreds of years old with deeply furrowed bark that seemed to lead to the sky.

Well, for many of my students, this power of the trees was discovered about week six of the trees and shrub identification class I taught. This was just about the time they started recognizing the trees and shrubs by their name. And trust me, their families told me they were tired of hearing cries from the car, "That's an Elm *Ulmus*, a Maple *Acer*," and the like. Suddenly, their neighborhood was alive, and they realized that the unique beauty of the trees and shrubs were providing wonderful majesty, air-cleaning qualities, cleansing the air, taking care of storm water, and providing beauty for their community, neighborhood, and even their backyard.

Now, what connection do you feel with these grand plants of our landscape? And if you don't have one yet, I hope this course will help you see trees and shrubs through a new and appreciative set of eyes. Here's what I'm going to do to make this happen. I'll take you to a variety of landscapes to share ways to incorporate trees and shrubs. I will also demonstrate some gardening techniques to keep your plants healthy or expand your collection. And we'll visit my garden, where we'll plant a few trees and shrubs. And by the end, I hope you'll feel the power of the trees, just like my students. And these beauties, how they've been around longer than all of us, providing shade, food, lumber, and cleaner air and water.

So let's get started finding why a beautiful landscape is good for your mind, body, and spirit, not to mention the value of your home. Trees and shrubs create the framework that we can build our landscape around. So whether you're gardening on a balcony or a multi-acre lot, there's always room for a tree, shrub, or more. Trees and shrubs are the constant in the landscape. They're always present, though always changing with the seasons and over time. They provide the structure your landscape is built around, that framework. In this class, we take the journey of creating a beautiful, long-lasting framework for your landscape, the one that's in your dreams and you'd like to see made a reality. And we'll look at the different design roles of these plants in our landscape.

So let's get started looking at a few possibilities. Trees and shrubs help you create that outdoor living space, so whether you're creating small rooms on a large acreage, or, maybe creating an outdoor living space on a deck, balcony, or patio, trees and shrubs can help. As you can see here, the trees are providing the shade; they're protecting that space, making the ceiling for that outdoor living space. And, even if it's just one bench and one tree, it can accomplish the same thing; instead of a shade umbrella, how about a small shade tree?

Now, we figured out how to decorate and create our indoor living space; think about trees and shrubs as that structure that we use outdoors. We'll use some of our smaller-scale trees and shrubs to be the walls or dividers in our outdoor space, just like they've done here. They can create small sitting areas outside. They can help screen noise and views from your neighbors, traffic, and the like. So look for ways that you can use them to create that small getaway; it's a great place to go. And then we'll add maybe a few vines and flowers and maybe dwarf plants to create a beautiful outdoor space that changes throughout the seasons, much like this home gardener did.

Now, if you were gardening in the '80s, you may have experienced the perennial craze, like many of us. I was one of those. We were ripping out our front lawns and replacing the grass with perennials. Now, I only had a small city lot at the time, and I packed it full of a beautiful, blooming garden. And I live in a northern climate, so winters can be long in my neck of the woods, and I enjoy looking at the seed pods, the seed heads of the grasses blowing in the wind, the birds that eat the seeds from my perennials. But even I got tired of looking at that dead stuff in the landscape and found that I needed some dwarf conifers, cone-bearing evergreens, or deciduous shrubs, those that drop their leaves, to really add some structure and framework to the landscape.

And that's what my friend Dorothy did here. Isn't this a beautiful mixed garden? This garden screens the area between her yard and her neighbor's. And what a lucky neighbor to have such a beautiful barrier or screen to look at. As you can see, she incorporated dwarf evergreens; they're kind of peeking through the garden. She's got some colorful shrubs that provide colorful foliage in the summer, flowers in the spring, and some interesting fruit over winter. Lots of perennials, and even some bulbs, as you see those *Alliums* peeking through during the summer. So mixing it up a bit but using trees and shrubs to provide that constant is a great way to add beauty while adding structure to the landscape.

Now, no matter the size of your landscape, you can find a plant, tree and shrub-wise, to fit. Now hopefully, it's not this small, like this railroad garden. But there are lots of dwarf evergreens and shrubs on the market. More and more breeders are developing these, knowing that people are looking for ways to incorporate these beauties into their landscape, even when their space is limited. But keep in mind that dwarf plants aren't always as dwarf as we expect, so check the tags. In fact, dwarf plans just mean they're smaller than the straight species. So let's think about an American Arborvitae. They typically grow 60 to 80 feet tall, depending on the environment, so a dwarf variety just needs to be shorter, and that provided a surprise for many gardeners, who put techny, a dwarf variety of arborvitae, in their yard. Thinking dwarf, it would be eight feet, it really grew 12 to 15 feet tall, so many people were surprised. So always check the tag. It will give you the ultimate size of that plant, give or take a few inches or feet, depending on the growing conditions, but it's a much better place to start, than the word dwarf.

And as you can see here, dwarf evergreens, those are the beauties in here, not only provide structure, but color in the garden. We've got a blue spruce, a dwarf blue spruce. We've got some golden junipers. Lots of colors, lots of forms, lots of texture. Add in a few perennials, and we've got a beautiful garden. And look at the texture of this Cedar; nothing can beat that. And you can see some of the other forms that are available out there. So take a look for interesting plants that will fit the available space.

And that's important, the available space. One of the things we'll talk about throughout this course is making sure your trees and shrubs will fit when they reach mature size. You know, when you go to the nursery, that little tree or shrub in the pot looks very tiny, but quickly will grow to full size. And I think that was the surprise this homeowner had; those shrubs outgrew the space provided. And now, they're blocking the front door. Not quite the welcome sight they may have hoped for for their visitors. So their choice? Prune them down into submission, where they may lose their natural beauty, or replace them. Lost time, lost money, because now they're starting over.

Now this is a much larger-scale landscape, a bigger building and bigger shrubs. And they've pruned them partly for their geometric size and their more formal look, but they're also pruning them to try to keep them from blocking the window. But despite all the pruning, you can see the windows are tucked behind many of these shrubs, blocking some of the beauty of the brickwork on this, the land and stone, trim, and the leaded glass windows. So again, make sure your plants provide the beauty you want, but in the right size. And as I keep saying, they are beautiful, but, it can be challenging to put trees and shrubs in the landscape. They change over the season, and over time. So that young pine tree you planted that was nice and pyramidal, as it ages, it becomes more open, broad, and picturesque with age, beautiful, but a little different in the overall landscape design.

This baroque is one of my favorites, at a local botanic garden. It's been around for several hundred years, and the majesty of this tree is amazing. And we go from bare trunk to wonderful leaves, some fall color, and look at that against the winter sky. Now, after several hundred years, that overall form is not changing much, but it does provide a lot of different looks throughout the season.

Now, we often think of flowers as being the beautiful part of our landscape, and trees and shrubs can provide those, just like this Dogwood. So we want to look for plants that have multiple seasons of interest, flowers like this, or one of my favorite Magnolias, the Butterfly Magnolia.

Now one of the things to consider about flowers is, will they be consistent in your area? I love Magnolias, but as a spring bloomer, they're often damaged by late spring frost in my area. So the Butterfly Magnolia not only provides that unique yellow flower, but it blooms a little later and is seldom nipped by frost, so it's a reliable bloomer in my part of the country. So you might want to consider that as well—timing.

Colorful foliage is another thing to consider. Some trees and shrubs have colorful foliage that gives them interest all year round, like many of the beeches that we saw at Northwind Perennial Farm here. And isn't this a beauty? It's a beautiful addition to the landscape and provides color throughout the season.

Fruit is another thing, or colorful foliage as well, not only in the summer, but also in the fall. So, many plants have beautiful flowers, but their leaves change, so they may emerge green with a tinge of red, turn green, or maybe chartreuse. Color up in the fall, much like this high bush cranberry viburnam; it's starting to color up for the fall, and you can see the fruit, which will persist over winter. Now if you've ever eaten a cranberry bush viburnam fruit, some people love them. Boy, I think I'd need a lot of sugar to make them tasty, but they do persist on the plant, providing winner interest, ferment a little, and the birds come through and enjoy that little treat come spring.

This is a Korean Mountain ash, and if you experience hot dry summers and have tried a European Mountain ash, this is a little more heat and humidity tolerant, and a little different look. Notice that beautiful pink fruit, and when the leaves turn from green to almost an amber or apricot, sounds crazy, but it is a beautiful combination. And the birds love the fruit, so you get to enjoy them, and it'll bring the birds in, so you can enjoy them.

But when you're selecting a plant for fruit, is it going to create a mess? Anybody that's grown a *ginkgo* and found out it was a female may have experienced this scene. Now, you may have heard of *ginkgos*, good for the memory, a prize dish in many Asian foods, but the fruit smells, kind of like dog droppings or baby vomit, so not a good thing. So if it's in your front yard, you want to make sure you get a male *gingko* and skip the fruit, unless of course, you know someone who will come out and harvest it for you. So make sure that fruit is not a mess that you need to clean up.

Many new varieties of Crabapples have been bred for small, persistent fruit, because people were tired of fighting the yellow jackets in fall that were swarming around the fallen fruit or cleaning up the mess. So that small, persistent fruit hangs on the tree until the birds clean it up, so it's a win-win for both of you.

And Crape myrtle, look at that beautiful bark. Bark is one of the things we often overlook, and that beautiful bark is there year round. Sometimes hidden by the foliage, sometimes overpowered by flowers, but bark is a nice consistent feature.

This is a *Pinus sylvestris*, or Scotch pine. Look at that beautiful orange bark. As that tree gets older, it's gorgeous, more intense. And the green needles against it really stand out in the landscape. And red twig dogwood, a favorite of many gardeners, because those bright red twigs really stand out against the winter sky. And look at how it brightens that landscape that's otherwise a lot of brown and white. And my baroque, again, that I love so much. It's got that deeply furrowed bark, just really is amazing. And here we have a Paperbark maple. And a closer look, you would see that orange exfoliating bark. It's a nice specimen plant in this garden, but that bark adds nice, subtle color in the growing season, and then really becomes the star of the show come winter.

Now, form is something else we want to consider when we're looking at our trees and shrubs. Form in the landscape design can be very powerful. You know, if we take a look at those large shade trees, those that tend to have more spreading or horizontal branches, really provide a canopy to our landscape. They're also very soothing, because they mimic the way our eye moves across the landscape. The spruce in the middle are very pyramidal, and point to the sky. Now, we've grouped them together here, which really softens that impact. One pyramidal plant on the corner of your house emphasizes the height of the house, instead of anchoring it to the ground. So use pyramidal plants carefully. They really grab your attention and direct your eye upward. The round bushes on the ground are often the common shape in the landscape and used often by gardeners. Easy to repeat, easy to use for unity, and very soothing on the eye. So those are some shapes to consider.

You may want to consider some vase-shaped trees, like the elm trees that used to line many urban cities. Wonderful, reaching to the sky, providing a canopy, kind of a security blanket for those of us below, and definitely shade. Beautiful scenes, maybe, from the past, so consider some vase-shaped trees, as well. Weeping trees anchor structures to the ground, tie the plants maybe to a water feature below or your house to the ground, create a nice focal point, pointing you downward.

Now, the other thing you want to know to do is consider the added value. We've talked about flowers, fruit, foliage, color. But what about the birds and butterflies trees and shrubs can bring to your landscape, flowers that the hummingbirds like to nectar upon, or the butterflies like to visit? That motion and color really adds interest to the landscape. Or, maybe it's a songbird or two you want to bring in. This European Mountain ash was one I'd always used with my students in the fall, when we'd go out and they'd have to identify trees and shrubs with no leaves. And it was always loaded with fruit, and the cedar waxwings would move through, clean out the fruit, usually in the middle of the exam. I enjoyed the visit. Most of my students were a little too obsessed with passing the test, but it's an amazing experience to watch birds feeding on your landscape plants. And the good news, about 86 percent or so of birds eat insects, so they help control the bad guys that attack our garden plants.

Fragrance is another one you'll want to consider. Daphne is a wonderful shrub, with fragrant flowers in the spring. And this is Carol Mackie; notice that really nice variegated foliage. So it's evergreen during mild winters, even in colder climates, and, if it's a cold winter, the leaves brown out and are replaced by new leaves. But the fragrance is what always gets me. I like to put these by a front entrance, a patio, a deck, so that I can enjoy the fragrance when they are in bloom. A little aromatherapy. And I always say gardeners were into aromatherapy way before it was the hip and trendy thing.

You may always think of lilacs when you think of fragrants. The hummingbirds love them. In fact, I usually put my hummingbird feeder by my lilac to make sure they find that feeder. Beautiful bloom, and good news for lilac lovers, there's a repeat bloomer out there now. The Bloomerang® lilac blooms in spring, rests, and then blooms late season until frost. And those in warmer climates? There are a few that will bloom even in warmer climates, and those of you with hot winters or warm winters that don't get a chill, you've got some other beauties with wonderful fragrance to consider.

Texture is something else we want to consider. And when we think of texture, fine-textured plants have narrow leaves, tiny flowers, smaller leaves, things like that, bark that's smooth, fine branches. Coarse-textured plants have big, round leaves, much bolder texture, coarser bark. Grab our attention. So we want to look at texture when we're selecting our trees and shrubs. And that's one feature that definitely changes, especially with deciduous plants, leaves on, leaves off, very different looking plant. And this garden is a great example. So in the back we have Arborvitae; you can see a hint of that evergreen, a nice backdrop that's there year round. We've got some round flowered *aliums*, or flowering onions. The light, airy plant is a perennial called *Amsonia*, or blue star. And in front, we have Tiger Eyea sumac. Look at the lacy leaves on that plant. They emerge kind of a yellow-green, turn to a bright green, and drop off, leaving nothing but sticks in the landscape. So we go from a nice, delicate plant to just sticks over winter. So keep texture in mind, and keep in mind that it can change drastically.

Another plant that's gained a lot of popularity is Ninebark. And Ninebark is great for hot, dry areas. But why it's gained popularity is the breeders have introduced varieties with colorful foliage. And that's one thing you may want to look for, a favorite plant, but different varieties for different attributes. So we've got some with purple leaves like Summer Wine and Diablo, and look at those pinkish white flowers. Coppertino, which is a cross between the yellow- and purple-leaf varieties, for that more coppery-color foliage. But in any case, in winter, when the leaves drop, you have that shreddy bark that looks great against the winter sky. Now, if you're in an area with Crape myrtles, you might go, oh, that's not the prettiest bark, but if you can't grow Crape myrtle, this is a good alternative.

The other thing you want to consider as you're selecting your trees and shrubs is what brings you pleasure. This is a Serviceberry, also known as a Juneberry, one of my favorite trees, white flowers in the spring, fruit in June; they start out pink and turn blue, look just like a blueberry. In fact, they taste like a nutty blueberry to me. Great fall color, and when the leaves drop, it exposes smooth, gray bark. I love to grab a handful as I weed my garden.

They make great pies, and the birds love them. So they're great for eating and cooking, if you can beat the birds. In fact, I had one in my backyard, and I would watch the robins line up on my fence; one would jump in, grab a berry, go off, munch on it. Another would come in. Great entertainment, as well as tasty fruit.

Now, you know with the edible craze, you may be looking at getting something a little more edible than those tiny Juneberries, maybe apples, and pears, and citrus, and avocado. And incorporating those into your landscape as part of the framework is a great way to have something edible and beautiful. And we'll talk more about that in our next class.

Now, how can we use these plants in the landscape in other ways? Mixed planting beds I showed you, and they're great for trees and shrubs, less maintenance for you, because if you've got your trees and shrubs in one planting bed, maybe mulched in with woodchip mulch or ground cover, or mixed in with perennials, like you see here, it means you have one big bed to mow around, versus 20 individual plants. And, it's better for the health of the plants. The roots are mulched; they're cool and moist; less competition from the grass; better for the trees and shrubs.

You may want to consider elevating your trees and shrubs in a berm. And elevating the planting is a great way to deal with poorly drained soils. You lift those plants above that poorly drained soil. It's also better for screening bad views and noise. You'll increase that noise barrier by lifting the plant, and you'll get faster results, because you're elevating those small plants right from the beginning.

Or maybe you want to create a mini forest. A friend of mine loves to put these Dwarf Alberta spruce together in groupings. For those with small spaces, it may be three in a pot. For those with larger landscapes, it might be 10 or 15. Can't you just picture a small gnome with an ax coming out of that forest of dwarf Alberta spruce? So it may be something to consider. Or if you have more space, using some of the larger blue spruce, like you see here, to create the feel of a forest in your backyard.

We also want to make sure that we design with health and longevity for our framework. Picking the right size plant, as I mentioned before. The reason being is, when that plant outgrows that landscape, you either have to mutilate it and spend time and energy reducing it in size, or replacing it. Make sure that it's not only the right size up, but also spreading. You want to space your plants properly, because as those plants grow, it will be very difficult to control all of them and keep them all looking their best. That'll be less work for you, less pruning, and better for the plants. And you don't want to have your tree surrounded by grass right up to the trunk. Grass is a huge competitor, especially for young trees. They steal the water and nutrients from the tree and slow down growth.

In fact, we had a Catalpa tree on campus, and I was taking my students around, and it was only about six feet tall. And my students said, that's a tree? So we expanded the mulch bed by five feet, got rid of the grass, and I'll tell you how to do that later, and we covered it with mulch. It was a hot, dry summer, and nobody was on campus to water. But that tree put on an additional foot of growth, just by expanding the mulch bed. So you might want to think about doing that. Less hand trimming for you, better for your plant.

Well, now that you have a handle on the how and where to create your framework. You're probably thinking, but I don't want to wait for that little tree to grow into that big plant. Or maybe you're thinking, I'm not going to live in this house long enough, or I won't live long enough to see that tree reach full size. Well keep these things in mind; you could increase the value of your house. You'll sell your house faster; Realtors say that people who had a good landscape, their houses go faster, even in tough economic times. And, you want to plant for the future. Somebody planted that big old Bur oak, even if it was a squirrel. People left it for hundreds of years, so I can enjoy the shade beneath that tree. I think we need to plant trees for our great grandchildren. And if we don't have grandchildren, for our friends' grandchildren, the next generation. You know, planting a tree for the future is a very powerful statement on your philosophy in life.

So why not cram these plants in together to speed up the results? Well, as I keep saying, it's more work for you when we don't give plants room to grow. You'll be trying to keep that big tree small, or you'll have to remove those excess plants, and that's more money spent replacing trees, as they outgrow their location. And probably, even more importantly, you've lost time. You plant a tree, five years later, have to remove it, or 10 years later. You're starting from scratch; you're going to start over and need 10 more years to get that tree up to size. So select the right plant for the location, and that means fitting into the available space—no conflict with overhead utilities, no conflict with underground utilities, and space it right.

I had a landscape architect one time tell me that he told people to put their plants together twice as close as normal, because his philosophy is, as they grow, you remove every other shrub, and then, you have quick results and long-term benefit. And I said, I don't think you've talked to gardeners before, because they can't thin their beans. Removing every other shrub they've paid $30, $40, $50 for is going to be hard, and by the time they finally realize they have to do it, the trees they're leaving will be distorted, and they'll end up removing those. So, unless you're going to be good at thinning your trees and shrubs, plant it right to start with.

But I do have some tricks you can use. Use staggered rows. By staggering your rows, but properly spacing the plants, it appears to be a good, solid screen, and as those trees grow, they'll still fit in that location. You'll get short term benefits with long term results. And one of my favorites is, put the right size plant in the location, space them correctly, and then fill in those voids with annuals and perennials. And that's what we did here. I do talks at the state fair in my area, and I was charged with getting this garden looking its best. There had been some construction damage, and we had to start over. Of course, we're planting in June for an August fair. And the grounds manager said, it has to look good by fair time. Now, I think she wanted me to overplant, but I said, we'll make this a learning opportunity.

So if you look closely, you may be able to see a Black lace elderberry, some rainbow Knock Out® roses, some broccoli plants, some cabbage plants, some coralbells, and a variety of annuals and perennials. So, this is what it looked like come fair time. Everything filled in annual-, perennial-wise, and vegetables, and that gave us our quick impact. That was in three months. And then three years later, this is what we're looking at. The shrubs reached full size, I just had less annuals to plant every year, and I moved a couple of perennials, but moving an ornamental grass or Coralbells is a lot easier than moving a tree or shrub. So you can have good short-term impact with long-term value. So you can see quick results from these plants, and we can get that, even when we select carefully and provide the proper space.

Now throughout this course, we'll discuss strategies for extending the life of your trees and shrubs. We'll spend some time outside digging, some time inside chatting, and visiting beautiful landscapes. I want to thank Meadows Farms for helping us landscape our studio to help set the mood and inspire you as we go through this class. So what I'd like you to do now, is to take a look around your existing landscape. Make a few notes on what's working, and what's not. Maybe list those plants you want to keep that maybe need a little helping hand from you, and we'll give you some guidance on that.

Maybe some plants you've been trying to consider whether to remove them or not. We'll help you decide if they're healthy enough, or if you can prune them back into shape, or give them the proper care they need. And as you're making that list, we'll revisit your list and your landscape throughout this course. And together, we'll find ways to use or amend your landscape, to create the look and feel you desire. And once you take a closer look and are thinking about this living framework of trees and shrubs, we'll dig a bit deeper about their functional value and how to take care of these beauties.

Form and Function in the Landscape
Lesson 2

Creating the landscape of your dreams in less-than-ideal conditions can be challenging—and most of us have less-than-ideal conditions. Trees and shrubs can help, whether for screening a bad view, adding year-round appeal, or creating an outdoor living space. Select plants that are suited to the climate where you live and to the growing conditions in your garden. Choosing the right plant for the prevailing conditions will pay dividends in beauty, energy conservation, storm water management, and pollution reduction.

Consider Growing Conditions

- Match the plants you choose to the extremes of heat and cold where you live. Plants that are cold hardy will tolerate average minimum winter temperatures. Most tags will tell you, and cold hardiness maps are available online. At the other extreme is heat hardiness— whether a plant can tolerate an average number of days with temperatures above 86 degrees. Once temperatures climb above that level, plants can suffer physiological disorder or damage. They may decline, function less well, and burn up more energy than they produce. They're also more susceptible to insects and disease problems.

- Soil drainage, rainfall, and light are the essential growing conditions for any plant.
  - Heavy clay with poor drainage can drown a sensitive plant. Sandy, rocky soil lets moisture through.

  - A Seattle garden requires different plants from one in Phoenix; the plants you choose must be suited to the amount of rainfall you get.

○ You also need to consider whether plants need full sun, partial sun, or shade. Think about any other growing conditions unique to your backyard, your neighborhood, and your community.

Plant to Conserve Energy

- To conserve energy, place trees to shade the east and west windows of your home to screen solar heat and reduce cooling costs. Use large, mature trees to shade the roof and keep the attic cool: This can reduce the inside temperature by as much as 40 degrees. Three properly placed trees can save up to 30 percent of energy use; thus, it's worth the effort to select, plant, and properly care for trees.

- Those who live in the north need sunlight to help warm the house in winter. Keep large shade trees away from the south, southeast, and southwest of the house to minimize winter shading. Deciduous plants that lose their leaves in winter give you the benefit of dappled shade in the summer and sunshine through the bare branches in winter.

The type and placement of trees in your yard can greatly influence heating and cooling costs.

- Use a green roof—plants on the roof—to conserve energy and extend the life of the roof; green walls also help reduce energy costs. You can place a tree espalier at the side of the house to absorb heat and insulate the house, keeping it cooler in summer. In some cases, you can use vines to keep the house warmer in winter.

- If you have a window-unit air conditioner, you can reduce cooling costs by as much as 10 percent by shading it. In fact, you can shade it and camouflage it all in one by using an arbor and a perennial vine. This arrangement also maintains the air flow in the unit.

- Consider foundation plantings. The original idea of these was to mask the foundations of homes, which in older houses were much higher than they are now. Although foundations are less of an aesthetic issue now, foundation plantings can cool the landscape by 15 degrees around your house. That means less money spent on air conditioning.

- Break away from the tradition of sheared evergreens pushed up against the house and use a variety of plants to achieve seasonal and year-round beauty, while creating outdoor living space and conserving energy.

- Using deciduous plants by outdoor living spaces, especially if you're in a cold climate, takes advantage of their leaf drop when you need solar heat in winter and spring and of their leafy shade in warmer months. A redbud is a good example. It has blossoms in the spring, right on the branches and stems. In summer, it has heart-shaped leaves that turn a beautiful yellow in fall, and winter exposes the nice form and scaly bark.

- Windbreaks are another way to save energy. Plant trees away from the house at a distance of one to two times their height. Keep in mind, though, that snow will pile up on the windward side, so be careful where you place a windbreak. You don't want it next to a driveway where you need to shovel or plow. Staggering trees in rows will hasten results, increase the beauty of the landscape, and be more efficient.

- Include mixed plantings in a windbreak to minimize damage should one of the plant species succumb to disease. Mixing it up a bit—including some pine, some spruce, and some deciduous plants—increases disease resistance and resistance to pests. Also include some perennials or deciduous shrubs, perhaps some that flower, form fruit, or have great fall color, to ensure that the windbreak is both beautiful and functional.

- Storm water can be a problem, especially in urban areas. Because pavement and buildings occupy land that once absorbed runoff, the water flows into storm sewers, which can overflow and cause flooding. Adding a few trees can help reduce runoff by 2 percent to 7 percent.
  - Even one tree in front of your house absorbs hundreds of gallons of water, preventing overflow into the storm sewer.

  - In addition to keeping water on your property, which is great for your lawn and garden, trees also reduce the cost of wastewater treatment, absorb carbon dioxide, and improve air quality.

Divide and Screen
- Trees and shrubs help define space, protect privacy, and outline "rooms" within a larger landscape. They have long been used to delineate property lines, but you can also use them to separate places to sit quietly in the yard from play spaces for children, for example, or to screen your vegetable garden. If your property abuts a landscape change, such as a natural wetland, trees and shrubs help soften the transition from the garden to a natural space.

- One of the least favorite questions for a landscaper is: "How many arborvitaes, pines, spruces, and junipers do I need to create a screen between my yard and my neighbor's?" Before you make a wall of evergreens, think about where you really need that screen.

- Carefully consider the views you want to keep and those you'd like to screen. Go indoors and look out your windows. Then go outside and sit down in a few spots. If there's an area where you spend a lot of time standing, stand up and look around.

- This exercise is a good way to decide how many trees and shrubs you really need for screening. You may want to leave some space open for a view of your neighbor's garden while you mask the dog kennel on the other side.

- Make sure you include wildlife in the screen. Evergreens are great shelter for birds, protecting them from predators and the weather. Berry-producing plants attract birds, and flowering plants attract hummingbirds and butterflies.

- Look for creative solutions. It's a safe bet that you don't need a wall of evergreens but, rather, strategically placed plantings.

- A typical hedge or divider is a row of yews. There's nothing wrong with this arrangement, but it often could be more attractive. Mix in some deciduous plants, such as a black chokeberry aronia. This plant has white flowers in the spring, black or red fruit that persists through the winter, and beautiful fall color, plus it tolerates some shade and moisture. It's a real beauty for the landscape and a favorite of birds.

- If you need a tall screen, you can use bald cypress. It's a little formal but interesting and provides a different texture. Be aware that bald cypresses are deciduous conifers; they produce cones and drop their needles in the fall. If the needles turn rusty, the plant hasn't died; it's just moving into its winter phase.

- If space is limited, try espalier-style pruning, which results in a kind of living artwork. *Espalier* is the process of training plants to grow flat against a wall. This technique is wonderful for softening the view of a house or in an area that you want to screen but still be able to see through.

- You can use shrubs and trees to anchor structures, artwork, arbors, and gazebos into the landscape and make them look as if they are a part of it, as well making them focal points. If you do this, make sure that your plants are in scale—not oversized or undersized compared to the rest of the landscape.

- You may want to include some edibles in your landscape. Blueberries are a healthy choice even in a small area, and dwarf berries are available for small-space gardeners. When you're looking at edibles, think substitution: Instead of a Japanese maple, consider a black lace elderberry. These trees have beautiful foliage, as well as flowers that butterflies enjoy and fruit to make jams, jellies, and—of course—wine.

Questions to Consider

1. Are your trees and shrubs planted to maximize their energy-saving potential? How does foliage size and placement relate to the sun and your light preferences?

2. Do any of your trees or shrubs serve as a natural focal point? What might work well? How might espalier-style pruning—teaching your tree or shrub to grow flat against a wall or fence—work around the home? Would a gazebo or trellis be appropriate?

Form and Function in the Landscape
Lesson 2—Transcript

Creating the landscape of your dreams in less-than-ideal conditions can be challenging, and most of us have less-than-ideal conditions. But trees and shrubs can help. Now whether it's screening a bad view, or adding year-round appeal, or creating an outdoor living space, trees and shrubs can be that framework to help you develop the landscape of your dreams.

Now as we discussed in the first session, we always want to consider the plants' mature size when developing your landscape. Make sure that those small plants you bought in a nursery will still fit the landscape when they reach their full size. Sometimes it's hard to imagine those tiny little plants can get as big as the tag says, but trust them: It will.

You also want to select those plants that are cold hardy, and that means they'll tolerate the average minimum winter temperatures of your area. For example, camellias. Beautiful plants, but not hardy in my neck of the woods. If I put one out in the garden, it's sure to die after the first winter. So I want to look for plants that are cold hardy to my region. Most tags will tell you, and there are cold hardiness maps available online.

Now on the other extreme, you also want to consider heat hardiness. Is that plant able to tolerate the average number of days with temperatures over 86 degrees? Now, once temperatures are over 86 degrees, plants can suffer physiological disorder or damage. They can suffer decline. They don't function as well. They burn up more energy than they produce, and so they can start declining and not looking as good.

Now birch trees are a great example. If you know the paperbark birch, they're native to northern areas, where the summers are cool and the soils are cool and moist. We bring them down south of their natural region, put them in short-mown grass. It's like a prairie there, with short grass. The grass and the soil are warm and hot. The temperature is too hot. Those plants not only suffer, but they're also more susceptible to other insect and disease problems. So match the plant to the cold and the heat of your region.

And of course, the plant needs to be suited to the other growing conditions. Will it tolerate the existing soil? Do you have heavy clay that's poorly drained? Or maybe sandy, rocky soil where the moisture just goes right through? How about rainfall? You want to get plants that will tolerate the rainfall, so you're not out there watering a lot once they're established. And how about the light? Does it need full sun, part sun, or shade? And any other growing conditions unique to your backyard, your neighborhood, and your community.

Now let's consider how this living framework can also help with things like energy conservation, storm water management, and reducing pollution. You may remember some of your lessons from Arbor Day celebrations of the past, where trees are good for the environment. But we've found they're even better than we suspected.

So let's start with energy conservation. Consider, evaluate, and make the most of the angle of the sun throughout the day and the year. Take a look at these helpful animations. As you can see, in the summer, the sun is high in the sky. So as it travels across your house, it rises in the east, so trees planted on the east cast a shade, or shadow, on your house, and then, the west, shining in through the windows. In the winter, the angle of the sun is aimed more from the south, so, the light getting to your home is different.

Now, as you can see, those trees greatly impacted the sun light reaching your house. So we want to design the layout of our plantings to take advantage of that. Use that framework to take advantage of solar impact. Now, what that means is you want the sun to come in during the cooler months, but you really want to shade it out from coming through the windows during the warmer months of summer. So placement and type of tree you select, can greatly influence your heating and cooling costs. So we're going to place trees to shade the east and west windows, so that during the hot months, we don't gain a lot of solar heat from the sun. This reduces our cooling costs. We want to use large, mature trees to shade the roof of our house so that we can keep the attic cool by reducing the temperatures by as much as 40 degrees; with large shade trees, we can reduce the cooling costs, as well.

Now this is a picture of my city home that I used to live in. And as you can see, I have quite a few plantings. You can see just the edge of the street tree on the west side of my house. Now, I never had air conditioning in that home, except for my street tree. It blocked the sun, the west sun, from reaching my living room and dining room, and most importantly, my bedroom. Without that tree, I would have never survived without air conditioning. In the morning, the sun would come through the east, but that was great; it wasn't as hot or intense, and I used some other seasonal plantings to help with that.

Now we don't want to forget to shade the walks, the drives, and the patios. If we keep our cars cooler when they're parked, it means less energy spent cooling them off. We want our patio shaded during the summer so that we're not sweltering in heat and actually getting to enjoy our outdoor living space that we've taken time and energy to design, and we want to enjoy it.

Now three properly placed trees can save up to 30 percent energy use, so it's really worth your effort to select, plant, and properly care for these trees. Now, if you live in the north and you need sunlight to help warm your home in winter, you want to avoid placing trees so that they block the sunlight in winter where the sunlight can help warm the house and reduce your heating costs. That's my situation.

Use fine-textured, deciduous plants that minimize shading in the winter. Now, fine-textured are plants that have tiny leaves. They tend to have thin stems, something like a Honeylocust. Deciduous plants lose their leaves in winter, so the benefit here is we get the shade from that dappled shade from, say, a Honeylocust for the summer, so that's great. They drop their leaves, and in winter, the sun can shine through and warm up our house. So it's a great way to have the best of both worlds. Now obviously you wouldn't want evergreens in that situation, because they're holding their needles and providing shade year-round.

Now you may have heard of green roofs, where people are putting plants on the roof to conserve energy, extend the life of their roof, but we're also finding that green walls help reduce energy costs. And here we have a tree espaliate on the side of this brick home. And what happens is it absorbs the heat, insulates the house, keeping it cooler in summer. And in some cases, we can use vines to keep things warmer in winter. So, that may be your next step in your landscape. But if space is limited, this is a way to have trees, seasonal interest, and some energy conservation even in small spaces.

Now keep large shade trees away from the south, southeast, and southwest side of the house to minimize winter shading. Remember those big trees have a big impact on blocking the sunlight, so we don't want to shade the house in the winter, again, to let the sun shine through. Now you can also reduce cooling costs by shading the air conditioner. Here what we've done is we've shaded the air conditioner and camouflaged it all in one. Now, not only did we camouflage it with the arbor, but we used a vine to cover. This is an annual vine, but soon, the perennial sweet autumn clematis will cover that trellis, and it was a way to shade the air conditioner, to reduce the amount of energy used to run it, so saving energy, and also mask the view in that outdoor living space.

Now use small trees or vines, as I mentioned, but we want to make sure that we maintain air flow. That's very important. So maybe a small tree limbed up that casts shade on the air conditioner, or a few shrubs placed away for air flow, or, as I showed you before, the vines that cast shade. Now you can reduce your cooling costs by as much as 10 percent just by shading your air conditioner. And as I mentioned, you'll mask view and it will improve it much more.

Now, foundation plantings are something that are, maybe it changed over time. You may have heard the term, or you may have made some foundation plantings. The idea behind foundation plantings was to mask the foundation of the house. You may remember seeing or still see old homes where you see cement block as the foundation and the siding, or the brick work starts much higher. So landscape architects used to put shrubs in front of there to mask that view. Now, we don't necessarily have to mask the view, because new homes usually have the siding to the ground, or brick to the ground, or the foundation is less of an issue from aesthetics. But, foundation plantings, plantings near your home, can cool that landscape by 15 degrees around your house. That means less money spent on air conditioning.

These are just a few examples of what gardeners have done, break away from the tradition of sheared evergreens pushed up against the house, but using a variety of plants to achieve the same thing, but provides seasonal and year-round beauty.

Now you also want to shade for you. As I mentioned, shading walks and drives and patios. Here a red bud, it's beautiful. It has blooms in the spring, right on the branches and the stems, and so they really stand out in the spring. They're edible, too. They have got kind of a sweet flavor; you can add them on salads. In the summer, they'll have heart-shaped leaves that provide shade. In fall, those leaves turn a beautiful yellow, and in winter it exposes the nice form and that scaly bark. So a good four-season plant, and here it's providing shade through an entryway and an outdoor sitting area.

Now the benefit of using deciduous plants for areas like this is it makes grilling a lot easier and a cooler experience. And the other benefit of using deciduous plants by outdoor living spaces or dining areas or places you gather and sit, especially if you're in a cold climate, is the plants don't have any leaves on them in the spring when we need that solar heat to keep us warm when we're outdoors. Then, when it starts to get hot, those leaves are out there providing shade. And when the cooler temperatures of fall return, the leaves drop, and we have the sun shining through to help keep us warm. So it's a great way to get seasonal change, in terms of solar heat benefit or shading, whichever you need.

Now, windbreaks are another way that we can help save and reduce energy costs. And the idea here is to plant trees that block the cold winter wind, maybe create shelter for some nearby plantings, or if you're in a windy area, you may need that windbreak year round. This animation shows how those winds travel over the trees and down. Keep the trees, at least one to two times their height, away from the house, because that will give you the protection you need. The snow is going to dump on the downwind side of those plantings, so be careful where you place your windbreak. You don't want it next to a driveway where the snow goes up and over and lands right where you need to shovel or plow. So keep in mind the placement of those trees for greatest value, from snow management, as well as wind control.

Now, you want to also be aware that you'll speed up your results for your windbreak, and you can increase the beauty by staggering your rows, much like we talked about before about getting quick results with trees and shrubs. By having several layers to your windbreak, you'll have better impact with that windbreak, quicker results, and it will look better sooner. Have some mixed plantings, and here's a couple reasons why. If you have nothing but spruce in that windbreak, and a disease comes in that attacks spruce trees, you could lose the whole windbreak. So mixing it up a bit, maybe some pine, some spruce, don't forget to add some deciduous plants, you'll increase your disease resistance, and resistance to pests as well. And you want to add some perennials or deciduous shrubs, those that lose their leaves, maybe that flour, maybe that form fruit or have great fall color so that it's a beautiful addition to the landscape, not just functional.

Now those of you in the city who are like me may go, well, I don't have a large area to plant, to create a windbreak in your own yard. But more and more municipalities are using plantings to reduce the overall heating and cooling costs for our communities. A lot of places, like Los Angeles, are doing the Million Tree Initiative, where they're trying to plant a million trees to greatly reduce hydrocarbons, cool the city, and make a difference.

What happens in a city is, with all that pavement and all those buildings, they absorb the heat. And the temperatures are much higher during the day, and significantly higher, even up to 20 degrees or more, at night. So here they've used green roofs, and you notice they're even some trees on the rooftop. Now, before you start planting your roof, make sure you have an architect or engineer come in and make sure your house can support that and your roof. But, if your whole community is planting street trees, filling green spaces with trees and shrubs, the impact overall is great. You're going to reduce the whole overall temperature of that urban heat island in the city by several degrees during the day. So if we all work together, we can have great impact. You might want to contact your local municipality; find out if they have any initiatives that you can get involved with.

Now storm water has another problem that especially in urban areas we're seeing. We've got all this pavement, all these buildings, and no place for the water to go, except the storm sewer. So here's what happens. It rains. The water rolls off our roof, down the drives, and into the storm sewer, and then it overflows. So we have flooding, we have pressure on our water treatment plants, and it's a big problem. Adding a few trees can help reduce runoff by as much as 2 to 7 percent. So that street tree in front of my house was absorbing hundreds of gallons of water and preventing them from going into the storm sewer. So it kept the water on my property, which was great; it took care of the trees' needs; and it kept it out the storm sewer. So it also reduced money spent treating water and pollution as well. So trees have a big impact in that way.

Trees will also help define our space, and we talked a little bit about that. As you're doing your outdoor living space, we can use trees and shrubs to create privacy, or maybe create small rooms within larger landscapes. Or, maybe block those views we don't want to see. So trees and shrubs have long been used to delineate property lines, typically hedges often sheared. So you know this is my yard. Here's the hedge. That's the neighbor's yard. And sometimes it's abrupt, but it could be, this is the place I want to sit and read quietly, and there's the place for the kids to play. And my vegetable garden is in the back, kind of strategically placed behind some beautiful plants.

Now, on this landscape they've used some trees to separate a garden area from a natural area. So in this beautiful perennial garden you'll see some shrub and trees in the background. And what's nice about that is those trees then separate it from that natural wetland. So there's a delineation, a big change in the landscape, but the trees help soften it and make it a more gentle transition from a more informal perennial garden to a natural space.

One of my least favorite questions I get and I'm often asked is, how many arborvitae, pines, spruces, junipers, do I need to create a screen between my yard and my neighbor's? And that screen needs go from the front curve to the back alley. Now, in my book, that's a pretty nasty neighbor, if you're worried about that. Well, what I usually try to say is before you make a wall of green evergreens, think about where you really need that screening. Now here they've used arborvitae to create a screen. They threw in some ornamental grasses to break things up. But, if a disease moves in, guess what? What do you do? One plant dies, how do you repair that space? So you've got eight-foot arborvitae, because that one tree never dies right away. One plant dies, what do you do? Do you buy a little arborvitae and put it in the middle? Do you buy a big one and then kill the other two on either side?

Do you do what this gardener did? Very creative solution, maybe not the best in terms of visual, but I think they took a bad situation and made it better. They filled that void with a trellis, trained some vines, put some annuals in front, and they repeated those annuals in front of the remaining arborvitae. So they filled the gap, made it look somewhat intentional, and solved their problem. But, I'm going to try to help you avoid that in your landscape.

So start by looking at what views you need to keep and which views you really need to screen. This is my balcony for my home in the city. And what I found is people loved going on my balcony and I couldn't figure out why. So I spent some time really trying to figure it out. Well, it was above the noise and bustle of the city, so that was positive. And it was a great place, right? My office was right inside, I'd step outside, and I took a look at the views. So, standing there when I'd look to the south, you can kind of see my neighbor's house. I was looking right into the second-floor bathroom window. Maybe not the best view. To the east, behind the chair that you see, was a view into the alley, a little noisy, a little messy, not really my favorite view. The view you can't see, to the north, was into the park easement. And my house was right in the canopy of the county easement, and so it was like being in the canopy of a forest. It was wonderful.

So what I decided to do was keep the view of the forest, because I did feel like I was right in the treetops. But as you can see, I put a palm and some hanging baskets, so that my neighbor, who I enjoy chatting with, had a little sense of privacy when she was in her bathroom upstairs. And I also didn't have to look into it. And then on the east, I put hanging baskets, so when I sat on my balcony, I could look at those, but if I wanted to look at my garden when I was standing up, I looked down.

Now this is a very small-scale example, but a good example of looking for those views you want to keep, and those you want to hide. So think carefully as you're looking around and wandering around your house and yard. Go indoors, look out your windows. Look throughout the yard and over to your neighbor's. Which views do you want to mask? Then go outside. Sit down in a few places. Is this a place you're going to sit and read? What are the views that you want to keep, that you want to mask?

Maybe there's an area where you spend a lot of time standing. Stand up and look out. It's a great way to really decide that maybe you need three arborvitae, a few deciduous plants, and some grasses here. Leave that space open so you can see your neighbor's garden. Mask the dog kennel on the other side. Look for those creative solutions, because I bet you don't need a wall of green evergreens, but rather, really strategically-placed gardens. Otherwise, a fence might work.

Now you may recognize this if you've purchased our container class, but this was a screening opportunity we used from a deck situation. We wanted to create privacy for the two individuals. So, we used boxwoods as our evergreen, elevated on empty shrub pots, and in front of it we used Shenandoah switchgrass and pretty colorful pots, and tucked in you may just see a little glimmer of Black lace elderberry and a few other shrubs. The cool part about this is they had a big deck, very empty. It provided screening and privacy for them, as well as their neighbor, and so both people benefited by a beautiful screen. And the best part is, the person we are redoing their deck, didn't lose any valuable space.

And mix it up. I've been talking a lot about that, but mixing it up also is visually beautiful, as well. And so here we have blue spruce, and we have some perennials, and we have some colorful shrubs that really give us a very attractive screen as well. And then also make sure that you include wildlife in that screening. Evergreens are great for shelter for the birds. It protects them from predators and the weather. Maybe some berry-producing plants that bring them in or flowering plants for the hummingbirds and butterflies. And you can see a great example of this. We've got a nice mix. We've got a purple-leaf Ninebark, we've got alliums that are bulbs, we've got some black-eyed Susans, a nice variety, and a few ornamental grasses peeking in for some added texture as well.

Now here is kind of your typical hedge or divider. It's a row of Yews. And it's OK, and that magnolia behind, it's a beauty. But that hedge of Yews just could use a little something. How about mixing in some deciduous plants like this Black chokeberry *Aronia*. It has white flowers in the spring, black or red fruit that persists through the winter, beautiful fall color that you can see here, tolerates some shade and moisture. And if you know about *Aronia* or chokeberries, you know they're very high in antioxidants. And we're seeing more and more jams, jellies, and wine made from this medicinal plant. But it's a real beauty for your landscape and a favorite of birds, but they wait for the fruit to ferment a bit before they clean them off the plant. You get to enjoy them all winter, and you get to enjoy the birds as they feed on the fruit in the spring.

Now, this is your kind of more formal hedge, but using a different plant. These are Bald cypress, so if you need a tall screen, looking for something formal, look at this. A little bit formal, but interesting, a different texture. But be aware, Bald cypress are deciduous conifers. Conifers are plants that produce cones, not necessarily evergreen, and deciduous means they drop their leaves or needles. So this plant produces cones, but drops its needles in the fall. So when those needles turn a nice, rusty color, don't think your plant died. It's just moving into its winter interest.

Now these are some Musclewoods, beautiful native plant to woodland areas across North America. Look at that beautiful fall color. Not your typical screen, but the twiggy branches will provide some screening, or perhaps this is a solution for areas that you only look upon during the warmer months. So it's a great way to screen not only the views that you need to, but at the time you want. And here we've added some low-growing shrubs in front of the fence that'll eventually fill in. Mixed it with some taller trees for an upper canopy, and then throw in some perennials underneath for added color. And again, the texture and the color of your conifers, dwarf or big cone-bearing evergreens, great for the landscape.

Now, if space is limited, you might want to try espaliering, kind of living artwork. And we're going to talk a little bit more about that when we talk pruning, but espalier is training plants to be somewhat flat and one dimensional right up against the wall. Here they've espaliered on a decorative fence, so it's softened the view, great up against a house to soften the view, or maybe an area where you want to screen, but still want to be able to see through. Maybe the entertaining area overlooking the play area where the kids are. You want to be able to keep an eye on them, but you want a sense of division or separation. Something like this will work well, and again, that green-wall effect that's good for energy, also a living artwork and great for small spaces.

We can also use shrubs and trees to anchor structures, artwork, arbors, and gazebos into the landscape. Look at how nicely this gazebo is nestled in amongst those trees; it looks like it belongs there, versus out in the middle of the lawn with no plantings around it. So use your trees and shrubs to anchor those structures and artwork to the ground. Make them look like it's a part of it.

You know, and here we've got a foundation planting and some mixed beds in the garden. Now remember I mentioned the foundation plantings, a common way to use trees and shrubs around the house, shrubs in particular. Well, this gardener took that idea out, went further away, included a variety of plants and her foundation planting, echoed or repeated them in other beds to really make a cohesive landscape, beautiful, fit into the neighborhood nicely, but had that added seasonal interest.

And if you look closely at this landscape, you may spot a tomato, a pepper, a strawberry, and a hanging basket, along with some peonies, some evergreens, and other deciduous shrubs. It's a wonderful, changing foundation, not what we typically would expect, but one that makes your visitors stop, take a second look, especially helpful in a small landscape where we're trying to make the most of every square foot.

Now we can also use our trees and shrubs as focal points in the landscape. There's no missing this Tricolor Beech. It really grabs your attention in this landscape. As it gets bigger, it will be more impressive. And here this Tricolor Beech is more on its own, nice, horizontal branching. And remember, we talked about how form really impacts. Doesn't it just make you want to look around that landscape? And that unique foliage color is beautiful. The Beeches tend to hold their leaves after they turn kind of a beige color for winter. They'll hold some of their leaves close to the trunk, which makes them rattle in the wind, very nice sound for the winter interest.

You want to make sure that your plants are in scale. I said they're good at anchoring, but we don't want the plants to look oversized or undersized next to the landscape. You want it to be in scale, much like this Japanese maple is with this small bungalow home.

We talked a little bit about edibles, mainly thinking about birds and butterflies. But you may want to include some edibles in your landscape. Blueberries are a healthy choice, and many of us are trying to grow our own food so that we can have fresher-from-the-garden flavor, more nutritional food, and control what goes on our plants and the food that we eat. Well, you can include edibles in your landscape. And even if you have a small space, look at this container of blueberries. There are lots of dwarf berries out on the market now that are available for small-space gardeners. But even if you have a large garden, you may want a pot of blueberries for your patio or deck, so you can pluck them off when you're having your morning oatmeal.

I can't think of a better barrier plant than a raspberry, but, they may be a little too big for some areas. So if you have room, consider using raspberries and blackberries as your barrier plants. They'll do well in full sun. You will have to protect the harvest from the birds if you want to enjoy it. But you can also try one of the dwarf varieties, like this Raspberry shortcake in a pot. The other benefit? Only grows two to three feet tall, and it's thornless, and it produces most of the summer long, so you'll be able to enjoy the fruit.

So when you're looking at edibles for your landscape, think substitution. Instead of a Japanese maple, how about a Black lace elderberry? Not only do they have beautiful foliage, but flowers that the butterflies and you can enjoy and fruit that you can enjoy, make make jams, jellies, and of course, wine. Or, the birds can enjoy them, and you'll enjoy the birds feeding on them. Instead of a Crabapple, how about an apple? Here they've been pleached over the arbor to make a very dramatic accent in the landscape.

I mentioned my favorite Juneberry before, so there are ornamentals that are edible as well. So a Juneberry, good for the birds, edible for you, just as Corneliancherry Dogwood is. Cornish moss, it has yellow flowers early in the season, even before Forsythia bloom, those yellow shrubs we often see in the spring. Good, red fruit that we can enjoy, the birds will eat them. It's a little astringent, makes you pucker, but add a little sugar. They make great jams and good wine, as well, purple fall color and nice, kind of scaly bark for winter—seasonal interest, edible fruit for you and birds to enjoy. So check it out. There's a lot of options.

Now we've looked at traditional and perhaps new ways to you of using and integrating trees and shrubs in the landscape, creating that framework that not only increases the beauty, but also the function in your design. So take another look at your landscape and see if there are any ways you can help reduce energy costs and increase the beauty with the use of trees and shrubs. And while you're surveying the landscape, look at some of the challenges that exist, light and moisture. Next class we'll explore ways to incorporate trees and shrubs in these challenging conditions.

Trees and Shrubs for Challenging Conditions
Lesson 3

Most plants thrive in full sun to partial shade with moist, well-drained soil. Unfortunately, most of us don't have those ideal conditions for our trees and shrubs. But understanding the needs of your plants, as well as the impact of existing plantings, buildings, and our neighbors' structures and plants, can help you create a healthy and long-lasting landscape, no matter what the growing conditions.

Observe the Sunlight
- Plants need light to produce energy in order to can grow and thrive. Many have larger leaves, more leaves, or both, providing more surface area and increasing efficiency in absorbing light.

- Observe the shade patterns in your landscape throughout the year and throughout the day. In spring, many trees have not leafed out, allowing the plants growing beneath to get sunlight; as the leaves come in, those plants adapt to the shade.

- Notice the position of the sun over time. The angle changes how much light reaches the plants. If you observe carefully, you'll notice different types of shade.
  - *Dappled shade*, which lets in light sun throughout the day, is probably best for both sun- and shade-loving plants.

  - *Open shade* is heavy shade with full sun on summer afternoons. Finding the right plant for open shade can be challenging because even in the shade, sunlight can cause a great deal of heat during the day.

  - *Medium shade* occurs in areas that get no direct sunlight; the shade is constant.

○ *Dense shade* occurs next to walls, fences, or dense-canopy trees, where almost all the light is blocked.

○ *Dry shade* can be any of the above. It occurs when trees casting shade act as umbrellas, blocking water from reaching the soil; if water does hit the ground, the trees absorb it before the plants beneath can. You also find dry shade under overhangs or under decks, where water and light are limited.

Select Shade-Loving Plants

- Once you know the best shade conditions for a particular plant, you can use that plant as an indicator to identify others that need the same conditions. Start with a few shade-tolerant perennials or annuals and match them with trees and shrubs that thrive in shade.

- To identify shade-tolerant plants, look to nature for clues. Understory trees and shrubs naturally grow under the large canopy of a forest and are well suited to shady conditions. Most evergreens, with the exception of hemlock, prefer full sun or light shade. Boxwood and, to some extent, yews also grow in shade.

- If your planting area is too shady for trees and shrubs, consider shade-tolerant ground covers, mulch, or moss.

If you're considering thinning your trees to allow light to reach plants below, it's probably best to call a certified arborist.

Select Sun-Loving Plants

- Too much light is usually related to extreme temperature and lack of moisture. The more sunlight you have, the faster the plants grow and the more resources—water and nutrients—they need. Selecting plants that tolerate these conditions in your growing environment will reduce your workload and increase the beauty and success of your garden.

    o Junipers are famous for their heat and drought tolerance, and they come in several varieties: trees, spreading forms, and ground cover. Some have blue-green needles, and some have golden needles; all are heat and drought tolerant.

    o Rugosa roses are tough and hardy. Not only will they take the heat, drought, and salt from deicing or ocean spray, but they also produce beautiful edible rose hips, high in vitamin C.

- To create shade during the hot, dry months and during the hottest part of the day, look for areas where you can build an arbor or a pergola to cast some shade on plants that may need a little protection.

- Mulch is an aid to any plants, especially in hot, dry conditions. Spreading an organic mulch, such as shredded bark or wood chips, over the soil surface will help keep roots cool and moist.

- It's also a good idea to plant perennial ground covers under trees because, just like mulch, they help keep roots cool and moist but, unlike grass, don't compete for water.

Water Carefully

- Water is a critical factor in growing conditions. If you understand the science behind plant growth and soil moisture, you can do a better job of managing both.

- Excess water displaces oxygen that roots need to absorb water nutrients. Instead, other harmful gases collect and can cause root rot. Make sure that the soil is well drained and you don't overwater.

- The age of a plant also affects its ability to absorb water nutrients. Established plants are most tolerant. Overwatering older plants and younger plants that don't have strong root systems can be deadly. It's not always easy to detect overwatering because the impact is underground. A few of the above-ground symptoms that may indicate excess water include the following:
  - Because wilting usually indicates a lack of water, when you see that your plant is wilting, your first instinct is to water it. But if it's already overwatered, you'll make the problem worse. Look carefully at the plant; check the soil before you add more water.

  - Leaves turning yellow in between the veins, a little decay, and even some soft spots can also be caused by nutrient deficiencies, diseases, or physical damage to the roots through construction or cultivation. Again, check the soil moisture, evaluate recent rainfall, and examine how you're watering to decide where the problem lies.

  - Flooding, which is obviously out of your control, can seriously damage plants. The longer they are submerged, the greater the risk of decline and death. Some plants, such as willows and alders, are more able to tolerate flooding than others; if your area is prone to flooding, you may want to use these in your landscape.

  - Root rot is a problem secondary to flooding or overwatering. After your plants start declining or when you're removing a dead plant, you'll see that the roots have rotted and died back.

- We tend to kill our plants with kindness, so be careful.
  - Water thoroughly—to ensure that the whole root zone is moist—but less often to encourage deep roots that will be drought tolerant when necessary.

o   Grab a handful of soil and run it through your fingers. If it's cool, crumbly, and moist, then it's time to water thoroughly for plants that like damp soil. For those that prefer dry soil, wait a little longer before watering.

o   Always dig beneath the mulch and a few inches down to make sure you're checking the area where the roots grow.

o   Take special care with new plantings. Because they have small root systems, they need water more often. As they get established, you can gradually extend the period between waterings.

Ensure Good Drainage

- Another cause of waterlogged plants is poor drainage. If you have heavy soil that feels like pottery clay when you rub it through your fingers, you can see that it compacts; it can prevent water from draining and allow it to collect around your plants' roots. With trees and shrubs that have extensive root systems, you need to think about ways to amend the soil or deal with the drainage problem.
    o   For shrubs, amend the whole planting bed, not just the planting hole. If you amend only the planting hole, the roots won't explore the soil around it, and they'll end up growing in circles.

    o   If you can't amend the soil, create a berm and elevate the plants above the waterlogged soil.

    o   You can also try a French drain, which is a trench filled with gravel and covered with about a foot of soil. When the water collects, it slowly drains through to the groundwater and away from your planting beds.

    o   Design a rain garden to capture water running off patios, decks, or the roof. The rainwater slowly recharges the groundwater and goes where it's intended, not flooding the other parts of your landscape.

- Flooding can cause other problems, as well. For example, it can wash away soil from the roots of trees and shrubs, or it can pile soil on top of them.
  - When roots are exposed, they are subject to drying and damage.

  - Excess soil impedes air flow to roots and can kill trees. For some species, as little as an inch of soil over the root system is deadly.

  - After a flood, you may observe debris on leaves. That soil on leaves blocks sunlight and prevents photosynthesis. A mature, established plant will recover, but a young plant is susceptible to damage in these conditions.

Protect against Drought

- At the other extreme from flooding is drought. Plants are 80 percent water and must have water for all their essential functions. Drought can be the result of factors other than lack of rainfall: High temperatures and strong winds, for example, increase loss of moisture through the pores in leaves; this process is called *transpiration*.
  - Plants that are heat intolerant scorch because they're losing water faster than they can absorb it.

  - If winds are an issue and you're watering properly but your plants experience a great deal of drying, a windbreak may be the answer.

  - Plants often wilt and curl their leaves to conserve moisture at midday; by the time the temperature lowers and the sun is setting, the leaves open back up.

- *Scorch* is the leaf margins turning brown. On evergreens, you'll see brown needles, usually on new growth, and you may see an increase in seasonal needle drop. Always keep an eye on your plants, taking notes, and you'll be better able to diagnose problems.

- Drought-stress symptoms often appear years after a drought, and you may not always make the connection. For example, 2 to 4 years after an extreme drought, you may find that your trees are being attacked by bores—insects feeding under the bark—or a disease may move in and finish off trees that are already stressed.

- Drought is more than just a lack of water, and getting to the cause will help you resolve the issue. Select drought-tolerant plants, and look for heat hardiness, that is, the plant's ability to tolerate temperatures higher than 86 degrees. Make sure the plant's characteristics match the growing conditions in your area.

Questions to Consider

1. Analyze the effects of vegetation growth and adjacent structures on the well-being of your trees and shrubs. Are they receiving adequate light? What adjustments need to be made?

2. Identify open, dappled, medium, and densely shaded areas.

3. Would your trees and shrubs benefit from mulching, whether to preserve moisture around the roots or to keep grass from growing up the trunks?

4. What causes waterlogged soil?

Trees and Shrubs for Challenging Conditions
Lesson 3—Transcript

Most plants thrive in full sun to partial shade with moist, well-drained soil. Unfortunately, most of us don't have those ideal conditions for our trees and shrubs. But understanding the needs of our plants will help us create healthy and long-lasting frameworks no matter what the growing conditions. Well let's start with sunlight. Plants need light to produce energy to grow and thrive. And if you take a look at shade-tolerant plants, they've adapted over time. Many have larger leaves or more leaves or both, and that gives them more surface area to absorb the light so they can be very efficient in absorbing the light to produce the energy they need.

Now, matching plants to the growing conditions and the light is very important. We spoke earlier about sunlight as it relates to energy conservation. Now we need to evaluate the sunlight based on plant growth. Now once again, we need to look at the sun and shade patterns throughout the year and throughout the day. When you think about your garden or your landscape in the spring, often many trees haven't leafed out, so the plants growing beneath get more sunlight, but as the trees leaf out there's more shade, so they need to adjust. And also the position of the sun in the sky throughout the day and throughout the year really changes how much light is reaching the plants below. So take a little time to look at your landscape throughout the year—spring, summer, fall, and even winter—and throughout the day, morning through night. You know, many of us work during the day and only see our garden in the evening, so make sure that when you have a day off, you check the light patterns and shade patterns at that time.

We also need to consider the impact of existing plantings, buildings, our neighbors' structures and plants that impact the light conditions, and changes in any of those. Often people put up a shed or a structure and don't think about the impact on the sunlight that reaches the surrounding plants.

So as we take a look, you'll notice that there are different types of shade. Dappled shade is probably the best for plants, good for sun and shade lovers, just light sun throughout the day, nothing blazing hot, it really doesn't burn the plants, but enough for the plants to grow and thrive. Now, open shade is heavy shade with the full sun in the summer in the afternoon, the hot part of the day. So sometimes this can be very challenging, because we've got shade, but we have sunlight during those really hot times, so it makes hard to find just the right plant to survive.

Now, medium shade, under decks or south-facing entrances with no direct sun, those are things that get shade but no sun, so we don't have the blazing sunlight that we did in open shade, but we have a more constant shade, so even though it's challenging, at least it's consistent, making it a bit easier to find plants to survive those conditions. And dense shade happens next to walls or fences or dense canopy trees, where almost all the light is blocked, and I bet you can find a few spots like that in your yard or your neighbor's yard as well.

Now, dry shade is any of the above. Often it's when trees are casting the shade and they block the water reaching the soil. And, if any does, they absorb it before the plants beneath can. I always tell people, go out after a heavy rain under, say, a Norway Maple or an oak tree with big leaves that blocks the light, and also the water, and see how dry your soil is beneath that. We also find dry shade under overhangs or under decks where water is limited, and those are solid structures that may make it a little difficult to deal with because of the lack of light and because of the lack of water.

Now, one thing I like to do is I like to use indicator plants. You know, you find a plant that you know that thrives in these growing conditions, and then you know all the other related plants that need that same kind of light or shade. It makes it easier to identify the growing conditions and the suitable plants. So you might want to try that, plus you can start with maybe a few perennials or annuals that are shade tolerant and match it with the trees and shrubs you often find growing associated with those plants.

Here we've got a Pagoda Dogwood, and this is a wonderful plant that really thrives in partial shade; it likes its roots cool and moist. Really doesn't like hot afternoon sun, but it will tolerate full sun. If you look at the plants surrounding it, you'll notice some viburnums, also plants that like a little bit of shade, especially from the heat of the afternoon, Coralbells, which could take shade as well as some sunlight, and so you can see that these plants all require the same growing conditions. They'll all thrive, but you know, if one of them thrives, the others will, if you have another garden you're starting in a new location.

Well, we've talked about identifying shade, but now, how do we deal with it? We've defined it. You've identified where it's occurring in your landscape. What do you do next? Well, the best thing? Select shade-tolerant plants. And I always like to look to nature for my clues. Understory trees and shrubs are those plants that naturally grow under the large canopy of a forest, and so those are plants that are really suited and have developed in shady conditions. Those are good shade-tolerant plants to consider. Plus, if they're native in your area, and the soil conditions are the same in the other growing conditions that they developed in, you'll have good success.

Ironwood is an understory tree, a small-scale tree that's slow growing. It tolerates shade to full sun, moist to well-drained soils. It's called ironwood because the wood is really very strong. It kind of looks flaky, almost like old paint peeling off a post, which gives it some winter interest. The flowers are unique, but the fruit will persist all winter, almost looking like little ornaments in the winter time. So you might want to try an ironwood if you've got a small space, shade, and need something that's kind of growing and spreading to fill that area.

As far as evergreens, most really prefer full sun or light shade; Hemlocks are the exception. Gentsch white Hemlock is a dwarf variety. It grows about eight feet tall at maturity. But why it's called Gentsch White? It's got white new growth, so the new leaves, needles, come out white and then turn to green. Look at that graceful, delicate texture. So if you have a shady location, one evergreen choice could be a Gentsch's white Hemlock. Boxwood, and to some extent, Yews will also take the shade, Arborvitaes somewhat.

If you want something with some seasonal interest in the shade, try Oakleaf hydrangea. The leaves are shaped like an oak leaf, thus the name. They flower in the summer, beautiful panicles of white flowers that turn to pink and then beige. And in the fall, the leaves turn a beautiful red, yellow, and purple. It's a great plant. Once the leaves drop, it exposes the orange exfoliating bark for winter interest—Oakleaf hydrangea.

Fothergilla is a wonderful plant that's great for the shade. It's a relative of witch hazel. The rabbits, unfortunately, like it just about as much as we do, so you'll need a little added protection. Fragrant white flowers in the spring, nice foliage in the summer, some varieties have a blue-green cast to them, and look at that fall color. It's a great plant for small spaces. There are dwarf varieties, and the straight species gets to be five- or six-feet tall. So you might want to try that in some partial shade.

One of my new favorites is Garden Glow Dogwood. Look at that foliage. Those leaves come out kind of a bright lime green or chartreuse in the spring, and it really brightens up the garden. As the summer continues, it goes into a more of a bright green, white flowers the butterflies like, white fruit for the birds to enjoy, and red stems for winter interest. Now, avoid hot afternoon sun as this plant will scorch. And we'll describe scorch in just a minute.

Now, another thing you may want to try is to increase the light that reaches those plants below. You can't do it if it's caused by a building or a deck, but if it is a tree, you can thin out the crown of the tree that's casting the shade. Now, thinning is selectively removing branches to let more light through to the ground below. But before you get out the pruning saw and ladder, consider hiring a certified arborist. A certified arborist has voluntarily gone through a testing through the International Society of Arboriculture to show their level of knowledge and skill. Make sure they're insured. But you want to make sure that you have a qualified person taking care of your tree. Because if you want to keep it, you want to make sure it's around for a long time. And a certified arborist can come in and do a good job. You can contact your local extension service, go to [www.treesaregood.com], and find a certified arborist in your area.

Now, we'll address some of the challenges of planting under trees a bit later. But, if it is too shady for trees and shrubs to grow in that existing area, you may look for shade-tolerant ground covers. You may be forced to do some mulching, or you may consider moss. That's what nature does. And, if you look in the woods, you'll see that those spring ephemerals come up, those wild flowers that emerge early, and then disappear in the shredded natural litter of the forest. You may be forced to do something like that. But instead of thinking of it as something bad, think of it as mimicking nature. Embrace it and enjoy it, and you'll save yourself a lot of frustration and work. Now, too much light is usually related to extreme temperature as well. So when you have a lot of light, you often have high temperatures and a lack of moisture. They're all somewhat inter-related. The more sunlight you have, the faster the plants grow and the more resources—water and nutrients—they'll need. So you're going to need to beef up your plant care in some cases.

Now, again, selecting plants that tolerate full sun, as well as the temperatures related to that full sun, and the moisture in your growing environment, will help reduce a lot of your workload and increase the beauty and success. Junipers are notorious for their heat and drought tolerance. This Red cedar, *Juniperus virginiana*, is a wonderful example. They have awls and scaly needles, so they're kind of prickly, so you certainly can identify them, but they really add a lot of interest to the landscape. There are tree forms, spreading forms, and ground covers. So, one that you could imagine. Some with blue-green needles and some with golden needles. And all are heat and drought tolerant.

Crabapples are a favorite of many. Now, if you've had an older crabapple, you're probably thinking, ugh, what a mess from the fruit. The leaves always drop off midsummer. Why is she recommending these? Well, the good news is, the new varieties, the new cultivars, tend to be more disease resistant, so they hold their leaves and don't develop apple scab, the disease the causes those leaves to drop, or fire blight that causes the tree to die. And you want to look for one with small, persistent fruit so it stays on the tree until the birds come and clean it off. Select for the flower color you like, but honestly, the fruit will give you more value. So, the flowers may last a week or two in the spring, but pick a fruit that you like, because you'll enjoy it throughout the winter and one the birds will enjoy as well.

Hawthorn's a close relative of Crabapple, interesting foliage, nice fruit. Again, the birds will help clean it up. Many have thorns, and so you'll want to place it carefully in the landscape so it's not causing a problem for people passing through. They do produce white flowers in the spring that smell, not fragrant, but they do smell. So again, place it carefully. It may not be a tree you want by your bedroom window in spring when you're trying to enjoy the fresh fragrances of spring, but it is a beauty for the landscape. Rugosa roses, tough and hardy, not only will they take the heat and drought and salt from deicing or ocean spray, but they also produce beautiful, edible rose hips, high in vitamin C, great for us to enjoy. You can use them to make tea; you can use them for jams and jellies; but, the birds will also enjoy them as well, and a bit of winter interest for you too.

One plant you may or may not be aware of is Blue mist spirea, sometimes called Bluebeard or *Caryopteris*. It's a late summer bloomer with blue flowers, something so many gardeners are seeking, gray-green leaves, blue flowers that the bees love. Now, before you panic, they're going to be so happy nectaring on those flowers, they are not going to bother you at all. Now, you may also want to create shade during the hot, dry months and during the hottest part of the day. Look for areas where you can create maybe an arbor, pergola, or perhaps grow a vine over that structure to add some shade to those plants that maybe need a little protection from the hot afternoon sun. Or if you're in an area where your summers are hot and the sun is intense, you may need a little bit of a canopy to help those plants get a little bit of the shade that they need.

One of the easy things we can do to help any of our plants, but especially in hot, dry conditions, is mulching. Putting an organic mulch, like shredded bark or wood chips, over the soil surface will help keep the roots cool and moist. Just be sure not to pile them up against the trunk of the tree. The old saying about Clematis, it likes it's face in the sun and the feet in the shade. That vine likes full sun, but you need to mulch the base of the plant or cover it to keep the roots cool and moist. And that's one way you can grow that pagoda dogwood I mentioned earlier, in sun, as long as you keep the roots cool and moist in sufficient water. And this is just one example of mulching.

Now you may remember my story about the Catalpa, not only does that conserve moisture, but it also keeps the grass away from the trunk of the tree, so it's less competitive so the water goes to the tree and not to the grass. So it makes your job easier, less watering, better for the tree, easier to mow around. And here we've mulched a bed with ground cover. It's a good idea to plant ground covers under trees, perennial ground covers, that is, that stay in place, because just like the mulch, they help keep the roots cool and moist. But unlike grass, they don't really compete with the trees and shrubs for those water nutrients. It's easier for them to live together in that mulched bed.

As you can see, growing conditions are all interrelated. The amount of light, moisture, and temperatures all impact the plant's need for and ability to tolerate light, moisture, and temperature extremes. So let's talk about water. It's the second critical factor that I want to discuss. Too much or not enough can make it challenging to develop the landscape you desire. You know you've got to either supplement or pick plants that tolerate it. Now, if you understand the science behind plant growth and soil moisture, it can help us do a better job to manage both. Excess water displaces oxygen that's needed by the roots to absorb water nutrients. So basically, what happens, the water fills all the soil pores and the plants can't pull it up. And instead of the plants pulling up the moisture and oxygen being available, other harmful gases will collect and can actually cause root rot and kill those roots. So you want to make sure that your soil is well drained and you don't over water.

The age of the plant can impact the ability. Established plants are most tolerant. Over watering older plants can be deadly and younger plants that don't have the root system. But it's not always easy to detect if it's over watering, because the cause may not be available or easy to detect, and the impact is underground. I always say that my patients, as the plant doctor, are already half buried and they can't talk to me. So I have to do a little detective work, and so will you.

Here are few of the above ground symptoms that may indicate the plant problems due to excess water or poor drainage. Wilting, now, when we think of wilting, we usually think of a lack of water, and that kind of gets this bad syndrome going. A gardener, you may see that your plant's wilting, so what's the first thing you want to do? Go out and water it. But if it's already over watered, it can't pull the moisture up, no oxygen, remember? We're adding more and making the problem worse, so we really need to look at the plant, check the soil before you add more. That may be a good indication of whether it's time to water or not.

Now you may also see that the leaves on your plants turn yellow in between the veins. So you'll get a little bit of yellowing, and you may get a little decay, and you may even get some soft spots. Now, these kind of symptoms can also be caused by nutrient deficiencies, diseases, physical damage to the roots through construction or cultivation or who knows what. So all those things can cause that same symptom. So, this is a clue that you need to do a little more research. Again, check the soil moisture, evaluate the rainfall recently, look at how you're watering, and decide where the problem lies.

Now, flooding is something we really can't stop. You know, nature's in control of that, and the duration of the flooding really impacts how your plants will survive. The longer the plant's submerged, the greater the risk of decline and death, so timing is an issue. Also, some plants are more able to tolerate flooding than others. Think of those trees that we often see growing beside or in the water, things like Willows and Alders and things like that, and we want to really kind of keep an eye on those and use those appropriately in those areas.

Now, root rot is a secondary problem. It usually is caused by damage to the roots, too much water. We discover that after our plants start declining, or when we're removing it, we'll see that the roots are rotted. Die back, again, there are many causes that result in our trees and shrubs dying back, but over watering and flood damage can be two of them.

So let's start out with what's too much water. What causes waterlogged soils? Well, as I mentioned, over watering is probably the biggest cause. We want to be kind to our plants, and we tend to kill them with kindness, so we want to be careful. Water thoroughly so we moisten that whole root zone, but less often to encourage good, deep roots that will be drought tolerant during those periods when water's not available. So grab a handful of soil and run it through your fingers. If it's cool, crumbly, and moist, then it's time to water thoroughly again for plants that like it moist. For those that like it dry, let it get a little bit dryer. Always dig beneath the mulch and a few inches down to make sure you're checking the area where the roots grow.

Now, with new plantings, you really need to give them special care. They have a small root system, so you're going to need to water them more often. But as they get established over the next few years, you could extend the period between watering, always thorough but less frequently, until they're established. But don't forget about established trees. They do need care during extended drought.

But back to poor drainage and wet soils. Heavy clay soils are those that are compacted, also can prevent water from draining and collecting right around the roots. Heavy clay soil feels like pottery clay when you grab it and rub it through your fingers. The soil drains slowly. Compacted soil results from construction or equipment running over the soil, and it pushes those particles together so the water can't drain. A high water table is a problem for many where the water's just below the planting surface.

So the challenge with trees and shrubs is they have an extensive root system. So if we're trying to fix problem soil, how are we going to do that? Tree roots go two to five times the height of the tree beyond the tree trunk. There's no way you could amend it, plus half of that may be in your neighbor's yard. So we have to think about ways we can amend that soil or deal with the problem with water, especially when it comes to trees.

For shrubs, it's easy. Amend the whole planting bed, the whole planting bed, not just the planting hole. When we amend the planting hole, the plant roots won't explore the soil around. They end up growing in circles; it's like a pot in the ground, so we want to amend that whole area. For trees and shrubs, we can create a berm and elevate them above that waterlogged soil. So dealing with poorly drained soils when amending is not possible, we could do the raised berm. But we could also try to do a French drain to get that water away. It's basically a trench filled with gravel covered with about a foot of soil so the water collects, slowly drains through to the ground water but away from our planting beds.

We'll talk a little bit about cisterns and rain barrels in a minute, but the idea is to collect water from hard surfaces, like your roof, collect it for times during drought, but keep it off of the garden where it tends to collect. Rain gardens are gardens that are designed to capture water running off of patios, decks, the roof. Run it through a garden with soil that's been amended, planted with plants that tolerate flooding and drought so that it slowly recharges the ground water and it's going where it's intended, not flooding out the other parts of your landscape. But before you do any of this, you always want to check with your municipality, because there may be some concerns or restrictions for redirecting or capturing water. And you also don't want to create a problem for your neighbors.

Now heavy rainfall and flooding, obviously, it causes excess moisture, but there's some other effects that we need to consider. The soil can be washed off or on to the roots of the trees and shrubs. So obviously, when the roots are exposed, they're more subject to drying, damage, and things like that. Excess soil piled over the roots impacts air flow to the roots and that can also kill the trees. For some species, as little as an inch of soil over the root system can kill them, so that's another downside.

Soil on the leaves. If you've seen trees and shrubs after a terrible flood, you'll see there's often a lot of debris on the leaves. That soil on the leaf blocks the sunlight and prevents photosynthesis. It doesn't allow the plants to capture the sunlight it needs to produce energy to grow and thrive. Now the plant's age is also something to consider as well. If you've got a mature, established plant, it's going to be OK. A young plant? More susceptible to damage. If your flood's a one-time event, most trees and shrubs will usually tolerate short periods under water, less than a week. The longer the period of flooding, the less likely they are to tolerate it. And if you have an area that's regularly flooded, avoid planting trees in this area. You want to manage that excess water in the ways we mentioned, with swales and French drains and other strategies. Again, checking with your municipality first.

I mentioned a couple of those plants that tolerate wet soils and flooding, but here are a few more. River birches have exfoliating bark. They're native to river basins, so they tolerate those wet conditions. Larches, which are deciduous conifers that have nice, delicate needles that drop off in fall. Bald cypress, you may know for their knees. In areas that are flooded, they tend to produce these knees, or woody protrusions from their root system, so that's a way they can capture oxygen. Red maples, I mentioned Alders, and even chockeberries and elder berries will take it a little wet.

Well let's look at the other extreme, insufficient water or drought conditions. We all know that water is essential for plant growth. Plants are made up of 80 percent or more of water, so they are needed for all the essential plant functions. But a lack of water can be caused by many other factors. You know it's a lack of water or rainfall, right? Warmer temperatures. So even if we're getting decent rain, if the temperatures are high and the winds are strong, it increases transpiration. And transpiration is what plants do. They lose moisture through the pores in their leaves. It's like sweating. OK, so if the winds come and blow that moisture off the leaves, as it transpires, they lose more.

If you've ever seen plants that don't tolerate the heat, you may notice they scorch. You water and water, but it seems like they just can't pull up enough water because they're losing it faster than they can absorb it. So higher temperatures, as I mentioned, increase also the energy that's produced and used; that means more water. So we want to keep all those factors in mind. If winds are an issue and you're getting a lot of drying and watering properly, maybe a wind break is the answer.

Maybe if you're seeing your plans wilt, again, it could be too much water, but it might also be insufficient water. But before you break out the watering can, wait. Plants often wilt and curl their leaves to conserve moisture. I often see plants look very wilted mid day, and by the time that temperature is reduced and the light's reduced, sun is setting, those leaves are opened back up. So often, that's a defense mechanism. So before you break out the sprinkler, check that out.

I mentioned scorch before, and that's really the leaf margins turning brown. And what happens is there's either not enough water, or as I mentioned before, the plants can't pull up enough; they lose that moisture; and often the leaf margin turns brown. Now, again, heat, wind, or a lack of moisture can cause that.

On evergreen's you'll often see brown needles, usually on the new growth from a lack of moisture, maybe on the windward side from wind damage. And you may see an increase in seasonal needle drop. Now seasonal needle drop is a normal occurrence. Evergreens lose their older needles. That's normal. The inside needles will yellow and brown when they are three, four, five years of age. But after an extreme drought or an insect infestation, they often drop more needles than usual. So it may be an indication there's a problem, or it could be seasonal needle drop, the normal amount. So always keep an eye on your plants. Start taking notes, and you'll be a better observer and better able to diagnose problems.

Now, drought stress symptoms often appear years after a drought, and that's kind of a tricky thing. We have an extreme drought, the trees survive, maybe don't look so good, but year two, three, or four, maybe they are attacked by bores, insects feeding under the bark. They can eventually kill them. Or maybe a disease, a deadly disease, moves in and finishes off that stressed plant. So managing water is very important.

So as you can see, drought is more than just a lack of water. It could be wind, it could be some of those other factors, like extreme heat. And getting to the cause will help you resolve the issue. And select drought tolerant plants as well. Look for heat hardiness as one of the other underlying issues. I mentioned that before, and those are plant's ability to tolerate temperatures over 86 degrees. So when you look at a heat hardiness rating for a plant done by the American Horticulture Society, you'll see that it says it'll tolerate x number of days. Make sure it matches those growing conditions in your area.

Now, heat and drought tolerant plants usually have smaller leaves with hairy or waxy coverings to help them conserve moisture. We're going to water right. We're going to mulch correctly. We'll talk more about this later. And set your priorities when water is limited. New plantings, moisture lovers like the birch, evergreens, especially prior to winter, and even mature trees during an extended drought, in that order is how we want to water them with drought-tolerant species being at the end.

Now, hot and dry conditions, we can conserve the moisture by amending the soil, adding compost or organic matter to the whole bed, not just the planting hole. And we can use mulches, as I mentioned earlier, to conserve that moisture. It also helps suppress weeds and improves soil over time.

But, you might want to do something like harvesting rain water. I mentioned rain harvesting earlier, and it's really a good way to collect water when it's abundant and then use it when it's lacking. But before you get a rain barrel or a cistern, check with your municipality. Rain harvesting is not allowed in some communities and states, so you want to make sure it's an OK thing to do. But on the other hand, many places are offering rebates or giving away rain barrels to help you install these systems. The idea is to keep it out of the storm sewer.

So let's take a look. I have a rain barrel here, and let's take a look at some of the things to look for, whether you're making your own or purchasing it. Make sure that your rain barrel has an overflow, because you're going to collect a lot of water in this rain barrel. Notice that it has a screen on top to help keep debris and insects out, and that's good for keeping that water flowing. You want to make sure the spigot is located low on your rain barrel, because that rain water is going to collect, and if it doesn't all empty, it stagnates, and it's not a good thing. We've also elevated our rain barrel, because they do empty by gravity. So you want to make sure you elevate it so it empties more efficiently. Also, it's easier to get the sprinkling can underneath there, or, hook up a hose so that you can then hook it up to a soaker hose and water gardens nearby.

Now, you can collect as much as 623 gallons of water from one inch of rain off of 1,000 square foot of roof. That's a lot of water, so you're going to want to set up your system so that it either overflows away from your house or into another rain barrel. When we collect water, we often worry about mosquitoes that love standing water. Fortunately, there's a good solution for that. It's a product called Bacillus thuringiensis israelensis. It's a bacteria that only kills the larva of mosquitoes, black flies, and fungus gnats, and we just can put one of these mosquito dunks or the flakes in our rain barrel. If there are mosquitoes that lay their eggs and the eggs hatch and turn to larva, they eat this and die. The good news. It won't hurt kids, pets, or your plants. It's totally organic and safe, so it's a great solution if you're worried about mosquitoes.

Now, cisterns are just larger forms of rain barrels that can be above or below ground. Both are ancient systems, and we're rediscovering them as we're trying to conserve our precious resource, water. Now, if you're really a sustainable gardener and you want to take it one step further, how about a five-gallon bucket. Very simple technology. Place this bucket under the faucet while you're waiting for the water to warm for your bath or shower, then use that water to water containers or plantings outside. It's a great and easy way to conserve water. Now you can also collect water dripping from the air conditioner or dehumidifier. I empty my dehumidifier every day and use it for containers indoors and out. It's simple, it's easy, it's a great way to recycle that water.

Well, we've explored some of the climatic challenges that our trees and shrubs face. Next session, we'll look at some of the things that people do that impact the health and beauty of our trees and shrubs.

Shopping for the Best Trees and Shrubs
Lesson 4

Going to the garden center and nursery can be overwhelming and tempting at the same time. So many plants to choose from—where do you begin? More important, where do you stop? Once you have your destination in mind, prepare for your shopping trip. Shopping without a plant list is like going to the grocery store hungry, and we all know that can be an expensive mistake. Make a list of plants you need or locations you want to fill. Make sure that the plants you choose are sound and healthy; transport and unload them carefully; and keep a record of what you bought, where you bought it, when and how you planted it, and how it thrived (or didn't).

Choose Your Destination

- Begin by deciding where to shop. Because most independent garden centers grow their own plants, they usually have a reasonably good selection of plants that perform well in your area.

- Nurseries are more focused on trees and shrubs, and if you are looking for something special, you may want to visit one near you. If the shrubs or trees have been locally grown, you know they will thrive in your growing conditions.

© moodboard/Thinkstock.

Independent garden centers often have well-trained staff who can help you make wise selections.

- Big-box stores offer discount prices because they usually buy plants in large quantities and sell them in stores across the country. That means that the plants may not be suited to your growing conditions, so be sure to check the tag. Always make sure that plants are in good health before purchasing, no matter where you shop.

- Mail order is becoming popular not just for bulbs but also for trees and shrubs. Because you're buying plants sight unseen, check the seller's customer satisfaction rating to make sure that other customers have been satisfied with the plants they received.

Prepare to Shop
- When you're making your plant list, consider the following:
  - Envision each plant's function: how you want to use it.

  - Weigh the growing conditions, including light, moisture, drainage, and soil.

  - Make sure the plants you choose are hardy.

  - Measure your available space and anticipate the size of full-grown plants.

- Avoid invasive plants. These are plants that were originally introduced because they were low maintenance, tolerated difficult situations, and performed well but then escaped the garden and invaded natural areas; honeysuckle is a good example.

- When selecting plants, consider the size as it relates to your budget and your ability to handle your selections if you plan to plant them yourself.
  - Because smaller plants are cheaper, you may be able to plant more at one time if you buy small and let them grow.

  - The size of the tree or shrub you're buying is a consideration because if you drop it and break the root ball, you'll end up with problems.

  - Often, a small plant put in at the same time as a larger one does better over time. The larger the plant, the larger the root system, which means that more roots are lost in transplanting. The root system in the smaller plant is less susceptible to damage in transplanting; thus, it grows stronger, larger, and better able to support the tree or shrub.

- Consider how the tree or shrub was grown: bare root, container grown, or containerized and balled in burlap.
  - ○ *Bare-root* plants are grown in the field. They are dug, the soil is removed, and they're transported immediately to you or placed in cold storage to ensure they stay dormant until they're ready for planting.

  - ○ Bare-root plants are challenging to manage because the roots can dry out quickly. You must keep them cool and moist. They are usually available only in the spring and for a very short period; once the temperature gets warm, the heat stresses the plant. Make sure you can get bare-root plants in the ground quickly or store them safely to ensure that they don't dry out. Most bare-root plants need staking because their root systems are so small they have trouble anchoring and supporting the top growth.

  - ○ *Container-grown* trees and shrubs are the most common in garden centers and nurseries. They're available throughout the season because they're potted, which means they're easy to water and maintain. One of the concerns about container-grown plants is girdling roots. This condition occurs when plants stay in a container too long, and the roots, constrained by the side of the pot, start growing in a circle.

  - ○ The other concern is that most container-grown plants are grown in soilless mixes of peat moss, bark, and vermiculite and perlite with no mineral matter; these mixes tend to dry out quickly. The interface between this mix at the root ball and your surrounding soil may mean that you need to water the root ball a little more frequently than the surrounding soil, especially if you have heavy clay.

o *Field-grown* trees and shrubs are dug, wrapped in burlap, and often placed in wire cages. Such "balled-and-burlapped" plants are very heavy to manage. Some species must be balled and burlapped to survive the transplanting process. They are typically dug in the spring, but they can be planted throughout the growing season because their roots are intact. When you see them in a nursery or garden center, you'll notice that the root base is buried in wood chips to keep it cool and moist. You'll need to do the same if you don't have time to plant your selection right away.

Examine Plant Purchases Thoroughly

- At the garden center or nursery, you want to make sure that plants are structurally sound and free of damage from insects, disease, or stress.

- If you're considering buying a tree, take a look at the trunk.
  o If the tree has been grafted, as is common with ornamentals, the graft should be aboveground.

  o The trunk should be straight and should lead to a single dominant trunk with one stem taller than the rest. If multiple stems are fighting to be the leader, you must prune early in the plant's life to select a leader. Otherwise, several branches will grow upright and have narrow crotch angles; when a storm comes through, the trunk will split.

- Check the leaves for signs of insect damage, which would be speckling, holes, or browning; disease, which would be spotted leaves and brown edges, as well as cankers or sunken or discolored areas on the stem; and stress. Avoid a plant with any of these signs.

- Look for clean pruning cuts and minimal branches growing into the center. Make sure that basic pruning has been done during growth and development.

- Look at the base of the plant to make sure that the stems are evenly distributed; as the plant gets larger, the stems should grow outward, not crossing, bending, or rubbing, which will create future problems. Look for limited breakage, which tells you that the plant or shrub has been handled properly.

Transport and Unload Carefully

- Transporting plants is as important as buying healthy ones. You don't want to spend time and money picking out a great tree and ruin it on the ride home. Transporting plants can be more challenging than you think. Nursery staff will often gather the plants, put them on a tractor or skid loader, and load them for you.
  - You need a large vehicle—a pickup truck or a trailer—if you plan to transport trees or large plants yourself. Do not cram a large plant into a small space. The branches will break and you will damage the plant.

  - Bring some tarps to line your trunk or truck bed to keep the soil contained.

  - Wrap the trunk with carpet or some other fabric or material to protect the plant from damage as you're moving. Secure it in place using bungee cords or tarps.

  - Wrap the leaves. If you don't, the wind will dry them out, and they'll brown and die. Evergreens lose moisture through the needles, so make sure to wrap those, too.

  - If the plants will extend beyond the back of your vehicle by more than 3 feet, hang a red tag for safety's sake.

- Unloading a tree requires help. If you try to do it on your own, chances are you'll drop it, break it, or damage it.
  - One way to unload is to slide the tree or shrub down a ramp, either into a wheelbarrow or right into the planting hole.

- If you have someone to help you manage the root ball and tree, you may want to lift it into a wheelbarrow and wheel it to the planting site.

- Other ingenious moving strategies include pot lifters, which are straps that go around the plant with handles on each end for lifting, or a child's snow saucer that you can drag.

- You may decide it's worth paying the nursery to deliver your plant: Nursery staffers are experienced and have the right equipment for the job.

Protect before Planting

- Once your plants are unloaded, give them proper care until you can plant them. Store them in a sheltered location.

- If they're bare root, dig a trench, set the roots in place, and cover them temporarily to keep them from drying out. This is called *heeling in.* Even though the roots are covered, you must water them often enough to keep the soil moist.

- If you have a balled-and-burlapped plant, keep the root ball moist; cover it with wood chips to reduce the frequency of watering.

- Treat container plants from the nursery as you would container plants you already own. Check the soil daily and water thoroughly whenever the soil is slightly moist and crumbling.

Keep a Garden Journal

- A garden journal is a record of your plants: where you purchased them, when you planted them, and whether or not they thrived; insect or disease problems; droughts or floods; and extreme temperatures. It's a place to record the planting and care of your garden.

- Keeping a journal is especially useful if you're starting a new landscape, but even if you're just adding a few new plants, start a journal now. Use whatever method feels right for you and that you will maintain:
    - Use your cell phone to take pictures and record information in the notes.

    - Buy a spiral notebook to jot down information.

    - Create a spreadsheet on your computer.

    - Inspire yourself to keep records by buying a beautiful book.

    - Keep your tags in a three-ring binder, using page protectors to keep them in place. Some gardeners tape or staple tags to a page, along with information about each particular plant.

Questions to Consider

1. How do you decide where to shop for plants? What is the difference between a nursery and a garden center?

2. What is a plant list, and why should you make one?

3. List four factors to consider before buying a plant.

Shopping for the Best Trees and Shrubs
Lesson 4—Transcript

Now that you've taken a close look at the growing conditions and decided how to use those trees and shrubs to create a landscape that's functional and beautiful and that long-lasting framework, it's time to go shopping. And going to the garden center and nursery can be overwhelming and very tempting all at the same time. So many plants to choose from, where do you begin? And more importantly, where do you stop?

We'll first start by deciding where to shop. Most independent garden centers have a decent selection of plants that perform well in your area. They also have staff quite often trained to assist you in your selection process. Nurseries are more focused on trees and shrubs. Many of them grow their own, and so that gives you a wider selection. So if you're looking for something special, you may want to visit a local nursery as well. And, if they've been grown in the area, you know they'll thrive in your growing conditions.

Now, big box stores offer discount prices; they usually buy in large quantities, and so they buy a large number of plants that are sold throughout their stores across the country. And so that means they may or may not be suited to your growing conditions, so check the tag. And often, they have limited resources to take care of the plants properly, so you always want to make sure the plant is in good health before purchasing, no matter where you shop.

Now, mail order is becoming more and more popular, not just for bulbs, but also for trees and shrubs. Now, you can find more unusual plants when shopping online, and they're not always bare root. They may even be grown in a container, in a pot, and sent through the mail. So you want to check their customer service satisfaction rating, however, to make sure that other customers have been satisfied with the plants they received, only because you can't see them in person, which makes shopping a little more challenging.

Now, once you have your destination, or in my case, it's usually multiple destinations, in mind, you need to prepare. Now, be sure you have your list of plants you need or locations you want to fill, because shopping without a plant list is like going to the grocery store hungry. Now, let's just take a few minutes to review factors to consider when selecting a tree or shrub. As we mentioned before, plant function, how do you want to use it? Are you looking for something that's going to screen a bad view, so you want multiple stems. Or are you looking for something you could look under to see the neighbor's perennial garden? And what are those growing conditions that you have in that location? How much light, moisture? Make sure it's hardy. What's the soil like? And don't forget about the size.

Measure and do another accounting of the available space. You know, guessing isn't always a good idea, because once that plant gets home and in the ground, you don't want to find out it's not suited for that area. And the other thing you're going to want to do is check about with your utility companies. But you want to look above for any overhead lines, and also reconfirm where those underground utilities are. And since you can't see them, one of the things you're going to want to do is call the free utility locating service available across the country. In the U.S. you call 811; in Canada, it's One Call, and they'll mark the underground utilities with flags like this. It takes them several days, so call ahead. A good thing to do before you go shopping, maybe even before you put your plan in place, because then you know what spaces to avoid.

Now, once you're at the store, you can reconfirm your plant selection. You know, I often change my mind once I see what's available, or if something isn't available. And I always double-check the tag, because there's so many new varieties out there, it's hard to keep track. So you're going to want to check the tag for size, growing conditions, hardiness, and just reconfirm that the plant you choose will fit that location and also so that it will grow in your area. So you might check that, too, as well.

And avoid invasive plants when you're shopping. This happens because plants were introduced that were low maintenance, they tolerated difficult situations, and they were great performers. Sound too good to be true? Well, it was. Many of them escaped the gardener landscape and invaded our natural areas. Things like Buckthorn and Honeysuckle and Tree of Heaven left the garden and now are taking over our woodlands and wetlands, and crowding out our native plants. And that's bad for the whole ecosystem, because that's the food and habitat for many of our native birds and water fowl and other wildlife. So we want stop planting those.

Some are banned for sale, so that takes that choice away. Others are on a watch list. And invasiveness varies with location, so you're going to want to check with some local sources or online. And one good example is the Butterfly bush; it's invasive in some parts of the world, and barely survives in others, like my garden—short-lived, doesn't reseed, doesn't cause a problem. But where does, it's crowding out the native plants. Now, some gardeners choose not to buy these plants, even if it's not a problem in their location. They don't want to support or encourage nurseries to grow plants that are invasive in other areas or perhaps even where they're raising them.

Now the good news? Breeders are working on developing noninvasive varieties of Butterfly bush, like Lo and Behold, the blue chip series of Butterfly bush. It's a plant that's a little smaller, does not reseed, and has actually been cleared for areas where Butterfly bush was banned. So keep a watch out for varieties of your favorite plants that may be invasive, but new introductions that aren't.

Now there are few others to watch. Buckthorn and Honeysuckle, both shrubs that have gone into our woodlands and crowded things out. They leaf out early, hold their leaves later, so that gives them an advantage over our native plants. Tree of Heaven is the tree you often see in urban areas, lots of seeds produced, grows just about anywhere, cracks in sidewalks and the like. So you can guess, it's very invasive. Nandina, Broom, and Multiflora rose are just a few others to consider.

So what are you to do? Well, check the tag again. If it sounds too good to be true, it probably is. If it says spreads rapidly, grows just about anywhere, flowers readily, might be something to give a second look. Do a bit more research if you're not sure. Ask the sales clerk or go online. It may not be invasive, but it may be aggressive, meaning it grows and spreads and fills in the garden, crowding out the more timid plants it shares its space with. So even though it's not invasive, it's not leaving the garden and invading our native spaces, it's just crowding out its neighbors, it may be a plant that you want to take a pass on. Why? Because you'll spend a lot of time weeding it out, pruning it out, and doing a lot of work to keep it in check. So, save yourself some work in the end. Well, there's lots of helpful sites, as I mentioned, so just do an Internet search; type in the plant of concern; or maybe ask for a list of invasive plants.

When you're at the garden center, you want to take a close look at the plant. You want to remember that this Forsythia that's only a couple feet tall right now is going to grow eight feet tall when it's mature. That's a big difference. So you want to make sure that it's not in front of a window, it doesn't a block a view, but it serves a purpose in your landscape. Now, this is a good graphic of looking at mature tree sizes. It gives you an idea of where they fit in relationship to a house and each other, so you may want to take a look at that. You may, again, want to look online, and, again, start visualizing how tall and wide that plant's going to be.

Now remember the strategies we discussed in Lesson 1 on how to create quick impact while maintaining the long-term health and beauty of your trees and shrubs. This may help quell that need to over buy and cram lots of plants in to get quick results. Now, when selecting plants, you also need to consider the size as it relates to your budget, OK? Smaller plants are cheaper, so you may be able to plant more at one time if you buy smaller and let them grow. Plus, you get the enjoyment of watching that tiny little plant grow into a bigger plant.

Also, make sure that you can manage it if you plan to plant it yourself. I have this beautiful candymint crab that I bought for my now ex-husband. And we went to the nursery, a former student gave us a great deal. So that tree we bought had a 2½-inch diameter trunk at 4½-feet high, very big tree, very big root ball, and very heavy. And two plant people trying to plant a tree in a small front yard was pretty entertaining. We ended up rigging up a ramp to slide it down and put it in place. It was heavy for us, and I was much younger then. So make sure that you can manage the size of the tree or shrub that you're buying. Big consideration, because if you drop the plant, break the root ball, you're going to end up with problems.

And from a plant-health standpoint, bigger isn't always better. Instant results you'll get with larger plants. They'll be big when you buy them, but they kind of stay that size over a long period of time. Plus it's a huge shock—the bigger the plant, the bigger the root system, so more roots were lost during transplanting. So what you'll find often is we put a small plant in at the same time as one that's larger in diameter, and guess what, at the end of five, or six, or seven years, they're the same size. But the root system in the smaller one is much better. It's larger, better able to handle and support that tree. So starting small, as you can see by this diagram, really pays off in the long run. If you want instant results, you can get them with bigger plants, just remember, good TLC and patience are needed no matter what size you start with.

Now trees and shrubs are available bare root, container grown, or containerized and balled in burlap. Now, bare-root plants are grown in the field. They're dug up, the soil is removed, and they're transported immediately to you, the end result, or stored over winter in cold storage. And that way, they stay dormant until they're ready for planting. Now, they are usually only available in the spring, most of the time, and for a very short period of time.

Now, bare root are less expensive, so that's a good thing, lighter to maneuver, and once we plant our balled and burlap tree, you may go, hmm, not a bad idea. But they're a little more challenging to manage; there's no soil on those roots, so those roots will dry out quickly. You must keep them cool and moist. So when you buy bare root, you need to make sure you can get them in the ground or store them safely so that they don't dry out. They're not as forgiving once planted. Remember, very small root system to support that plant. So, you will have to give them extra special attention to make sure they get sufficient water, important for any tree and shrub you plant, but especially so for bare root. Most of them will need staking, because they've got a very small root system that's really hard for them to anchor in and support the top growth, so you need to be prepared to do that.

Some trees and some shrubs are field-grown, dug, wrapped in burlap, and often placed in a wire cage, and those are called balled and burlap. And those trees are very heavy to manage. Some species need to be balled and burlapped to survive the transplanting process, and so that's why you'll see some in containers and some that are balled in burlap. They tend to be more expensive. They're heavier to move—very heavy to move—and typically dug in the spring, but they can be planted throughout the growing season, because they've got their roots intact. When you go to a nursery or garden center, you'll often see that balled-and-burlap root base buried in wood chips to keep it cool and moist, and you'll need to do the same if you buy it and don't have time to plant it right away.

Now, there's some great debate about removing burlap and cages, and we'll talk a little bit more about this when we actually plant a few trees. Container-grown trees and shrubs are probably the most common that you see in garden centers and nurseries. They're usually a lot easier to handle. They're usually smaller pots one or two people can carry, and so that makes them easier for you to manage. They're available throughout the season because they're in a pot, easy to water, easy to maintain. But, just like any of the others, you need to keep them watered. But because they're in the soil and they've been grown in there, they're a little more forgiving. They're moderately priced, and so that makes them an affordable option for many people.

One of the concerns we have about container-grown plant is girdling roots. When plants stay in a container too long, the roots hit the side of the pot and start growing in a circle. And even though we're putting them in the ground, they continue to grow into a circle unless we do something about it. So let's take a look at the roots here. So you can see we've got lots of nice, white, healthy roots. And we've got one that's just starting to circle around the pot. This really isn't too bad, and we can easily fix that before we put it in the ground. And we'll show you how to do that at planting.

So, we want to check for that at planting time, but just want to make you aware. Now the other concern we have is most of these plants are grown in soilless mixes, meaning there's no mineral matter; it's peat moss, and bark, and vermiculite or perlite. Now, that dries how quickly. It's like a container mix versus the surrounding soil. So that interface between this, where the root ball is, and your surrounding soil may mean you need to adjust your watering a bit, watering the root ball a little more frequently than the surrounding soil, especially if you have heavy clay.

Now, plants that are containerized or potted, those are plants that were bare root, maybe received by the garden center or nursery, potted up, maybe in late winter, grown for a couple of months, and sold in the spring. They don't have time to develop a root system that fills that container, so you're going to need to handle that carefully, slice away the pot when you do your planting. And I'll show you that in just a little bit.

Now, the selection process isn't quite over. We want to make sure that those plants are structurally sound. So let's take a look at this dogwood. One of the things when we're looking at trees is we want to take a look at the trunk. This tree has been grafted, and that's very common with ornamental trees. One of the things they do with ornamental trees in the nursery is something like this Variegated dogwood tends to be a little slower, or maybe we don't have as much plant material to start new plants. So to speed up the process, they'll take a piece, or a bud, or something like that from the desired plant, in this case, the Variegated dogwood, and graft it to a hardy root system. That graft should be above ground. We also want to look at the trunk, nice and straight.

And, it should lead into a one, single dominated trunk with one central leader. And that means one stem that's taller than the rest. Now, if you take a look at that, this isn't quite the case here. We've got multiple stems fighting to be the leader. Now, it's not too bad as long as you do some pruning early in this plant's life so that we have one main leader. If we don't, we'll have several branches growing upright, and what happens there is those branches are co-dominant leaders, they have narrow crotch angles, so when a storm comes through, it splits apart. So, during pruning, we can correct this. Not too bad, just keep that on your list.

The other thing you want to look for are wide crotch angles. Now, this tree tends to have somewhat narrow crotch angles, and you want to make sure we have a lot that are evenly distributed. So, because it's opposite, meaning leaves and stems come opposite, the branches are opposite, but then the next set are up further. We want to make sure they're somewhat evenly spaced going up the trunk of the tree.

Then we're going to check the leaves. Make sure they're good and healthy. Any signs of insect, disease, or stress, we'll want to avoid that plant. Look for good, clean pruning cuts, proper pruning cuts, we'll learn more about that later, so that they're getting that tree off to a good start. And minimal branches growing into the center, we want to make sure that basic pruning has been done during the growth and development of this tree, because we want it off to a good start before we start growing.

Now let's take a look at the shrub. Some similar things, we want to make sure the leaves are good and healthy, nice and dark green, free of insect and disease damage. But we also want to take a look at the base of the plant. So we want to make sure that those stems are evenly distributed, because as the plant grows, we want to make sure it's growing outward, not crossing, not bending, not rubbing, creating future problems. Again, we're going to look for good cuts by the nursery. Limited breakage, because if there's a limited breakage, it means that they've been handled properly and don't really cause a problem. So we want to make sure those pruning cuts have been made properly in the nursery. That's a good indication of care, as well.

In addition to checking the structure, we also want to make sure that the plants are healthy. And I mentioned a few things to look for, but just a bit of a review. Make sure the plants are free of pests—insects and diseases. Look for signs of insect damage, which would be speckling of the leaves, maybe a lot of holes in the leaves, browning as well. Look for signs of disease, spotted leaves and brown edges; that can indicate a disease problem. And brown edges, as we've already learned, can mean too much or not enough water, which means no proper care or insufficient care, so avoid those plants. Cankers or sunken or discolored areas on the stem, that could be a serious disease problem. Any other signs that the plants haven't been handled well means you should leave them at the garden center, or the big box store, or wherever you're shopping, and look for something healthier.

And, when you're transporting the tree, it's just as important as buying a healthy tree. You don't want to spend all that time and money picking out a great tree and ruin it on the ride home. So once you've made your selection, we're going to need to get these big plants home, which can be a little more challenging than you think. You're going to need a large vehicle, a pickup truck or a trailer if you plan to transport it yourself. The last thing you want to do is cram a big plant into a small space. Again, you'll break branches, damage this tree or shrub that you so carefully selected. Consider bringing some tarps to keep things clean. You can line your trunk, line your back of your pickup truck or whatever, and keep the soil out of the car or out of the area. I like to use an old child's swimming pool. When I'm buying lots of small shrubs, I stick that in the back of my car, and then I can pop them in there so the soil stays contained.

Now, at the nursery, they often load the plants. They'll often go gather the plants and put them on their tractor or their skid loader and bring it out to the yard for you to load. And many times, they'll load them for you. As you can see here, these trees were carefully lifted to safely put them in and load them and bring them to the homeowners here. They loaded them into the back of the pickup truck for them, as well. So hopefully you'll go to a nursery that does the same for you.

But whether they're loading the tree or you're loading it, a couple things to keep in mind. Wrap the trunk. You want to make sure that that trunk, if it's leaning up against the back of your pickup or trailer or the trunk of your car, wrap it with carpet or some other fabric or material so that if it does bounce on the trunk of the tree, that it doesn't damage or doesn't rub as you're moving. Secure it in place. You may want to use bungee cords or tarps to do that, as well. And then, make sure to wrap the leaves. If the plant has leafed out already, you want to make sure that you wrap those leaves. The worst thing I hate to see is a tree standing up in a pickup truck, fully leafed out, going down the freeway. All the wind is drying out those leaves, and they'll end up browning out and drying up and dying. So wrap those up, and keep them in control. So you want to make sure that they're protected. Same goes with evergreens. Those needle plants loose lots of moisture through the needles, so you want to make sure to wrap those too. Give them plenty of room. Cramming several plants into a small space can end up in some breakage in branches, so you want to wrap them; you want to move them so that you have the least amount of damage. If the plants are going to hang over the end of your vehicle by more than three feet, you need to hang a red tag over it for safety's sake.

Now, unloading your tree is just as important. And guess what? You won't have the help of equipment and the nursery workers to get it out of your vehicle and into the planting hole. So a couple things you want to keep in mind. When you're unloading that tree, ask for some help. Don't be embarrassed to go to your neighbor or friend and get some help, because you don't want to drop or drag that plant. You spent a lot of money; you're investing in the future; and if you try to do this on your own, chances are you'll drop it, break it, or damage it.

Now you can slide it down a ramp, like you see here. That's one way of getting that big tree out of the pickup truck, just kind of slide it down. That's what we ended up doing with our candymint crabapple. It was too big for the two of us to do. And you can see that works quite nicely. You may back your pickup truck right to the planting hole and slide it in place, or slide it into a wheelbarrow.

If you can manage that plant, that root ball, and tree, and you've got a good, strong friend to help, you may want to lift it off the tailgate or out of the trailer and set it into a wheelbarrow, and then wheel it to the planting site. A lot of it depends on what that space is. If you're in a small, tight city lot, like I used to live, I didn't have much room to negotiate big equipment or vehicles in my yard, and really had to use a lot of ingenious ways to move big plants. Pot lifters or an old child's saucer works great, too. Pot lifters are devices that use straps to go around the plant, whether it's a pot or balled and burlap, handles on either end so you can haul that to the next spot. An old child's snow saucer works great. You can set the tree there and drag it across to the planting site. Either way, it works quite well to get the plant from your vehicle safely to the planting hole.

Now, after listening to all this and watching this heavy duty work, you may decide it's worth paying the nursery to deliver your plant. They're experienced; they have the equipment to do it right. So considering paying that extra delivery charge; it's a good insurance policy. They'll get your tree there safely to your home. And most places offered two options. One, they'll deliver the plant and plant it for you, so you don't have to do any of the digging. The other option is you prepare the planting hole, they deliver it, often set it in the planting hole for you, and you finish off the job. Either way, it's a great way to get your plant in place with a little less back-breaking work on your part.

Now, once your tree's at home, you're going to need to give it proper care until you're able to plant it. Often, you go shopping, you buy lots of plants, and something comes up, and you can't get them in the ground. Not a problem as long as you store them properly. So store those plants in a sheltered location. Make sure that if they're bare root, they need to be heeled in. And heeled in means you're going to dig a trench, set those roots in place, and cover them temporarily. And that's just to keep them from drying out. Now if you have a balled and burlap plant, you're going to want to keep that root ball moist, so cover it with wood chips to reduce the frequency of watering needed. And for your container plants, treat them just like your other container plants. Water thoroughly whenever that soil is slightly moist and crumbling, so check it daily. Water as needed. And don't forget about those bare-root plants that you have heeled in. Even though the roots are covered, you're going to need to water them often enough to keep that soil moist. So water is important.

Now, whether you planted your trees and shrubs right away, or you heeled in your bare-root plants, or you've got them stored somewhere safe, now is a good time to start a journal. Now, if you don't know what a garden journal is, it's basically a place to record plants, when you plant them; where you purchased them; how those plants did; any significant happenings; insect and disease problems; any weather occurrences, droughts and floods and extreme heat or extreme cold. It's just a place to record your planting and care of your garden, and this is a great time to start, especially if you're starting a new landscape. But even if you're just adding a few new plants, start a journal now. Many ways you can do it. A spiral notebook, take notes. Use your cell phone and take pictures and record information in the notes. How about on a spreadsheet on your computer? Or maybe you prefer a beautiful book so you're inspired to keep the records.

I always keep my tags. I often use a three-ring binder and use page protectors to put the tags in place. Some gardeners will tape or staple them to the page with information about that particular plant. So think about a system that works for you, something that you're going to keep up with. Now, Thomas Jefferson kept a journal of his gardening activities for more than 50 years, and he recorded every plant he put in and took out of his garden, when he planted, where he purchased it, how it did, and why it died. Now, I probably got 12 years under my belt, and probably not 12 total years, but I keep trying. And the older I get, and the worse my memory, the more important those notes are to keep. It can help guide you through future plantings, help you replace things as needed, and it's good information to pass along. Now, in our next session, we'll help you get your newly purchased plants, trees, and shrubs properly planted to ensure they provide years of beauty.

Planting Your Trees and Shrubs
Lesson 5

There's an old saying that you'll have better results planting a $10 tree in a $100 hole than a $100 tree in a $10 hole. The point is that planting correctly is as important as selecting the best tree or shrub for your landscape. Before you do any planting, call the free utility-locating service in your area at least three business days in advance. These services locate the below-ground utilities to make sure you avoid hitting gas, electric, phone, or cable lines when planting. In this lesson, we'll look at a number of other important considerations for planting, including timing and positioning.

Time Your Planting
- Timing is an issue for various types of nursery stock:
    - Bare-root plants usually go in at the start of the spring growing season. Try to get a bare-root plant in the ground as soon as you purchase it.

    - Some balled-and-burlapped trees can be dug in fall, and you can plant right away if they are properly mulched in wood chips.

    - Container plantings can be planted whenever you buy them or, if you've heeled them, whenever the ground is workable.

- Planting time can also vary with the type of plant, but because some are slow to put down new roots, they do better if they're planted in spring. Evergreens, for example, benefit from early-season planting because they lose moisture from their needles throughout the year; spring planting gives them time to get established before the winter.

- In areas with very hot summers, fall planting is best. The upper Midwest is a good example. In Milwaukee, research demonstrated that fall planting resulted in a better survival rate, probably because the weather was cooler, the soil was warmer, and the plants got established before winter.

Dig a Proper Hole

- Whenever you're planting a tree, find the root flare—the area where the trunk turns into roots and flares out like the bottom of a bell jar. Make sure that this area is at or slightly above the soil surface. That's important because the area above is trunk issue, and it's designed to be aboveground, not buried with the roots below ground. If you plant trees too deep, several serious problems can occur:

  ○ The tree may get root rot because the trunk is underground.

  ○ Deep planting encourages girdling roots that encircle and expand, choke the tree, stop the flow of water and nutrients from the roots to the top, cause dieback, and shorten the life of the tree.

  ○ Deeply planted trees are also susceptible to frost cracks, which occur when the south or west side of a tree is exposed to sunlight in the winter. The deep roots are frozen, but when the side of the trunk heats up during the day, the cells become active; when the side rapidly cools at night, the cells break and eventually crack.

- Measure the distance from the bottom of the root ball to the root flare. This will be the depth of your planting hole. Don't dig deeper. If you do, the soil will settle and your tree will be planted too deep.

- Dig your hole wide, preferably three to five times wider than the root ball, but at least twice its width.

  ○ Drive a post in the ground where you want the center of the hole to be.

  ○ Make a loop at the end of a ball of string and attach it to the post.

  ○ Pull the string out from the post to a distance of twice the width of the root ball and use marking paint to mark the perimeter. That way, you know the hole is centered properly.

- Rough in the sides of your planting hole. This step is especially important when you're working in clay soil or moist soil, because when soil compacts, the roots are unable to penetrate it, and they grow in a circle instead of exploring the soil beyond.

Situate the Tree Correctly
- Once the hole is ready for planting, select the best side to face the tree to its advantage. You may want to remove the tags now, especially if it's a tall tree. On a shorter tree, you can wait until it's in the hole, but either way, be sure to take the tags off and save them.

- Ask for help when planting larger trees to avoid damaging the tree and yourself. Root balls can be very heavy, and an extra set of hands can be useful. If a strong friend isn't available, look for a garden cart, a pot lifter, or an old saucer sled to help you drag and slide the tree into place.

- When you move a tree, move it by the root ball, not the trunk, and roll it in place. Hold onto the trunk for guidance but don't drag the tree by the trunk. That's very important: Using the trunk for leverage damages the roots.

- For balled-and-burlapped trees, cut off the bottom of the wire basket before setting the tree in the hole. If the root ball is crumbly and you are worried about keeping it intact, you can keep the bottom of the basket and compensate by removing the top of the basket and folding the bottom down. Because most of the roots are in the top 12 to 18 inches of soil, the basket will be out of the way. Remove the top part of the burlap, again folding it down below the root ball. That way, you can be sure that the roots won't stop growing.
  - Make sure you cut away any girdling roots. They will continue to grow and encircle the root ball if you don't prune them away or loosen them with a cultivator.

○ Water thoroughly. Some people water halfway through the planting: They backfill the hole with soil, water to help with settling, set the tree, and then fill the hole and water again. The key is making sure you have no air pockets; backfill with the existing soil, water thoroughly, and mulch.

○ Add a 2- to 3-inch layer of wood chips or shredded bark to help conserve moisture and keep grass away from the trunk. Be sure you don't pile the mulch over the trunk of the tree because mounting mulch can lead to adventitious roots and rot, which can shorten the lifespan of your tree.

• When planting a container-grown plant, prepare the hole the same way. Check for the root flare or, in the case of shrubs, the crown—the point where the roots meet the stem. That area should be at or slightly above the soil surface.

○ To remove a shrub from a pot, you can either roll the pot on the ground to help loosen the roots and then slide the plant out or remove the bottom of the pot, put the pot in the hole, and slice the side so you can peel it off. You definitely don't want to pull the shrub out by the stems.

© christingasner/iStock/Thinkstock.

Once the hole is ready, take a good look at the tree to determine its best face, then position it to take advantage of that view.

○ Again, look for, loosen, and remove any girdling roots.

- Bare-root plants may offer you a better choice, especially if your budget is limited. And if you're working alone, bare-root plants are much lighter. But you must be meticulous about their care.
  - Dig a hole large enough that you can spread out the roots to enable them to grow away from the trunk of the tree or shrub.

  - Prune off any broken, girdling, or damaged roots.

  - Make sure that the root flare is at or slightly above the soil surface.

- Many trees are grafted, especially ornamental and fruit trees, so make sure that you're lining up the root flare, not the graft. Depending on where you live, you may plant the graft above, at, or below the soil surface.
  - If temperatures in your area stay above 10 degrees, plant the graft 2 inches above the soil surface.

  - If winter temperatures range between 0 and 10 degrees, plant at the soil surface.

  - In much colder areas, plant the graft 2 inches below the soil surface to protect the graft.

Fertilizing, Pruning, and Staking
- Wait a year to fertilize. If you use high-nitrogen, fast-release fertilizer at planting, you can damage young, developing roots. Further, this fertilizer stimulates top growth, but what you want is root growth and development.

- Wait a couple of years to do major pruning, as well. The top growth has energy-producing leaves that help the tree develop and establish, and you don't want to prune those too soon. Remove only broken, damaged, or rubbing branches at planting, and wait a few more years to prune for structure.

- Staking is generally neither needed nor recommended because it can interfere with the normal development of a tree. The part of the tree above the stake moves more freely in the wind, which makes the trunk increase in girth. The portion beneath the stake doesn't grow at the same rate, which means that the tree will become top heavy and fall over when the stake is removed. Stake trees only in the following circumstances:
  - Stake when the tree is bare root and in need of support because of its small root system.

  - Stake trees with large canopies and small root systems.

  - Stake young trees exposed to high winds, traffic, and pedestrians to provide stability.

- If you must stake a tree, dig the hole wide and shallow, set the tree in place, and remove the burlap and wire cage. Pound the stakes deep into undisturbed soil so that they will be sturdy and hold on to the tree. Run canvas strips around the trunk and wire through the rivets. Never put wire through hose and wrap it around the trunk. Leave stakes in place for 1 year and definitely no more than 2 years. Remove as soon as possible.

Questions to Consider

1. How can you avoid severing a gas, electric, phone, or cable line when planting?

2. How can you use the root flare to calculate how deep to plant a tree?

3. What are two or more things that may happen if a tree is planted too deeply, and why?

Planting Your Trees and Shrubs
Lesson 5—Transcript

There's an old saying, and it goes something like this: You'll have better results planting a $10 tree in a $100 hole than a $100 tree in a $10 hole. While inflation may have changed the rates, and I think the real answer is $100 tree in a $100 hole, but the point is, planting correctly is as important as selecting the best tree or shrub for your landscape.

Now, before you do any planting, call the utility locating service in your area. In the United States, you're going to call 811 or One Call in the various provinces of Canada. And this service exists around the world. So call first. These services locate the below-ground utilities so you can avoid hitting gas, electric, phone, or cable lines when planting. Now, the good news is the services are for free, so you have no excuse not to call. Just call at least three business days in advance. They need about that much time for the crews to come out and mark the lines on your property. And those marks are good for about 10 days, so timing is somewhat critical. And if there's no conflict of where you want to plant and utility, they usually put a big OK at the spot so you know it's safe to go ahead and plant.

Now, calling in advance can save you money, because it's very expensive if you hit a line directly. And obviously, it can be deadly if you hit gas or electric, so call first. And saving money is what happened to me. When I was with the City of Milwaukee Forestry, we had a crew hit a fiber-optic line. Now, believe me, it's an expensive proposition. So when the crew called in, they said we have bad news and good news. I asked for the bad news first. They hit the line. The good news? It was mismarked. We weren't responsible for that big bill, which would have been thousands of dollars. So save yourself some money and take care of your health and safety by calling first.

Timing is also an issue when we're planting. There's various types of nursery stock that we've talked about before, and timing influences that. So if it's bare root, we usually plant at the start of the season. As I mentioned, they're dug and available immediately or in cold storage. But as soon as you purchase, try to get it in the ground. That's usually spring, the start of the growing season. Balled and burlapped trees are usually dug in spring.

Some can be dug in fall, and, they're placed in the nursery, and you can plant right away. Or, if they're held properly—mulched in wood chips either at the nursery, garden center, or your backyard—you can plant any time during the growing season.

Now, container plantings? Any time you can find container plants and they're available for purchase or you've heeled them in your backyard and the ground is workable, you can plant. Planting time can also vary with the type of plant you're growing. Some plants don't tolerate fall planting. They're slow to put down new roots, so, they do better if they're planted in spring. Now, I understand as a gardener, you may want to get that special deal on that fall sale and give it a shot. But if you have a choice, here are some trees that you want to consider, Red maples, birches, many of your fruit trees. Crabapples tend to be a little bit slower to put down their roots. Planting in the spring will give you that added advantage. Evergreens or borderline hardy plants benefit from early-season planting. I gives them a little more time to get established before the harsh winter because evergreens lose moisture from their needles throughout the year, even when the roots are frozen in the ground. So getting them a head start on the cold winter season will help.

Now those of you with the other extreme, hot Summers, may find that fall planting is your best bet. By planting in the fall, the soil is warm, the air is cool, and you have the mild winter for those plants to establish. Now, we also found this to be the case when I was at the City of Milwaukee as the assistant city forester. We kind of did a little bit of research on our planting, and we looked at our planting and survival rates from spring and fall. And one of the things that we found is that we had a higher survival rate in fall. And I think it had to do with a couple things, better whether, warmer soil, cooler air, and the plants got established before winter. And most importantly, our crew was happy. The weather was better, and if you feel comfortable planting, you're going to take your time and do a better job.

Now, let's walk through this process. When I planted a tree at my home, we picked an Ohio Buckeye. It was in memory of my mother, who passed away. And being from Ohio, the state tree—an Ohio Buckeye—seemed most appropriate. I picked a homestead variety. It's got excellent fall color, produces a little bit of fruit but not too much. I didn't mind the fruit because I have a lot of wildlife on my property that can enjoy it and help me clean it up.

We placed it near the place that I have for my grandkids so that it would be a little bit of shade for them and also a good memory and a tie to their great grandmother. We also wanted to block the view from the residential area over the hill. So as that tree grows and matures, we won't even notice the houses over that direction. And we placed it safely out of the way of the future sledding hill for my grandkids and me to enjoy, so we're sure we don't hit the tree on our way down the hill. So placement is important, but getting it in the ground was also an important consideration.

Whenever you're planting a tree, and in this case, we were planting a balled and burlapped tree, we need to find the root flare. And the root flare is the area where the trunk turns into roots, and it flares out. And we want to make sure that this area is at or slightly above the soil surface. And that's important, because the area above is trunk issue, and it's been developed, it's designed by the plant to be above ground, not buried below ground. And we want the roots below ground. Now, as you walk through the woods, you probably noticed this is how nature plants her trees. You'll see that root flare. You'll trip over those roots as you walk down the path, and that way, you know the tree's at the right height. That's what you're going for.

Now, if we plant our trees too deep, what happens is, not only will we get root rot because the trunk is underground, but it also encourages girdling roots. Those roots grow around as the trunk expands, the roots expand, it chokes the tree, stops the flow of water and nutrients from the roots to the top, and you end up getting die back, and it shortens the life of the tree.

Now, I went out with the crew from Wachtel Tree Science and Service, and we took a look at what was going underground with this Norway Maple. It was planted too deep. Now that was a common practice 30 some years ago. One is they thought if we plant it deep, we won't deal with those surface roots. Also, then we thought, OK, we'll plant it the depth at the nursery only to find that with different practices in the nursery, that root flare ended up being buried. So what happened is the folks at Wachtel Tree Science and

Service came out, used an air excavation tool to uncover and alleviate some of the girdling roots that resulted from deep planting of that Norway Maple. And you could see that that excavator blew the air away from the roots, exposing the roots so they could see what was going on underneath the ground without harming the tree. And then you can see some of those roots girdling. Later we'll check in with them and see how they alleviated the problem, but this is a great reminder to plant with the root flare at or slightly above the soil surface.

Now Norway Maples are particularly sensitive to deep planting and girdling root problems, so proper planting is even more critical for them. But it's critical for any plant, because when the trees are planted too deep, not only do we have problems with girdling roots, we also have problems with adventitious roots. Those are roots that develop from the root flare up along the trunk, and those are also more likely to girdle the tree. And we can see some of those in that same excavation. These too will enlarge and girdle the tree and cause problems.

And one of the things that happens when trees are planted too deep is we end up finding out that the trunk of the tree tends to rot, and it's more susceptible to storm damage, because it's very weak at that attachment. So strong winds blow in, we get an ice storm, a snowstorm, what happens is it blows over. And that's when you can definitely see the damage from planting too deeply. So, root flare at or slightly above the soil surface.

Deeply planted trees are also susceptible to frost cracks, and that's basically what happens when your tree on the south or west side of the yard is exposed to the sunlight in the winter. The roots are frozen, that side of the trunk heats up, starts to warm up, cells are active, sun sets, those cells break, and eventually leads to cracking. So proper planting will help with that as well.

Now, once you find that root flare, you want to measure the distance from the bottom of the root ball to that root flare. This will be the depth of your planting hole. You can use a tape measure, or what I like to use is the handle up my shovel and run another handle across, and that way I can compare the two. Whatever works for you works well. Don't dig deeper. If you dig deeper, what will happen is the soil will settle. Your tree ends up being planted too deep.

Now, you want to dig your hole wide, at least two, preferably three to five times wider than the root ball. Now, one of the things that you may have noticed is I used a little trick my friend Mark taught me. I took a string, made a loop, put it on the post, which is where I wanted my tree to go. I ran that out, a couple times the diameter of the root ball, and then used marking paint to mark that hole. That way I didn't have to think about it. I knew my hole was centered properly. It gave me my guidelines. It made the job much easier. So three times wider, five times wider even better, same depth as the root ball. Now that sounds like a lot of work, but keep in mind that it's shallow. You're going like a saucer or a bowl, a shallow bowl, so, you're not digging deep all the way around. And remember the $100 hole story, that we're actually preparing that planting hole so our tree is off to a good start.

One of the things that doctor Gary Watson at the Morton Arboretum found about digging a wide but shallow hole is the mere act of loosening that soil had great impact. It loosens the soil so the roots could go and explore the area beyond the planting hole, more important than amending the hole. In fact, we'll talk about that in a minute, the downside of amending the hole.

Rough in the sides of your planting hole? This is especially important when you have clay soil or you're working in moist soil, because when you dig and you can see it's kind of shiny and you glaze the soil on the edge of the planting hole, and when that happens, the roots are unable to penetrate the soil. So they hit the side, and it's just like a pot, and they grow in a circle instead of exploring the soil beyond.

Well now that we have the hole ready for planting, let's take one last look at our tree. We want to select the best side to face it to its advantage. Now, that may be your view or the public view. In my case, I'm looking at this tree from my house or when I'm in the yard. I wanted the best view, though they were all very nice. You may want to remove the tags now, especially if it's a tall tree you may need to have it leaned over. Remove the tags, or, on a shorter tree like this, you can wait until it's placed in the hole. Either way, just be sure to take those tags off, because as those stems get larger in diameter, they can actually girdle the tree and cause damage. Save your tags for future reference for that garden journal we talked about starting in our last session. It's a good reference; it will remind you of the cultivar that you planted, and it will serve you well in the future.

Now, ask for help when planting bigger trees. I did. You want to avoid damaging the tree and yourself. Those root balls can be very heavy, and an extra set of hands can be very useful. If a strong friend isn't available, you may want to look for a garden cart, a pot lifter, and old saucer sled to help you drag and slide it into place. But I think it's worth waiting until you can get some help.

Notice how we moved this tree. We moved it by the root ball, not the trunk. We rolled it in place. The trunk we just held on for guidance but didn't drag it by the trunk. And that's very important, because if you use your trunk for leverage, it damages the roots. Think about it. You're just moving it back and forth and the roots are stagnant. So definitely roll it into place. Don't drag it by the trunk of the tree.

Now, before we set this tree in place, there are a couple more things we need to look at, discuss, and prepare. For balled and burlapped trees, I recommend cutting the bottom of the wire basket off before setting it into the hole. Now, our root ball was pretty crumbly, so I was a little worried about keeping it intact, so I skipped it on this tree, but that's my usual practice. But I'll show you how I compensated. Set the tree in the hole. And notice we're removing that top portion of the wire basket with the bolt cutters. I've seen wire baskets left in place, removed five years later, and look as shiny as the day they went in the hole. The other problem, as those big roots near the surface expanded, the wire basket didn't, and it girdled some of those roots. So we removed the wire basket from the top, folded down the bottom because the majority of those roots are in the top 12 to 18 inches of soil. So that basket will be out of the way. We removed the burlap. We cut away the burlap, just leaving what was underneath and folding it down below the root ball. And that way we can be sure that the roots won't stop growing. I've also seen burlap fully intact 5, 10 15, even 20 years later when trees have been removed that were suffering and in decline. And when we pulled it out, the burlap was full of roots that were never able to penetrate and the burlap never decomposed, so it's very important.

Now, this is a controversial issue for some. Some of the growers are worried about compromising the root ball. They wrap it in burlap. Some even double wrap it. They put it in a wire cage to hold that root ball intact, so the last thing they want to see is us taking it off. But as I mentioned before, I found that years later those things are all intact. In fact, your assignment is to take a look at plantings in your neighborhood and community, and I bet you'll find some trees that have been in the ground for several years, and you'll find twine still around the trunk of the tree and burlap visible. So, if you do find that on your own property, cut that away, remove it from above the soil surface, and you'll have a better result in the long run. But from now on, remove those so this doesn't become a long-term problem.

We want to make sure that we remove all these things, and we want to look for girdling roots at this point. Make sure that you cut away any girdling roots, loosen them with a cultivator, because as we saw with the container plant, and we talked about before, these roots will continue to grow and encircle the root ball if you don't prune them away or loosen them. So take a little time to loosen those girdling roots that you may have discovered when pulling away the burlap.

Now, I mentioned before we're not going to amend the soil, we just loosened it. If we amend the soil with things like compost and peat moss, we create an in-ground container, something that those plant roots never want to leave. So if you have great soil in your planting hole, heavy clay around it, those roots aren't going to be able to penetrate, or, will stay where the growing conditions are better. On the other hand, if you have sandy, rocky soil beyond your planting hole, again, they're going to stay where the moisture is contained, not out in that dryer, sandy soil. The tree roots go two to five times the height of the tree away from the trunk, so, it'd be impossible to amend that whole planting hole, so get your tree off to a good start by loosening the soil but filling it with the existing soil. And that's very important.

So one of the other things that you're going to want to do is water thoroughly. Now some people water halfway through the planting so they backfill that planting hole with some soil, water to help with settling, and then completely fill the hole, and water at that point. You kind of decide what works best for you. The key is making sure you have no air pockets. So, backfill like we did with the existing soil, water thoroughly, and mulch. I like to mulch first and then water. I find I wash less soil away; it's more intact. You just want to make sure that you water thoroughly.

Add a two- to three-inch layer of wood chips or shredded bark. Now that will help conserve moisture. It also keeps the grass away from the trunk of the tree, and as we talked about earlier, grass is a big competitor with your young trees for growth. You'll also help conserve moisture so that the soil doesn't dry out but also moderate temperature extremes. You won't get hotter soils in the summer and colder in the winter. But be sure you don't pile the mulch over the trunk of the tree, because what happens is you end up with a little volcano. And just like mounting soil over the trunk of the tree, mounting mulch can lead to adventitious roots and rot, which can shorten the lifespan of your tree. So mulch, pull that mulch back, and only a two- to three-inch layer is all you need.

Now when planting a container-grown plant, you want to prepare the hole in the same way. Check for the root flare, or in the case of shrubs, the crown, the point where the roots meet the stem. That area needs to be at or slightly above the soil surface. Now, to get that shrub out of the pot, you can do one of two things. You can roll the pot on the ground, and that will help loosen the roots, and then you can slide it out of the container. You definitely don't want to pull it out by the stems. Again, you'll be damaging that area where the roots connect to the stems. So roll it and slide it.

Or you may want to remove the bottom of the pot, then slice the side of the container, and set it in the hole and peel it away. Now, this method works great for potted plants that may have been planted in late winter and don't have an established root system. Because if the soil's going to fall away, if it falls away in the planting hole, it's a lot easier to plant it in place than to move it once that root ball has fallen apart. Well no matter how you get it out of the pot, you want to look for and loosen and remove any girdling roots, just like we did with our balled and burlapped tree. Because again, they'll continue to grow in a circle. A good, sharp pruners will work, a cultivator is another way to do it.

Now let's talk a bit about bare root. After moving those heavy root balls or those big containers, you may decide that you know what? A bare root offers the gardener a better choice, especially if your budget's limited. They're cheaper. If you're working alone, it's a lot lighter. And we talked about some of the disadvantages, meaning you need to be really careful about care, just like with any new planting, but especially with bare root. Now we often find roses, mail-order plants, and fruit trees and a few shrubs used for hedges are often sold bare root. Again, available only during a limited time, usually in spring.

We're going to dig a hole large enough to accommodate those roots. So take a good look at the root system and dig a hole big enough that you can spread those roots out so they'll be headed in the right direction away from the trunk of the tree or shrub. Prune off any broken, girdling, or damaged roots. It's a little easier to find them here, so a good, clean cut will close up much more quickly. Make sure that root flare is at or slightly above the soil surface. We use the same measuring method with our bare root that we did with our balled and burlapped tree.

Now don't be fooled by the graft. Many trees are grafted, just like we looked at with the Variegated dogwood, and it's very common in both ornamental and especially fruit trees, so we want to make sure that graft is above ground, that we're lining up the root flare, not the graft. In the case of roses, it's just a bit different. Some roses are grafted. A small bud is grafted to a hardy root stock. Let's say you're growing a Peace rose. That bud from the Peace rose is grafted onto a hardy root stock. It helps the plant grow more vigorously, more quickly, and in some cases increases hardiness.

Now, depending on where you live, you may plant the graft above, at, or below the soil surface. So plant that graft—it looks like an knobby growth— two inches above the soil surface in areas where temperatures don't drop below 10 degrees during the winter at the soil surface, if the winter temperatures are below 10 degrees, but, above zero. And you'll plant that graft two inches below the soil surface in much colder areas, like mine. That protects the graft that can be winter killed in cold winter temperatures. And we'll talk a little bit more about winter protection, especially important for those grafted roses.

Now, many roses are now being grown on their own roots, so plant these at the crown, just like we looked at the other shrubs, at the soil surface. That's the place where the stems meet the roots. That's at the soil surface. So take a close look before planting your roses. The tag often will tell you if it's grafted. The garden center staff should be able to help, and if the graft is above the ground, you're sure to see it because it's that knobby little growth.

Now, once again, we're backfilling with the existing soil. So whether we're planting bare root, container, or balled and burlap. Water to settle the soil. Now, you can do this halfway through the process to help with settling, or, after you've filled the hole with soil, mulched, and watered. Just be sure to water thoroughly. I always go back, no matter how I do my watering, halfway through or after mulching. I always go back and make sure that my plant is at the right depth. And mulching with a two- to three-inch layer of wood chips. Again, pull it back from the trunk, and you'll have good success, and it'll give you that little edge about keeping that moisture in the soil.

Now wait a year to fertilize. What research has found that you'll get your biggest benefit by waiting a year. If you use high nitrogen, fast-release fertilizers at planting, you can damage those young developing roots, plus you stimulate top growth, and we really want the roots to take off. Wait a couple years to do your major pruning as well. Pruning now, you remove a lot of the top growth that has leaves, and those leaves produce energy that will help in the development and the establishment of that tree.

The old practice used to be to remove a third of the top growth when we planted. They thought, well, you're removing all those roots, you need to remove a third of that top growth. But what we found, it didn't work that way. So you want to remove just broken, damaged, or rubbing branches at planting, and then wait a few more years to do pruning for structure. And we'll talk a little bit more about pruning the next session to get that plant established for longevity.

Staking is generally not needed nor recommended. Staking can interfere with the normal development of a tree. What happens is, the part of the tree above where it's staked moves more freely in the wind. That makes the trunk increase in its girth and gets larger. The portion beneath the stake is held pretty steady, and so it doesn't grow at the same rate. If we leave our trees staked too long, they're top heavy and will flop over when the stake is removed. We only stake trees when they're bare root and in need of support because they have a small root system for the top growth. We also stake trees with large canopies and small root systems. This sometimes happens by the time we find the root flare and have removed some of that soil in balled and burlapped plants, or perhaps it was dug or transplanted and the root system is much smaller than the top. We need to stake to hold it and protect it that first year until it can root in.

We'll also do some staking when trees are exposed to high winds that are likely to blow them over. In cities, you'll often see trees staked, mainly because of the traffic and people. I once had a call from a citizen who had a kid climb up their street tree. Never saw a big enough tree in his neighborhood, so he thought, ah, it's a tree, I'll climb. Climb that 1½ inch diameter tree and the kid and the tree fell over. No one was hurt, but we did have to replace the tree. So staking provides some stabilization.

Now, I've this handy graphic that's a great way that shows you how to stake a tree. As you notice, we've dug the hole wide and shallow, set it in place, removed the burlap and wire cage. Notice the stakes are put in the ground and pounded into the ground beneath where the soil was disturbed. If we don't get them deep enough into undisturbed soil, they're not going to be sturdy and hold on to the tree. We're going to run canvas strips around the trunk, and I'll show you some in a minute, and the wire through the rivets. Never put wire through hose and wrap it around the trunk; it can damage it. We're going to leave these stakes in place for one, no more than two, years, until that tree's nice and sturdy. So, stake only if you need to. Remove as soon as possible.

Here's the canvas strap that I mentioned before. You notice it's nice and sturdy; there's a rivet on the end, and that's where the wire will be threaded through. And we've got a nice, sturdy wire to help hold the strapping around the tree and connect it to the stake. So if this was our tree, and of course, it was planted in the ground, we would wrap it around, run our wire through, and tie it to our post. Now, if we only used one stake, we'd want the stake here if the wind was blowing that direction, so the tree blows away from the stake, not into it. If we're using two stakes, we'd have them across from each other. It wouldn't be as big of an issue. And three stakes just gives you a little more security, but remember, we want some wiggle room in that, because we want the plants to sway and move in the breeze and thicken up their trunks. And be sure you remove it after one or two years.

Well now that we have safely tucked our plants into the ground, we've watered them properly at planting, we want to make sure we continue to water them properly for the next two to three years. That's how long it takes to get these plants to get established in your landscape. Water thoroughly, moistening the roots deep and the surrounding soil so that you can encourage deep and wide roots so that they'll be more drought tolerant and be established, so keep a special eye on those new plantings for the first couple years.

In our next session, we're going to talk about growing our trees and caring for them throughout the year. But in the meantime, grab that shovel and get busy planting.

Spring and Summer Care of Trees and Shrubs
Lesson 6

Trees and shrubs are the long-lived framework and some of the more expensive elements of your landscape. They require more effort to transport and plant than annuals, and they're expensive to remove if they fail. For all these reasons, you want to make sure they remain healthy. In this lesson, we will explore spring and summer care for your trees and shrubs. Providing early and ongoing care will help you minimize long-term maintenance efforts and costs, avoid storm damage, and reduce loss of trees and shrubs from environmental stress.

Water the Roots

- Roots absorb water and nutrients from the soil and store energy and water. They also help anchor plants. Trees and shrubs have several different types of roots.
  - First are the woody, perennial roots that make up the primary branches. Year after year, they increase in age and size, and they grow horizontally, raising above the soil surface. These important roots anchor your trees; they're connected to the finer roots that pull up water and nutrients.

  - Second are smaller, shorter-lived roots, only about $\frac{1}{16}$ inch in diameter, whose major function is to absorb water and nutrients. They grow outward and predominantly upward from the large roots near the soil surface because that's where the minerals, moisture, and oxygen are abundant and easy to retrieve. Water that area consistently. Slow, thorough watering, soaking the ground, moves water deeper into the soil.

- Botanists used to think that tree roots were as deep as the tree was tall. But recent science indicates that most of the roots are in the top 18 inches of soil and spread two to three times the height of the tree away from the trunk. When you're watering, keep the moisture in the top 12 inches of soil, where the fine feeder roots are growing.

- If you skimp on watering, you encourage shallow roots that can lead to drought damage. Trees need about 10 gallons of water per inch of trunk diameter. In general, it takes about 5 minutes to provide 10 gallons of water; multiply the diameter of the trunk by 5 to calculate how long to water your tree.

- For new plantings, water the planting hole and beyond to encourage a large, expansive root system. Many container-grown plants are planted in peat moss, bark, and vermiculite or perlite, which is very different from the surrounding soil; to allow for this difference, you may need to water at different times. You may water the root zone every couple of days, twice a week for sandy soil, or once a week for heavy clay soil.

- Many professionals use a *treegator* for new plantings. This is basically a bag filled with water and placed around the trunk of a tree. It slowly drips water into the soil, infiltrating deeply right around the plant where it's needed. You can purchase one at a garden center or nursery or make your own.
  - Measure the diameter of the tree. For every inch of diameter, you will need two 5-gallon buckets. Drill some ¼-inch holes into the bottoms and fill them with water.

  - The buckets allow you to apply water slowly to the soil, which encourages good, deep roots.

- Even established trees need watering during extended dry periods. Water the whole area below the drip line. Use a soaker hose, drip irrigation, or the treegator or bucket system.

- Deep watering means applying the water 8 inches below the soil, beneath the grass roots and breaking through the tough, compacted soil that often occurs during drought. Professionals use injectors, which you may find in garden centers. An injector is a probe you hook up to your hose and push through the soil. Don't dig holes to apply the water deeply. All that does is expose the roots and make them more subject to drying.

Think of remulching as improving the soil, not just adding another layer of mulch.

- For evergreens, water about 3 to 5 inches beyond the drip line on all sides of the tree to encourage the roots to grow outward. Water slowly, as you would with other trees.

Protect and Insulate
- Mulch is a layer of 2 to 3 inches of material that insulates between the soil and the air. It helps protect roots from weather extremes and retain moisture. It also helps protect tree trunks and shrub stems from mowers and weed whips, and it creates an environment conducive to healthy growth. Mulch also suppresses weeds and grass, competitors for water and nutrients.
  - Organic mulches include such material as wood chips and bark. These materials break down and improve the soil by adding organic matter and nutrients.

  - Inorganic mulches include stone and rock, which do not break down and improve the soil. They are decorative but not functional.

- Weed barriers are fabrics that let air, light, and water through but prevent weeds from sprouting. They should not be used with organic mulches because they turn the mulch to compost. They should definitely be used with inorganic mulch to prevent the stone from working its way into the soil.

- To apply mulch, spread a layer 2 to 3 inches deep around the tree or shrub and make it as wide as possible. The finer the mulch material, the thinner the layer should be; finer material knits together and is effective at conserving moisture and suppressing weeds.

- Applying new mulch every year or so is unnecessary and potentially harmful: Too much can slow down water and nutrients from reaching the roots of your plants. If you want a fresh look, lightly rake the mulch to turn it over and freshen it up.

- When you're converting grass to mulch, edge the area to disconnect the grass inside the mulch area from the grass and weeds outside. Cut the grass extra short to ensure that it will die quickly. Cover it with a layer of newspaper or cardboard to suffocate it, then cover it with shredded bark or wood chips.

Transplant

- Spring and fall are prime time for root growth; thus, transplantation, like fertilization, can occur either in spring, before growth begins, or in fall, as the plants enter dormancy. Before you start to transplant, make sure you can manage the plant. Large plants may be too big to handle. You can assume that the larger the plant, the larger the root system will be.
  - For example, a 2-foot-tall shrub will have a root ball 12 inches in diameter and 9 inches deep. A 6-foot shrub will have a 16-inch-diameter and 12-inch-deep root ball.

  - As a rule of thumb, a 15-inch-by-15-inch root ball may weigh 200 pounds or more, depending on the soil type.

- Root pruning is not always possible, but if you have time, you should do it. Tie up the branches to ease access to the roots; with a sharp spade, mark the edge of the intended root ball and dig a trench around the outside of the circle. Don't remove any soil; just cut through the roots. New roots will form on the cut ends. The idea is that when you transplant, you will have more roots near the trunk of the tree or the base of the stem. Do root pruning one season in advance: If you're going to transplant in spring, root prune in fall, and vice versa.

- If the root ball is properly sized, it will stay intact, although you may need loppers or a pruner to trim any tough roots. When you are ready to transplant, slide a piece of burlap underneath the root ball and—with help—lift it out of the old location and into the new one.

Fertilize

- Like transplanting, fertilizing is typically done in spring or fall. Resist the tendency to over-fertilize, and remember to wait a year before fertilizing new plantings. High-nitrogen fertilizer can damage young root systems and promote top growth at the expense of allowing plants to become established. Waiting a year also increases the fertilizer's value because the plants are more likely to pull it up.

- Established trees and shrubs have extensive root systems; they're always gaining nutrients from the surrounding area because they have more roots to absorb water and nutrients. As a result, they need little, if any, fertilizing. Furthermore, roots that are in planting beds or under the lawn get fertilizer when you fertilize the grass.

- Fertilize to promote or to speed up growth if your plants need a little nudge or when plants show signs of nutrient deficiency. Remember, nutrient deficiency can also look like over- and under-watering, so be sure to test the soil first. Often, nutrient deficiency is related to pH, rather than to the richness of the soil.

- If your plants are nutrient-deficient, a certified arborist might suggest tissue testing and take a sample of the leaves to see exactly what the plant is taking up. But this process is expensive and often not readily available.

- To fertilize a large tree, measure the tree's diameter at breast height—about 4 ½ feet above ground level. You'll need about 5 pounds of a low-nitrogen fertilizer for every inch of trunk diameter.
  - Remove small cores of soil or use a dandelion digger to punch holes about 6 inches deep in concentric circles around the tree, starting about 2 feet from the trunk and out to the drip line, covering the area under the canopy.

  - Apply the fertilizer deep in the holes, below the grass roots. Otherwise, you'll have plugs of green grass that will take up the fertilizer before it reaches the tree roots.

  - For mulch beds, evenly distribute the fertilizer throughout the area under the drip line right over the mulch. If necessary, rake the fertilizer in to make sure it goes to the soil below. Follow the label directions; some fertilizers don't need to be raked or watered in, while others do.

- Because many shrubs are included in planting beds, you fertilize them every time you fertilize your annuals and perennials. If they do need a nutrient boost, incorporate a low-nitrogen fertilizer around each shrub at a rate of about 5 pounds per 100 square feet. If you use a fertilizer recommended by your soil test, follow the label directions.

- Milorganite is an organic, slow-release, low-nitrogen fertilizer that also releases some of the phosphorus and potassium bound to the soil. Phosphorus is great for flowering, and potassium promotes disease resistance and hardiness.

Questions to Consider

1. Trees need about 10 gallons of water per inch of trunk diameter, and it takes about 5 minutes to deliver 10 gallons from a water hose. Using this rule of thumb, what are the watering requirements of your favorite trees? What about the largest tree in your yard?

2. Try making your own treegator. Remember, you'll need 10 gallons of water for every inch in the tree's diameter.

Spring and Summer Care of Trees and Shrubs
Lesson 6—Transcript

As you've discovered, trees and shrubs are the long-lived backbone, the framework of our landscapes. They're some of the more expensive elements of your garden. They require more effort to transport and plant than annuals, plus, they're expensive to remove if they fail. So we want to make sure they remain a beautiful, healthy asset in our landscape. So join me as we travel through a year of beauty and care for your trees and shrubs. You'll need to tweak the timing a bit based on where you live, but I can help you with that as well.

Now, providing early and ongoing care will help minimize long-term maintenance efforts and costs, will help you avoid storm damage to your trees, and reduce losses to trees and shrubs based on environmental stress. Water is something we need to monitor throughout the year in the life of the trees and shrubs. Too often, we water our plants, and then we walk away, assuming that nature will provide the necessary water and nutrients. Well, unfortunately, this isn't the case when we're establishing our plants, or even once they've rooted in and been in the landscape for several years. In addition, our weather patterns have changed. We're experiencing more droughts, and many communities are implementing water bans as well. So proper watering is critical in the establishment, longevity, and beauty of the trees and shrubs that form your framework. It's part of your season-long and ongoing need for your trees and shrubs. So it made sense we'd start with this task that you need to do.

Let's take a closer look at the science behind the trees and shrubs and the water use. Now, in the old days, we used to picture that tree roots were as deep as the tree was tall. But we've found out since that the majority of the tree roots are in the top 18 inches of the soil and go out two to three times the height of the tree away from the trunk, as you can see in this graphic rendition. The tree is more like a plate with the tree growing out of it. Keep that in mind, and that will help you take better care of your trees.

So, when you're watering your trees, keep in mind we want to keep the moisture in the top 12 inches of soil. That's where the majority of the fine feeder roots are growing. And let's talk about some of those roots and take a closer look at what's going on down below. Roots, as you may know, absorb moisture and water and nutrients from the soil into the plant. And so they're important in absorption and movement of these minerals and water. They store food, or energy, and water, and they also help anchor the plants.

Now, at least 90 percent of those roots, as I mentioned, are located in the top 12 inches of the soil. So we want to be careful what we do, but we also want to make sure we moisten that top 12 inches. Trees and shrubs have several different types of roots. They have woody, perennial roots that make up the primary branches. So if you think of roots almost like the top of the tree in terms of branching out from the trunk, those bigger, woody roots are perennial. They are year, after year, after year. They increase in age and size, and they grow horizontally.

Your framework also has smaller, shorter-lived roots. Their major function is to absorb the water and nutrients. They're much smaller, only about $\frac{1}{16}$ inch in diameter, but they make up the majority of the root system in that whole surface area, and that makes them critical to the plant's survival and longevity. And because they're so small, we often overlook their presence.

These smaller roots grow outward and predominately upward from those large roots near the soil surface, because that's where a lot of the minerals and moisture and oxygen are really abundant and easy for them to retrieve. So what does all this mean to you? Well, it means you need to make sure that we get the water where it's needed and used. By slowly moistening the top 8 to 12 inches of soil, we moisten that area consistently, providing water to the roots that will absorb it. Slow, thorough watering, soaking the ground, moves that water deeper into the soil, so we moisten the top 12 inches.

Now, if you water for a short period of time, you only encourage shallow roots, which can lead to more drought damage. I call it the one-beverage watering system. You get home from work, you open your favorite beverage, you water your trees, you water your shrubs, your vegetable garden, your flowers, your lawn. You're done. You're inside relaxing. You've done no good, but to encourage the roots of all those plants to go near the surface. You miss one day of watering, and guess what? They start declining and dying. Don't water overhead whenever possible. That wastes water. You lose a lot as the wind blows it away, and you also can promote disease by keeping the leaves of your trees and shrubs wet when it's not necessary.

Now, trees need about 10 gallons of water per inch of trunk diameter. And you can see that I'm measuring the trunk here to get an idea of how big that tree is, so I can do the math. Now, in general, it takes about five minutes to provide 10 gallons of water. But you want to check, because water pressure varies from house to house and municipality. So do a little test yourself and check it out, and then you can calibrate accordingly. Now, calculate that amount of water that you need by multiplying the tree diameter that we measured times 10 gallons for each inch diameter. And that will give you the total gallons of water. Or you can also do the math, tree diameter times five minutes, assuming that will give you 10 gallons, and that will be the time needed for watering.

For new plantings, you're going to want to water the planting hole and beyond to encourage those roots to go out of the planting hole into the soil beyond, to encourage a big, expansive root system. You'll also need to allow for the difference in the soilless mix, as I mentioned before, because many of our container-grown plants are in the soilless mix made up to peat moss and bark and vermiculite or perlite, very different than the surrounding soil. So for new plantings, you're going to need to keep that root ball in the soilless mix moist and the soil around it moist, but you may be watering at different times. It maybe every couple of days that you're watering the root zone but once a week for your heavy clay soil or twice a week for your sandy soil.

Now, many professionals use something called a treegator for new plantings. It's basically a bag that you filled with water and place around the trunk of the tree. It's slowly drips water into the soil, remember, infiltrating that soil deeply and right around the plant where it's needed. So you can purchase those as well at garden centers and nurseries, or make your own.

It's very simple. All you need is a five-gallon bucket. Simply drill some 1/4-inch holes into the bottom and fill it with water. You'll need two five-gallon buckets for every inch diameter of tree. That way, you can apply the water slowly to the soil, watering your plants, encouraging good, deep roots, and taking care of the job. When you take a look at a tree that hasn't been water properly, you can see over that period of time that it's slowly growing, putting out minimal root growth, and the top growth is not full and dense and really poorly formed, as opposed to a young plant that has been well watered and cared for. You've got better growth, bigger root system. And it's really off to a good start. And that means you'll have a mature specimen sooner that's going to look beautiful, providing shade or screening or whatever it is you're hoping that plant will do for you.

Now, even established trees need watering during extended dry periods. And you can see here that the grass is brown, so it's been a pretty dry summer. And we often overlook mature trees, thinking, nobody waters them in nature, why do I need to take care of them in my own yard? Well, guess what? If those trees in the forest die one or two here and there, it has a different impact than that one specimen tree in your front yard. So during extended dry periods, make sure even your mature trees are watered. Water the whole area below the drip line of that tree. Use a soaker hose or drip irrigation, or that bucket system I just described, and water that whole area beneath. You can see it works quite well.

You may have heard of the term deep watering. Now, that doesn't mean you apply the water several feet below the soil surface, but rather, just eight inches below the soil, down beneath the grassroots and breaking through that tough compacted hard soil that often occurs during drought. Now, professionals use injectors, and you may find those also in garden centers. And the idea is, you have a probe you hook up to your hose, and you push it through the soil about eight inches deep to apply the water. Again, you just want to get below those grassroots, breakthrough the compacted soil. Don't dig holes to apply the water deeply. All you do there is expose the roots and make them more subject to drying, so causing more problems than the drought.

Now, for evergreens, we're going to water about three to five inches beyond the drip line on all sides of the tree. We want to make sure that we encourage those roots to grow outward. We water slowly just like we did with the other trees. Now, mulching, like watering, is another task that can be done as time allows throughout the year. Watering we need to keep on top of. Mulching we can do when time allows, but usually is a task we do once a year, every few years, depending on the type of mulch.

Now, mulch is used. It's a layer of two to three inches of some type of material to create insulation between the soil in the air. Now, since those roots are near the soil surface, the ones that pull up the moisture and nutrients, mulching helps protect them from weather extremes, the heat of summer and the cold of winter. It also helps protect our tree trunks and shrub stems from mowers and weed whips, and it creates an environment that's conducive to healthy growth. It also conserves moisture, so you'll need to water less often. And that means less water used and less of your time spent watering. Mulch also suppresses weeds and grass. And if you remember, those are big competitors for water and nutrients for our new plantings. And so again, less work for you fertilizing and watering if we keep the competition at bay.

Now, I keep mentioning organic mulches. And these are things like wood chips and bark. Now, they break down and improve the soil. But most of us, I hear a lot of gardeners saying, "I have to apply them every few years. I don't want to do that." But the good news is, when you mulch, you're improving the soil, since they break down over a couple of years, it adds organic matter and nutrients to the soil. And since none of us have ideal soil, most of our trees and shrubs will benefit from this. So think of remulching as improving the soil, not just adding another layer of mulch.

The mulch zone also creates a buffer zone. As I mentioned, it protects your plants from weed whips and mowers, and that saves you time, less hand trimming involved. Plus, if you create a mulch bed, a combination of trees, shrubs, and perhaps perennials and ground covers, you have one large bed, better environment for your trees and shrubs, and only one big bed to mow around versus several different plants.

Let's look at a few of the mulches that you may be using in your landscape. I talk a lot about organic mulches, but there are things like inorganic mulches, stone and rock mulch. Many gardeners like these. They think they're decorative, ornamental. And they really liked the way they look in the landscape. They are an option, however, the problem is that these mulches don't improve the soil. They don't break down. And so they're decorative but not functional. In the summer, they tend to collect the heat. In the winter, they tend to cool off quickly. Now, I'm not a fan of weed barriers. And these are fabrics that let air, light, and water through. Now, the problem is, if you put organic mulches over top, it turns to compost, and it's a mess. But definitely, when you're using stone mulch, put weed barrier underneath. It prevents the stone from working its way into the soil where you need to replenish it. And if you ever change your mind and want to get rid of the stone mulch, you're digging rocks out of the top 12 inches.

So weed barrier only under stone mulch to make cleanup easier for you. Now, I've talked a lot about organic mulches, such as wood chips and bark. They moderate soil temperatures. They improve the soil, and we don't use weed barriers underneath, as I mentioned. This is pine bark. And you can see it's dark and it's rich in color, and nice organic mulch with a good smell. Two to three inch layer will last you a couple of years, and again, you'll need to replace it. But it's great for an informal, even a formal look, because of the dark color.

Now, shredded hardwood bark has some great values to the soil. They even think that maybe it has some disease-resistance value to the plants, helping create a good environment. I like the shredded because it knits together nicely, so it's great in an area where maybe you have a bit of a slope, or maybe where you want your mulch to tie together and not be so loose. A bit dusty but not bad at all. Will break down a few years, again, you're improving the soil.

Now, many of you may recognize this red Enviro-Mulch. And one of the things I always chuckle because it's basically ground oak pallets. So they've taken pallets, recycled them into mulch by grinding them, and then using a food dye to give them the color that you want. So here we have some red. This one's black. And I know a lot of gardeners like the black because it kind of blends in a little more naturally. I've seen this in yellow. I've seen it in green, turquoise, a wide variety of colors kind to match your gardening style design. This is a little slower to break down because oak is slower to decay, much like cedar mulches. So pick your mulch based on your landscape design, the function, the color you're looking for, and the longevity you desire.

Now, once you've selected your mulch, there are few things to keep in mind when you need to apply it. As you're applying your mulch, spread a layer two to three inches deep around the tree or shrub. Now, make that mulch ring as wide as you can stand. Wider is better for the tree, but it's usually an aesthetic issue for gardeners. Now, the finer the mulch material, the thinner the layer, because that finer material knits together and is very effective at conserving moisture and suppressing weeds. Coarser, thicker material leaves more spaces, so it dries out faster.

Now, you don't need to reapply the mulch every year. I've seen places where people have raked off the mulch and put fresh mulch on, or they add a new layer every year. So at the end of three or four years, their mulch layer's this high. Getting it too high is not necessary. Can kind of slow down water and nutrients from reaching the roots of your plants. Now, a lot of gardeners do this because they want a fresh look. Here are a couple things you can try. Lightly rake that mulch to kind of turn it over and get that fresher side up, freshen it up a bit. I've seen gardeners take cultivators and just lightly till the mulch, not the soil, but that turns it and refreshes up the look. And for those eco mulches, those Enviro-Mulches, you can get more dye to dye them as well. So, make it easy on you and good for the trees by mulching wisely.

Most importantly, don't pile the mulch against the trunk. Those volcano mulches, again, encourage adventitious roots, bad for the tree. Pull those back. And remember, when you're converting grass to mulch, there are things you can do without the use of chemicals. Here's what you do. Edge the area, because grass is interconnected and many of your weeds by rhizome. So you have a blade of grass, a rhizome, a blade of grass. So we edge to disconnect the grass inside the mulch area from the grass and weeds outside. We're going to cut the grass very, very short. We want that grass to be very short so that it's going to die quickly. Cover it with a layer of newspaper or cardboard; that helps to suffocate it, and then cover it with shredded bark or wood chips. Now, that cardboard and newspaper will eventually decompose. But in the short term, it helps suppress the grass and weeds and suffocate it, block the light, so it dies. You'll have the grass decomposing, you'll have the cardboard and newspaper decomposing, improving the soil, and your wood chips or bark in place. So you set that tree up for success without causing any issues.

Now, we talked a lot about those woody perennial roots of our trees and shrubs that are near the surface. And I mentioned that they grow every year. Well, those roots put on more growth on top of the roof surface. And they're often creating headaches for those of you mowing the grass or tripping over the surface roots. These are important roots. They anchor your trees. They're connected to the finer roots that pull up water and nutrients. We don't want to cut those roots. If we take an ax and cut the roots, we create entry ways for insect and disease problems. And that can be the end of our tree. We also don't want to bury the roots. Adding as little as an inch of soil can kill some trees if we cover those roots. And if we don't kill the tree, guess what? Those surface roots continue to put on new growth on top, and they're back in the way again. So mulch is one way that we can deal with that.

But maybe you don't want to mulch. How about ground covers? Look for perennial ground covers that are tolerant of dry shade, and that's important, because the tree canopy usually blocks the water as well as the light. So if you get a ground cover that tolerates dry shade, you'll have good success. We want to minimize our disturbance of the roots. Remember, the majority of roots are the top 12 inches, so don't get out the tiller and start tilling up that ground. Instead, take your ground covers and find areas in between those surface roots. Dig a hole a little bit larger than that perennial root ball, add a little compost, and plant it. And then, mulch on top.

Make sure you take good care, because you want to be certain that that plant gets well watered. You've got a lot of competition. The canopy preventing water from reaching the roots of that perennial, plus the tree absorbing the water before the perennial. So check on that regularly, especially in the first couple years to get it established. It'll be a beautiful look, good for the tree, and it'll be a nice planting addition to your landscape.

Now, we do want to minimize our root disturbance, and I mentioned using pocket planting in the newspaper. If you mulched your bed with the newspaper, short grass, you may want a year before you put in the ground cover, because it's hard to dig through that. But you'll have great success when you do it that way.

But you may decide, you know, ground covers are fine, but I want to add a little bit of seasonal color. Well, you can do that very easily. How about setting containers right on top of the ground covers? The other thing you could do is you can bury your pots in the ground. Now, you put your ground cover or mulch in place. You don't want to dig through those roots too often. So what we're going to do is take an old nursery pot, just as you can see here, dig a hole, and bury that nursery pot in the ground. Then, we're going to pot up our pansies, our mums, our other seasonal color that we want to set inside that buried pot. Now, the cool thing is, when the seasons change, you lift out the pot of pansies, say, in the spring, pot up something for the summer, maybe some coleus that's shade tolerant. Set that in the pot. When those are nipped by frost, lift them out and replace them with mums. It's easier on you and much easier on the tree.

Now, spring and fall are major times for root growth. So there's a few tasks that we can do either time, now in the spring or later in the fall. So whenever your schedule allows. Transplanting and fertilization are two of those. We transplant trees and shrubs that are growing in the wrong place, or maybe they outgrew their space, or maybe they need to be moved due to construction or a redesign in the landscape. So, if you're going to transplant in spring, do it before growth begins, or in fall, as the plants enter dormancy. These are the best times to do your transplanting.

But before you break out the shovel, make sure you can manage the plant. Large plants may be too big for you to handle, either to manage in terms of the root ball and the size and the weight, or for the plant to tolerate the move. This graphic shows you what roots look like and the size of a root ball when you're digging. Look at all the roots that are lost. So you can assume that the bigger the plant, the bigger the root system, the more roots left behind, the more stress on the tree. So think twice before you get out the shovel. You may be better off putting a new plant in that new location.

So, we want to take a look at the size of the plant to decide how big that root ball needs to be. So for shrubs, if you have a two-foot-tall shrub, your root ball is going to be 12 inches in diameter and about nine inches deep. On the other hand, if you have a six-foot-tall shrub, that root ball is going to be 16 inches in diameter and 12 inches deep. That's pretty good size to manage.

Now, keep in mind, a root ball that is 15 inches in diameter and 15 inches deep may weigh as much as 200 pounds or more, depending on your soil type. That's a lot of weight to move around.

Now, for trees, we're talking an even bigger root ball. So you want to keep that in mind. Now, we base our root ball on the tree at the diameter at breast height. Now, that's usually about 4½ feet tall. We measure the diameter of the tree. So if we have a tree with ½-inch diameter at breast height, 4½ feet tall, it would be 14 inches wide and 11 inches deep. On the other hand, if we had a two-inch diameter tree, that root ball is 28 inches in diameter and 19 inches deep. Now, that's a huge root ball that's going to weigh a lot. So keep that in mind as you're looking at moving trees and shrubs.

Now, the smaller the shrub, say, less than three feet tall, and a small tree, less than one inch in diameter, can be moved as bare root. We'd dig them up, wash the soil off, and move them to their new location. It makes it a little bit easier for you. And, with all of these types of transplanting, we plant it just like we described in the earlier lesson. Now, let's go step by step and go through how you can increase your success when you're transplanting.

Let's start with root pruning. Now, I know it's not always possible. Maybe you have a last-minute problem, you need to move the shrub, and you can't plan ahead. But if you have time, try root pruning. The idea behind root pruning is the season in advance, so, root prune in spring if you're going to transplant in fall. Or root prune in fall if you're going to transplant in spring. And the idea is you tie up the branches if need be for easier access to get them out of your way. Then, you mark the edge of the intended root ball. So let's say it needs to be 14 inches in diameter. Then, take a good sharp spade, a shovel, and dig just outside that circle. Don't remove any soil. What you're doing is cutting through the roots. New roots will form on those cut ends. The idea is, when you transplant, then you'll have more roots near the trunk of the tree or the base of the stem to go with the plant when you transplant. So that's something you could do in advance if you think about it and have time. But when it comes to transplanting, here's how you want to do it.

Now, you want to typically tie up the branches to keep them out of the way. Unfortunately, with this Korean spice viburnum, Sugar 'n Spice™, unfortunately, the rabbits did some pruning. Normally we do not prune before transplanting. Unfortunately, the wildlife took care of it. But, it got the branches out of the way. So, here's what we do. As you can see, we're going to dig about two inches away from the final root ball. That just gives us some space to work. Dig a trench all the way around that plant. Use a good, sharp spade so that you can cut through the roots. And then, come back, clean it off to the final size. Now, this is where you may want to call in for help. That is, if you already haven't. Now, if the root ball's properly sized, it will stay intact. You may need a loppers or a pruner to prune off any tough roots or a root underneath to help separate it. Slide a piece of burlap underneath the root ball, and either take one on each hand, or, in this case, we tied it up to hold the root ball in place. We both lifted it and moved it out to its new location.

Now, some trees are just too big for you to move. Now, if it has sentimental value, and you're willing to spend some money, you might want to hire one of the tree-care companies that specializes in moving big trees. Now, these companies will come in with a large tree spade. You've probably seen big trees in a tree spade traveling down the freeway. And they basically remove the plant. They'll dig the new hole, remove the plant, and set in place for you. There are people that move even larger trees that are dug and then moved by cranes. But make sure to do your research and hire a reliable company before you invest all that money in moving a large tree. Make sure they're insured, ask about their success in the past, and talk to some of their clients as well.

Now, fertilization is typically done in spring before growth begins, or fall, after the trees and shrubs have gone dormant. And generally, we tend to over fertilize all of our plants. And trees and shrubs are no exception. Remember to wait a year before you fertilize new tree and shrub plantings. High nitrogen fertilizer can damage the young root systems and promote top growth at the expense of putting down roots and getting established. Plus, you'll get greater value from the fertilizer if you wait a year. The plants are likely to pull it up.

Now, established plants need infrequent, if any, fertilizer. Trees and shrubs have extensive root systems, so they're always gaining nutrients from the area surrounding them. They have more roots to absorb that water and nutrients. And then, roots that are in planting beds or under the lawn are also getting fertilizer when you fertilize the grass, when you fertilize the plantings bed. And then if you leave your grass clippings on the lawn or use an organic mulch around your trees and shrubs, they're gaining nutrients that way.

So when should you fertilize? You can fertilize to promote or to speed up growth if your plants need a little nudge. You can also fertilize when plants show signs of nutrient deficiency. But I recommend you get a soil test first, because that will tell you what the problem is. Because, remember, nutrient deficiency can also look like over and under watering. And often, it's related to pH, not the amount of nutrients in the soil or what you can add with a fertilizer. You see, pH measures acidity and alkalinity of the soil, and it influences how nutrients are available to the plant. For example, on trees like red maples and white oaks, the leaves turn yellow with green veins when they're deficient in iron and manganese. And it's usually a problem that the pH is high, the soil sweet or alkaline, and even though there's plenty of iron and manganese in the soil, it's not available to the plant. So adding more fertilizer is not going to help because it's not available. And having excess nutrients can interfere with the uptake of others.

Now, it's very difficult to change pH, so we're better off selecting plant suited to the growing conditions, like blueberries for acidic soil to avoid them in alkaline soil. Now, if you work with a professional, they may suggest tissue testing. And they take a sample of the leaves, and that tells exactly what the plant is taking up. It's expensive and not readily accessible, and something you'd probably have a certified arborist to do and maybe use as a diagnostic tool.

Now, here's how we can fertilize a large tree. You can do it again in late fall after the leaves drop or early spring before growth begins. That will give you the biggest benefit. Measure the tree's diameter at breast height. Remember, that's about 4½ feet above the ground level, and you can see that's what we did here. You'll need about five pounds of a low-nitrogen fertilizer for every inch trunk diameter. So, apply that fertilizer in concentric circles around the tree starting about two feet from the trunk and go clear out to the drip line. You'll be covering the area under the canopy. Remove small cores of soil or use a dandelion digger like I did to punch holes so that you can get that fertilizer about six inches deep in the soil, right below the grassroots. Otherwise you'll have plugs of green grass, and they'll take up the fertilizer before it reaches the tree roots. You're just putting it underneath those grassroots. Place a small bit of fertilizer in that hole. And you do that in holes at two feet intervals around those concentric circles.

Now, for mulch beds, it's a lot easier. Just evenly distribute the fertilizer throughout the area under the drip line. I do it right over the mulch. And if need be, you can rake it in, so it goes to the soil below. Follow the label directions, because some fertilizers, like Milorganite, don't need to be raked or watered in, while others do. So read the packets. It's all the information you need.

Fertilizing shrubs is just a little different. Since many are included in planting beds, you're fertilizing them every time you fertilize your annuals and perennials. But if they do need a nutrient boost, incorporate a low-nitrogen fertilizer or one recommended by your soil test around each shrub or at a rate of about five pounds per 100 square feet of low nitrogen, slow-release fertilizer, or follow the label direction of the fertilizer you use.

Now some shrubs have special needs. Roses and other big, blooming shrubs may benefit from a little more frequent fertilizer applications. Endless summer hydrangea is a good example of that. Now, endless summer is a beautiful plant that was introduced because it's a big leaf hydrangea that blooms on not only old growth, but new growth. And that's important for northern gardeners, because one of the problems with big leaf hydrangeas in colder climates, they die back to the ground. The leaves come up, but you get no blooms. But if you bought an Endless Summer® and it's not flowering for you, here's the key to success—moisture, water properly spring through early summer. And then, you want to make sure you do a fertilization.

Now, one of the things that I found very useful is a product called Milorganite. It's low nitrogen. It's an organic nitrogen fertilizer, slow release. And what research found is that, when you apply the Milorganite, while the microorganisms break down those nutrients from that fertilizer, it also releases some of the phosphorus and potassium bound to the soil. And phosphorus is great for flowering. Potassium, disease resistance and hardiness. So by proper watering and use with that fertilizer, I've really seen great success getting those Endless Summers® to start to bloom. So give that a try.

Now, preparing for summer and the extreme heat and the droughts can be a stress on your plants, shade plants subject to drying during extreme heat. So things like Hostas, if they are in a hot spot, even if they're in shade, they'll lose a lot of moisture, and they'll get browning on the edges. The same with Coralbells. Now these are perennials, but they're good indicator plants.

Now, let's take that idea and look at some of our shrubs that prefer to be in the shade that may suffer from that heat and drought. We want to monitor the soil and the moisture and the water because that's going to help those plans when they're in those hot, dry areas, and of course, mulch the soil. Look at this is an opportunity. If you've got a plant struggling and you don't want to put in all that extra effort to keep it alive, consider replacing it and moving it to a better spot, maybe one with the little afternoon shade, or replacing it with something that's more heat and drought tolerant. It's a good opportunity to make those needed changes and reduce your maintenance.

Now, we've just made it through part of the year. As you can see, the tasks aren't difficult, but important in keeping our trees and shrubs healthy and looking good. Now, go out into your landscape, evaluate what's working and what isn't, make some notes in your garden journal. No journal? Now's the time to start. You can record not only those plantings as we mentioned before, but also your maintenance strategies. And, work on putting down what's working and your dreams for the future. In our next session, we'll cover the rest of the year.

Fall and Winter Care of Trees and Shrubs
Lesson 7

In our last lesson, we discussed the care of trees and shrubs through spring and summer. In this lesson, we'll pick up the year of care and beauty with fall, a time when many of us close down our landscapes for winter. Winter protection starts the day you plant your trees and shrubs: Proper planting and care increase your plants' ability to survive winter stress. Focus your efforts on evergreens, new plantings, and any borderline-hardy plants you just couldn't resist at the garden center. All will benefit from some additional care, especially as they're getting established.

Prepare for Winter

- You may want to start by shredding leaves with your mower and leaving them on your lawn. As long as you can see the grass blades through the pieces of leaves, the grass will be fine. The leaves break down, adding organic matter and nutrients to the soil and improving your lawn. You can also use them as mulch around trees, shrubs, and perennials or compost them.

- Roses are unique among the plants and shrubs we're discussing because some are grafted and because gardeners sometimes buy roses that aren't quite hardy enough for a particular area. Both types need protection in colder climates. The goal of winter protection is to keep the soil consistently cold to keep plants dormant; you can increase your success by waiting for a week of freezing temperatures before you add mulch.
  - To use the *soil mound method*, start by loosely tying the canes of your roses to keep them from whipping in the wind. Make a cylinder of hardware cloth, a wire mesh sturdier than chicken wire, to encircle the shrubs. Sink the bottom few inches into the soil to prevent rodents from crawling underneath and at least 4 feet high to block rabbits. Wait for the ground to freeze the framework in place. Put an 8- to 10-inch mound of soil over

the graft or the base of the plant. Once that freezes, cover it with straw, marsh hay, or evergreen boughs to further insulate your plant.

○ The *Minnesota tip method* involves digging a trench about a foot away from the base of the plant, then carefully tipping the plant over, being careful not to break the stem. Anchor the plant in place and cover it with soil. Once that soil is frozen, cover the whole thing with straw or evergreen branches.

○ The *leaf method* works well on rose beds with a volume of leaves to provide insulation. This is the only method that involves fall pruning. Prune your roses back to about 18 inches so you can cover them, and encircle the rose bed with hardware cloth as described above. Fill the cylinder with dried leaves, packed tightly to allow water to roll off and down the side. When temperatures start hovering around freezing in the spring, remove the hardware cloth, carefully rake the leaves away, and use them as mulch in the garden.

• No matter what method you use, start removing mulch as the spring temperatures start hovering around freezing. You may want to keep something handy to cover the roses in case of a surprise late-spring frost. Once the winter protection is removed, you can do the needed pruning for the type of rose you are growing.

• New plantings, as well as borderline-hardy trees, shrubs, and evergreens, may also benefit from winter mulch. Consider using the soil mound method for these plants.

• Broadleaf evergreens—such as rhododendrons, azaleas, and boxwoods that have wide leaves and hold them through winter— are often subject to winter winds and sun, and they benefit from windbreaks and shading to prevent desiccation, or drying of the needles and leaves. The reason this is a concern is that evergreen needles and broadleaf evergreen leaves continue to transpire throughout the winter. But the roots are frozen in the ground and can't pull up more moisture to replace what is lost. Use the soil mound method with hardware cloth or a burlap wrap during the first few years after planting.

- Remember that the winter sun comes from the south and the prevailing winds come from the west, so avoid placing broadleaf evergreens in those areas. Use them strategically, keeping in mind the weather conditions and the browning that can result from improper placement.

Prevent Damage

- Winter may mean snow, ice, and deicing salt, all of which can damage plants. If plants are properly pruned, they'll be less susceptible to storm damage.

- When snow falls on multi-stemmed, upright evergreens, it can split the plants open. As the snow and ice melt and the temperatures warm, these plants tend to right themselves. If the splitting occurs over the course of a couple of years, however, permanent damage can result. To prevent that, use cotton cloth or bird netting to loosely tie the stems together in fall; when the snow falls on the plant, it rolls off instead of splitting it apart.

- As the food supply dwindles over winter, your landscape looks even more inviting to rodents, rabbits, deer, and other creatures. Protect your plants from hungry animals with fencing and repellents. The key is being proactive: Start before the animals start feeding to increase your chances of success.

It's easier to keep animals away from your garden in the first place than to break them of the habit later.

- Cylinders of hardware cloth, useful for protecting plants from winds and from the cold, are also good for protecting them from animals, particularly voles. Those are tiny rodents that tend to eat the bark of trees and shrubs, the roots of hostas and daylilies, and the seeds of many plants.

- Fencing to keep out rabbits must be at least 4 feet high. If you're in an area that gets a great deal of snow, keep an extension handy; as the snow piles up, the rabbits can reach over the fence.

- For deer, moose, and other large animals, make your fence larger and farther away from your plants and secure the circle. Some gardeners even do double fences to ensure that large animals can't reach young, developing plants.

- Repellents are another option. You need to apply these early—before the animals start feeding—and repeat as necessary. Cayenne pepper works well, but some gardeners have noticed that deer seem to prefer the seasoned plants. Highly deodorant soaps also help repel animals, especially deer. Hang a bar from a tree or shrub, or spread slivers over the soil surface. Avoid soaps that are high in fat, because that can attract animals. Human or pet hair stuffed in an old stocking is another homemade remedy.

- There are also commercial repellents on the market. Some are based on herbs and have a minty fragrance. Others keep animals away with a strong, unpleasant smell. Whichever you choose, make sure you follow the label directions and replenish as needed.

- Scare tactics, such as clanging pans and motion-sensitive lights, are another option.

○ Try a variety of techniques, but always be sure to monitor for damage and adjust as needed. Fencing is effective but can be knocked over. Repellents may work for a while, but if enough animals are hungry enough, they'll plow through and eat just about anything. Keep an eye on all your plants throughout the winter.

• Salt damage is an issue for those living in cold climates, where snow and ice are common, as well as for those living along the ocean, where salt spray can affect the soil and plants.

○ Salt is hard on plants because water flows from areas of high concentration to areas of low concentration. As the salt dehydrates plants, water flows away from the roots, where the water concentration is high, into the soil, where the concentration is lower, leaving the roots laden with salt. This dehydration of the roots leaves the plants with a wilted appearance.

○ Salt in the soil also prevents the uptake of other nutrients that are important to plants, such as potassium, which is good for winter hardiness and disease resistance; calcium; and magnesium. When chloride is part of deicing salt, it prevents the chlorophyll production necessary for photosynthesis. That can result in leaf dieback, which will leave your plants looking as if they are drought stressed.

○ Often, those symptoms don't show up until spring, when you'll see browning of the leaf margin, called *scorch*. You may see actual dieback, or death of your plants, especially in areas that are close to sources of salt, such as driveways or walks. *Brooming* results when salt kills twigs and buds, causing fine, twiggy growth. Removing the source of salt or pruning out the damage will help.

- To prevent salt damage, look for the source and see if you can use barriers to salt spray. Use fabrics, such as burlap or weed barrier, or a salt-tolerant decorative planting to screen plants that are less tolerant of salt.
  - Sometimes prevention is simply a change of practices. If you salt your sidewalks, shovel first, then salt. If you salt when there's an inch or two of snow, then shovel after snow accumulates, you're tossing the salt-laden snow onto your plants.

  - Consider using plant-friendly deicing salt. It's a little pricier, but replacing damaged or dead plants can add up, too. Many new products in development use corn or even beet juice to help deal with the salt and ice issues.

  - In spring, wash the salt off your plants before growth to reduce damage. Leach the salt out of salt-laden soil by watering thoroughly, waiting, and watering thoroughly again. Spring rains will do the same thing, but if you have a dry spring, make sure your plants are watered and you've washed some of the salt past the plant roots below.

  - You may even want to consider re-landscaping. This could be as simple as adding mulch to create a barrier along areas that collect salt or moving trees and shrubs back and planting annuals in areas subject to winter damage.

- Enjoy the beauty of snow-covered plants, but resist the urge to help. To avoid damaging plants, don't shake off accumulated snow and ice but allow it to melt naturally.

Questions to Consider

1. Review the strategies for protecting your roses: the leaf, the soil mound, or the Minnesota tip method. Which ones might serve you?

2. Review the options for protecting your landscape from hungry animals. Which would be most effective for you?

Fall and Winter Care of Trees and Shrubs
Lesson 7—Transcript

In our last session, we discussed the care of our trees and shrubs through spring and summer. Now we need to forge ahead through the remainder of the year. So we pick up the year of care and beauty with fall. Now fall is a time when many of us are closing down our landscapes for winter and others are transitioning from extremely hot to milder weather. So let's talk about a few tasks we will be doing to manage throughout the season.

Now I'm always asked about managing leaves. My goal is to get you to look at these tasks as a free resource, not a problem to be tolerated. So let's start by looking at how nature manages her leaves in the forest. They drop from the tree, collect on the ground, and over time, decompose, creating that rich forest soil. Think about that as you deal with your leaves.

You may want to start by shredding them with your mower and leaving them on the lawn. As long as you can see the grass blades through the pieces of leaves, it will be fine. Your grass will be fine. Those leaves break down, adding organic matter and nutrients to the soil, improving your lawn. Or shred them and use them as a mulch around trees, shrubs, and perennials on the ground. Or shred them and compost them, and then you'll have plenty of compost to put into your gardens when you're starting new beds.

Now, for those in colder climates, it's time to prepare plants for the cold season ahead. And those of you who are lucky enough to be in a milder climate, enjoy the fact you don't have quite as much winter preparation and protection to do as those in more northerly, or colder regions. Now keep in mind that winter protection started the day you planted your trees and shrubs. Proper planting and care increases your plant's ability to survive the winter stress. And of course, using reliably hardy plants in the right growing conditions will give you that added preparation you need for winter, because healthy plants will survive the stresses of winter much better.

Now, we want to focus our efforts on evergreens, new plantings, and any of those borderline hardy plants you just couldn't resist at the garden center. All of these plants will benefit from some additional care, especially as they're getting established. Now we're going to start with Roses, because Roses are a little bit unique among our plants or shrubs that we're discussing. Some Roses are grafted, and often, gardeners buy Roses that aren't quite hardy for their area. Both types need a little protection in the colder climates. So let's take a few minutes to talk about the various methods for insulating Roses where the winters are quite cold.

Now, keep in mind that results of your winter protection can vary from year to year, just like the winters do. In extreme years, no matter what you do, you may lose your Roses. In milder years, you may have a lot more survival and less problems. But increase your success by waiting for a week of freezing temperature before you apply the mulch. Why? Our goal for winter protection is really to keep the soil consistently cold. We want to keep those plants dormant, and we're going to talk about keeping the animals out, because we're creating a nice habitat for them, as well as protecting our Roses.

Now, the soil mound method has long been used. And we'd start by loosely tying those canes to keep them from whipping in the wind and reducing damage that way. Now, some gardeners also add a circle of hardware cloth. Let me show you what that's about. Hardware cloth is basically this wire mesh, much sturdier and heavier duty than chicken wire. And you'll make a cylinder that encircles your shrubs. Now obviously, this isn't going to keep any hungry rabbits out, but we'd sink the bottom few inches into the soil to keep out rodents, like voles, that would try to crawl underneath, and make it at least four feet high to keep out the rabbits. So this will help hold all the mulch in place that we're going to use inside. So, here's the goal. After we tie our Rose canes, sink this hardware cloth, wait for the ground to freeze. That freezes this in place. Put an 8- to 10-inch mound of soil over the graft, that union where that bud was grafted onto a hardy root stock, or the base of the plant. Once that freezes, cover that mound of soil with straw, marsh hay, or evergreen boughs, and that will further insulate your plants. And as you can see, this cylinder of hardware cloth, great for keeping out the animals, but holding all that much in place so it doesn't blow away and end up in your neighbor's yard.

In Minnesota, where the temperatures are very extreme, they've developed a method they coined, the Minnesota Tip Method. They dig a trench about a foot away from the base of the plant and then carefully tip the plant over, being careful not to break the stem. Then they anchor it in place and cover it with soil. Once that soil is frozen, they cover the whole thing with straw or evergreen branches. It's worked quite well for them in their extremely cold winters.

Now this method also works well with Tree Roses like this, because Tree Roses are often grafted down at the soil line, and also up on top, to form that tree. Now with those two grafts and extremely cold temperatures, they're very susceptible to winter kill. So laying them over, covering with soil, and using the Minnesota Tip Method works quite well. You may also want to use this on climbers, because most climbers bloom on old wood, so if they die back to the ground, so go your flowers. So give that a try in those extremely cold areas.

A third method is the leaf method, and I like it because the leaves are free. And I find it works great on Rose beds where you have a volume of leaves to provide insulation. It's very simple. Just encircle the Rose bed with hardware cloth. Sink it several inches beneath the ground. So you want to do this before the ground freezes. It should be at least four feet high to keep those hungry rabbits at bay. Now this is the only method where I recommend pruning your Roses before winter. You're going to prune your Roses back to about 18 inches. And this is just so you can cover them. In general, we like to wait until spring, after we remove the winter protection, to do our pruning. So we've encircled, we've waited for the ground to freeze so that it locks that fencing in place, and we want to do that because we're keeping the animals out. By that time, when the ground freezes, guess what? They've found some place else to live, hopefully.

We're going to then, fill that with dried leaves. Pack it in tight. Some people cover it with plastic to keep them dry, but I find if they're packed in tight, the water usually rolls off and down the side. And the good news is, when temperatures start hovering around freezing in the spring, remove the hardware cloth, carefully rake the leaves away, and use them as mulch in the garden—great way to recycle, very little storage needed.

Now, some gardeners opt for Rose cones, and Rose cones are those white cones that you see out in the garden over winter. Personally, not my favorite. One of the reasons I don't like that method is I see people put them on too early, leave them on too late, and they actually cook their Roses over winter and have a lot of failure. But if you opt for Rose cones, wait for a week of freezing temperatures.

I would still recommend mounding the soil over the base of your grafted Roses. Then, if it's not ventilated, cut some holes in the side away from the prevailing winds. That way, on a sunny day, when the temperatures warm up inside that Rose cone, that hot air will blow out and vent the Roses so you don't cook them. Be sure to remove those when the temperatures hover around freezing in the spring.

Now, some years, doing nothing works just fine. But it's risky. You're taking a chance that you and nature are working in sync. But no matter what method used, start removing whatever mulch was applied as the spring temperatures start hovering around freezing. You may want to keep a little something handy to cover them in case you have a surprise late-spring frost. And then, as I mentioned before, once that winter protection is removed, you can do the needed pruning for the type of Rose you are growing.

Now, after this discussion, you may decide that you want to follow my strategy. I only grow hardy Roses in my landscape. I know that I'm not going to get around to winter protection. I'm not going to do all the fussing. My schedule is too crazy and busy. And, it's not that I'm lazy, I'm a low-input gardener. So I opt for hardy Roses that will survive in my climate quite well, with minimal care for me. And the other benefit? By not covering them, they provide winter interest that I love in my garden, and Rose hips for the birds to enjoy, and you too. They're high in vitamin C.

Now, some of the hardy Roses that are my favorite are the Explorer and Parkland series, developed in Canada, and known for their hardiness. William Baffin is a shrub Rose that grows large and is often trained as a climber because it needs no winter protection. If it's happy, though, it will send out runners, so you'll have large plants to contend with. But in my mind, that's worth the price. Buck Roses, developed in Iowa, tolerate the heat and humidity, as well as cold temperatures. And Knock Out® Roses have really taken the landscape Roses by storm, because they're so hardy, robust, good disease resistance, and developed by a friend of mine, Will Radler, who said he developed them for people like me who were tired of losing Roses to the winter, and I think he did a good job for all of us.

Now, some new plantings, not just Roses, as well as borderline hardy trees and shrubs and evergreens, may also benefit from some winter mulch. Now, consider using a cylinder of hardware cloth, sunk in the ground to keep out the voles and other rodents that tend to munch on the bark of trees and shrubs in winter, and at least four feet high to keep out the rabbits. We'll talk about deer and moose in a minute. Now again, you want to wait to apply any additional mulch after the ground freezes. By then, as I mentioned, the rabbits have found somewhere else to live, and our goal is to keep that soil temperature consistently cold throughout the winter to avoid freezing and thawing that can cause some damage.

Now, broadleaf evergreens, and those are plants like Rhododendrons, Azaleas and Boxwoods, that have wide leaves. They're not needled evergreens, but they hold their leaves through winter, are often subject to winter winds and sun, and they benefit from wind breaks and shading to prevent desiccation, or drying of the needles and leaves. Now, the reason this is a concern is, those needles on your evergreens, and the leaves on your broadleaf evergreens, continue to transpire, lose moisture from the leaves throughout the winter. But the roots are frozen in the ground and can't pull up more moisture to replace that.

So, again, you could do the cylinder of hardware cloth filled with evergreen boughs, or rap that cylinder in burlap. And many of you may have seen burlap in hardware stores or fabric stores, and it just helps cut the wind. It also provides some shade, as well, so that you can shade those broadleaf evergreens so they tend not to lose the moisture over winter. And other similar fabrics work as well. Now you can see a couple of examples here in Duluth and at Boerner Botanical Gardens. Now, it's not the prettiest thing to look at, but when spring rolls around, those evergreens will look great.

Now hopefully, though, this is just necessary the first few years, because in my book, why have evergreens wrapped in burlap or other fabric to look at all winter? And it brings to mind a story of one of my students. When I was teaching tree and shrub ID, one of my students had designed a landscape, and she put boxwoods on the south side of a house as a formal entrance. Now, if you think about the winter sun typically coming from the south, think about where the prevailing winds come in the winter, from the west. So we want to avoid placing broadleaf evergreens in those areas.

Well, Sandy learned about boxwoods and that I recommended not putting them on the south side where they tend to brown out from the winter sun. She went back to the nursery where she bought them, and they said, don't worry, we have green burlap to wrap them in. But again, do you want to look at green burlap, especially at your front entrance? So use your broadleaf evergreens strategically, keeping in mind the winter winds and the winter sun, and the browning that can result from improper placement.

Now, for many of you, winter may mean snow, ice, de-icing salts, and all of that can damage our plants. So, if we've properly pruned our plants, they're going to be less susceptible to damage by storms. And we'll talk more about that when we discuss pruning trees. And a good story comes to mind about my friends, Angie and Dean. They worked with arborists to keep their trees properly pruned. A big ice storm moved through their area, and they had the least amount of damage of all their neighbors, because they pruned properly to keep their plants in good shape so they're more resistant to damage.

Now, you may want to prevent damage on multi-stemmed, upright evergreens, things like junipers, or arborvitae. If you've experienced where the snow falls on top and splits the plant open, it's a very sad sight in the winter landscape, and you really need to just leave them in place. As the snow and ice melt and the temperatures warm, they tend to right themselves by spring. A couple years of this, however, and it can be more permanent damage. Now, once the damage occurs, I mentioned, just wait. That's all you can do. But, make a note on your calendar to do some preventive work next fall to prevent this damage. You could loosely tie the stems in fall and keep those stems together so when the snow falls on the plant, it rolls off instead of splitting it apart. Let me show you.

Tie those multiple stems up using strips of cotton cloth, or, I like to use that bird netting. You know that black plastic netting you use to cover your plants to protect it from birds? I like it because it blends in with the plants, and, if animals try to browse on your Arborvitae, they'll get a mouthful of plastic before they get to the plant. So let me show you how this works. I just have some cotton strips here, and I'm going to tie up those branches so the snow load falls off. And based on the height and size of your tree, just continue this all the way from bottom to top, and you'll protect your tree and prevent the damage, and it'll look beautiful come spring.

Speaking of animals, fall is a great time to protect your plants from hungry critters. As the food supply dwindles over winter, your landscape looks even more inviting to rodents, rabbits, deer, and other hungry critters that like to visit your garden. Protect your plants from hungry animals with fencing and repellents. Those are two of the options. The key is being proactive, starting before the animals start feeding, you'll increase your chances of success. It's easier to keep them away than to break the habit, because once they find there's good eats at your house, they'll be back for more. Now here are some of the plants that animals seem to prefer. New and young plantings, fruit trees, euonymus, members of the Rose family, witch hazel and Fothergilla, and many other plants you may have observed in the past, or your neighbors have had trouble with. If in doubt, provide some protection.

Now we've talked a lot about using cylinders of hardware cloth for protecting plants from winds and from the cold. It's also a useful tool to protect it from animals. Just like we did, we may make a small fence around our trees or shrubs by sinking that cylinder of hardware cloth into the ground, again, to keep the voles away. Those are tiny rodents that tend to eat the bark of trees and shrubs, the roots of Hostas and day lilies, and also the seeds of many plants. So sink that in the ground before the ground freezes. Once it freezes, it makes it harder for the voles to get through.

Now, moles are often blamed for the damage that the voles cause. So when you're talking to an expert or looking for solutions, don't use the word moles, because there are hibernating during the winter, while the voles are out busy, scurrying around under the snow looking for good eats. So, voles are the ones you want to keep away from your plants. They don't eat insects;

they eat seeds and plants. So keep an eye out on all those tasty morsels for them.

Now, when you're fencing to keep out rabbits, it needs to be at least four feet high. But keep an extension handy, because if you're in an area that gets lots of snow, as the snow piles up, it makes it easier for the rabbits to reach over that fence. Now for deer, moose, and other large animals, you may want to make your fence larger and even further away from your plants. And you need to secure that circle. I've seen dear knock down fencing to get to some Magnolias to do a little rubbing and munching, as well. And some gardeners even do double fences to really ensure that those big animals can't reach those young, developing plants. Usually once they're good size, it's a little easier to protect them and they're a little less appealing to the animals.

Now, repellents are another option. Now you need to apply early, and you need to start before they start eating, and repeat as necessary. Now I brought a few along with me. There are many homemade types of repellents available. Some gardeners find that cayenne pepper works very well. I had a landscaper that told me that he'd send his crew out early in the morning when the dew was on the plants to sprinkle the cayenne pepper. Now they wore safety glasses and respirators and gloves, because this stuff is hot and can really cause damage. I was sharing the story to a group of students and one of my students said, "Melinda, we found that the deer at the golf course preferred the seasoned plants over the unseasoned plants." So the moral of the story is, keep an eye on whatever repellent you're using.

There was research at several universities that found highly deodorant soaps really helped to repel animals, especially deer. You can hang a bar from a tree or shrub, or, spread slivers over the soil surface. Avoid those that are high in fat, because that can attract the animals. While they are munching on the soap, they'll then start to dine on your plants. Or you might want to try human hair or hair from your pets that you collect out of the brush. Human hair—next haircut, ask the beauty salon if you can keep the clippings, or visit your nearby barbershop, they'll be sure to remember you. Basically, place those in an old nylon stocking, and preferably one with a little human scent. The smell of humans helps deter the animals.

Now these are just a few of the many different home-made repellents you've probably heard about or read about. There are also commercial repellents on the market. Just be sure to read and follow label directions. Some smell good and they're based out of herbs and they have a minty fragrance. Other stink to help keep the animals away. Whichever you choose, make sure you follow the directions and replenish as needed.

Now scare tactics, like clanging pans and motion sensitive lights, are another option that you may find works for you as well. You might want to try a variety of techniques, but always be sure to monitor for damage and adjust as needed. Fencing is very effective, but often gets blown or knocked over during the winter, or by hungry animals. Repellents may work for a while, but if there's enough animals, and they're hungry enough, they'll plow through and eat just about anything. So keep an eye on all your plants.

Now some tactics will work in the rural areas better than urban areas, where animals are used to people. So things that rely on the scent of humans, like a handful of human hair, or pets, may not work well in the city, so again, adjust and monitor as needed. And when the snow and ice arrive, monitoring for your animal damage and managing the snow and ice is important, and you want to do it in a plant-friendly manner. Salt damage is an issue for those living in cold climates where snow and ice are common. It's also a year-round issue for those of you that live along the ocean, where salt spray can impact the soil and the plants you're trying to grow.

Now here's why salt is hard on plants. Water travels from areas of high concentration to low concentration, so, as the salt causes the dehydration of the roots, you have water moving from the roots into the soil, because there's less water where the salt's on the outside of the roots, than on the inside of the plants. So again, water moves from the roots, high concentration, out to the soil, laden with salt. So that's how it dehydrates your roots of your plant, which then looks like wilting.

Salt in the soil also prevents the uptake of other nutrients, things that are important to our plants, like potassium, good for winter hardiness and good for disease resistance, calcium and magnesium. And when chloride is part of that deicing salt, and the chloride is absorbed, it prevents the chlorophyll production. And chlorophyll is important for photosynthesis. And that can result in leaf dieback.

So your plants will appear to be drought stressed if the salt is in the soil. So often those symptoms don't show up until spring when things get up and growing. You'll see browning of the leaf margin, called scorch. You may see actual dieback, or death of your plants. And especially on the side closest to the source of salt, like drives or walks or areas where you tend to salt. And this is a good example of what leaf scorch looks like, just browning on your leaf margins. Now twigs and buds that are exposed to salt spray will dry and even die. And again, you first see the damage in areas that are exposed to the salt. So that's how you know it's salt damage, versus some other cause. You can tell where the walk is and the salt coming in draining off the salted sidewalk into the garden bed causing dieback.

Brooming can often happen because of salt damage. The salt kills these twigs and the buds, resulting in fine, twiggy growth like you see here. And that's called brooming. Removing the source of salt, or pruning out the damage will also help. Now you can prevent salt damage with a few items like barriers. We've talked a lot about fencing, but these barriers need to prevent the salt spray from the road and the cars going down the drive from hitting the plants. So you may want to use fabrics, like burlap, or weed barrier, like we showed before. Or maybe a decorative planting that's more salt tolerant to screen those that are less salt tolerant. So look at where the source of salt is coming from, and if you need to block it, that will help prevent the damage.

Sometimes it's just a simple change of practices. If you are the source of the salt because you're salting your sidewalks because of ice or snow, shovel first, and then salt. What happens is, we often go out, salt our walks when it's just an inch or two of snow. More snow piles up, we shovel the salt laden snow into our beds or onto our plants and cause problems. You may want to consider using plant-friendly deicing salt. They're a little pricier, but replacing damaged plants or dead plants can add up to a lot of money, too. The good news is there's lots of new products being investigated and developed using corn or even beet juice to help deal with the salt and ice issues.

In spring, wash the salt off your plants. Wash that off the plants, and often, if you do this before growth, you can reduce the amount of damage. And leach the salt out of salt-laden soils. And leaching is basically watering thoroughly, waiting, watering thoroughly again as that water is moving through. Now nature often does this. If you're in an area with spring rains, will wash that through the soil. But if you have a dry spring, make sure that those plants are watered and you've washed some of that salt past the plant roots down below.

Now you may even want to consider re-landscaping, because often we put plants in areas where salt is an issue, whether it's salt spray from the ocean, or salt from road salt, or where we tend to take care of our walks and drives. So maybe a little slight redesign will help. When I worked for the city of Milwaukee, we were responsible for replacing turf near all the police stations after winter. Now you can imagine anybody visiting a police station wasn't in a good mood. So the last thing they wanted is for that person to slip and fall. So they would heavily salt their walks. And every spring, we'd replace the turf along the side of the walk. So instead, I suggested we take pavers that matched the building brick, and create a barrier. So, they shoveled, salted, the salt-laden moisture went into the paver area, the buffer, and didn't damage surrounding plants, whether it's grass or trees or shrubs. That might be a solution. Maybe it's as simple as a mulch area along those areas, and then your plantings are further away. Or, move your trees and shrubs back a little further, put annuals in those areas subjected to winter damage so that you've got an additional buffer that's beautiful to look at.

You also can look for more salt-tolerant plants. There's lots of good lists available from your local university resource and garden centers. In coastal areas, Wax Myrtle, Oleander, and Sweet Gum are just a few to consider. Take a look at what's surviving on your city streets if you live in an area that uses a lot of road salt, Honeylocusts, Lilacs, Juniper, some, not all, Japanese tree lilacs, if they're not invasive in your area. So look around your neighborhood and see what's doing well and what's suffering, and add that to your list of plants to try. And enjoy the beauty of snow-covered plants, but resist the urge to help. I know we see snow and ice building up on our plants, and we want to get out there and shake it off. Don't shake, or don't knock the snow and ice off. You'll cause more damage. I see people out there, and I can hear the cracking going on underneath the snow and ice. You'll do more damage; just be patient, enjoy the view, and avoid that drive to go try to fix it. Let nature take care of it.

But you do want to make some notes of any changes that need to be made before next winter. And contact a certified arborist with the training and equipment to repair any large trees that are damaged over winter. They have the equipment to do it safely. And the money you save by trying to do it yourself, may be spend on a hospital or doctor visit, or missed work because you've fallen out of a tree or injured yourself.

I mentioned earlier that certified arborists, it's a voluntary certification, but it shows a level of competency. And so you might want to start by looking for a certified arborist. And consider developing a relationship with one, because spending time to find a quality tree-care professional will pay off in years of good service, healthy trees, and long-lived trees and shrubs. Plus, having a good working relationship with a professional arborist pays off, because when a storm occurs, the regular customers are the first to be served. But more importantly, they'll provide proper care and proactive pruning to reduce the risk of storm damage.

And the best news? Spring is on its way, and your landscape will soon be filled with new, beautiful blooms and the next cycle of tree and shrub care begins. So take some time to develop your own year-round maintenance program, record it in your calendar, include a few reminders in your journal so that you remember to do proactive care to keep your landscape looking its best.

Pruning Old and Young Trees
Lesson 8

Pruning is an important part of keeping your trees and shrubs beautiful and healthy. It's also one of those tasks that many gardeners fear and some even dread. They avoid it until there's a problem, at which point, they're looking at repair rather than prevention. Pruning paranoia is common, but tackling the pruning tasks you can handle and hiring a professional to do the rest is a good way to deal with it. Starting the pruning process early in the life of your trees will help reduce pruning needs and costs as your trees mature.

Use the Proper Tools
- Safety glasses protect your eyes as you prune. When you're reaching into a plant to cut, it's very easy to end up with a stick in the eye.

- A good pair of leather gauntlet-type gloves that fit tightly will protect your hands.

- Use bypass pruners that have removable blades, like scissors, that can be sharpened and a safety latch, as well as a sheath for carrying. Make sure they fit your hand and the job; they should be designed to cut stems of about ½ inch in diameter.

- Loppers extend your reach to branches that are hard to reach, and they can handle larger stems. Ratchet loppers have more power, which means you use less energy to make your cuts.

- A short-bladed saw allows you to get to tiny branches. A Sawzall with a pruning attachment is good for multi-stem shrubs.

Remove Codominant Stems
- Although it's unnecessary to prune until a tree has had a chance to root in, you should get it off to a good start by removing damaged or broken branches and pruning the major codominant stems. Ideally, one stem comes from the ground up and is the main trunk, or leader.

The side branches should not compete with it. Because that's not always the case, over time, you will prune side branches back to reinforce the leader.

- Prune young trees after a couple of years to establish a strong framework and direct growth evenly. By doing so, you avoid storm damage and hazards; furthermore, you will make much smaller cuts when the tree is young than when it reaches maturity, and those smaller wounds close more quickly.

- With a more mature tree, create a balanced, stronger structure by continuing to prune codominant stems. Start by evaluating the existing structure and identifying the leader, typically (though not always) the largest upright stem. If several stems are competing, pick the largest and closest to the center. Subordinate the others over time by pruning back about a third of their size initially.

Prune for Strength
- Strong branches and their attachments will stand up under wind, ice, and other stresses. Encourage branches with wide crotch angles and no included bark that spiral around the trunk. If the branches emerge across from each other or several at the same point, the tree will have a weak point that will tend to break apart in storms. Eliminate branches that cross or are parallel or touching because they will rub, causing open entry wounds for insects and diseases.

- Other branches you should remove include the following:
  - Stems growing out of the ground next to the trunk are called suckers. They don't compete for energy, but they can rub and cause damage. Cut them just below the soil surface; do not use herbicides because these can kill the main plant.

  - Stubs protruding from the trunk create entryways for insects and disease.

- Branches growing right above each other and branches with a narrow crotch angle eventually will grow into each other. When they do that, the bark comes together to form included bark, creating a weak connection. As they push against each other, cracks form, branches fail, and you end up with a split tree.

- Crossing branches will rub, causing damage and creating the potential for disease.

Prune for Balance

- Side branches should be less than half the diameter of the trunk. Also, know the form and mature size of the tree you're pruning to preserve its natural development. The lowest branches are temporary, so don't prune them right away: Their leaves produce energy to support the tree's growth and establishment.

- Choose the spot where you would eventually like the lowest permanent branch of the tree to be. Consider the tree's placement: Do people walk or drive underneath? Also consider its natural state: An ornamental tree can be limbed almost all the way to the ground. Keep these considerations in mind as you're establishing the framework.

- Balance the canopy. An unbalanced canopy has all or most of the branches on one side. To avoid this, shorten some of the branches on the heavy side or remove a few to balance out the crown. Over time, this will help the plant develop a more balanced crown as new branches grow and others slow down.

- New growth along the branch is called *lion's-tailing* or *over-lifting*. If you prune all those little stems, all the weight will be at the end of the branch, making it structurally weak and more likely to break. To deal with a tree that has been pruned in this way, first allow the tree to recover for 2 to 3 years to allow new growth to occur all along the stem. Then choose those stems you want to keep and shorten the others.

Maintain the Structure

- As you contemplate pruning mature trees over time, keep in mind what you are trying to accomplish. Maintaining the strong framework should always be the guiding principle.

  ○ Remove anything that's diseased, damaged, or dead. It's important to keep up with this type of pruning because damage and dying back occur throughout the life of the tree.

  ○ Remove any hazards, including branches that could fall and harm someone or damage property.

- Pruning improves flowering and fruiting. Occasionally, a fruit tree may need more light penetration; remove some of the stem to allow better flowering and more fruit occur.

- You may need to thin to allow more sun to reach plantings below. Thin carefully: The last thing you want is to sacrifice a beautiful tree to get some grass beneath it.

If you prune when plants are dormant, you can see the structure more easily to make better cuts.

141

Consider Timing

- If you prune in late winter, the wounds will close quickly as growth begins in spring. You'll get quicker healing and incur less risk to the plants from disease and insects.

- Avoid pruning during leaf expansion. As the leaves expand, sap flows and growth occurs. Pruning at this time could damage the trunk. In cold climates, pruning late in the season may also stimulate late-season growth that could be injured over winter.

- Evergreens are terminal growers; that is, they grow from the tip. If you watch a pine tree in the spring, you'll see the bud expands, called *candles*. You can prune those by half or two-thirds to eliminate some of the new growth. Spruces should be pruned above a healthy bud before the bud breaks.

Prune Thoughtfully

- Always take it slow when you're pruning. If you remove too much at one time, you stimulate growth and eliminate energy-producing leaves needed to support the tree.

- In general, remove no more than 5 percent to 20 percent of growth in the following situations: in a cold climate where plants tend to grow more slowly, in a landscape with mature or recently planted trees, and with trees that are prone to decay.

- Minimize the number of wounds.

- Remove no more than 35 percent of new growth at a time in the first 5 years of a tree's life. In trees between 5 and 20 years of age, remove no more than 25 percent to 30 percent of growth and any temporary or hazardous branches.

- Keep your pruning to a minimum as you continue developing and maintaining the structure of the tree. Continue to remove crossing and parallel branches and make sure nothing interferes with the main trunk.

Cut Properly

- The area where the branch meets the trunk contains energy reserves and chemicals that help prevent decay. Leave that intact; if your cut is round, not oval, it will close much more quickly.

- On finer branches, make cuts on a slant above an outward-facing bud, not too close to where the bud dries out but not so far that you leave a stub.

- To prune large branches, anything over 2 to 3 inches, say, use the double-cut method to prevent the weight of the branch from breaking and ripping the bark all along the trunk.
  - Make the first cut from the bottom, about a foot away from the trunk.

  - To remove the branch, cut from above and down so that if the branch were to break, it would not rip the trunk but break off by the first cut.

  - Make the final cut flush with the branch bark collar.

- One pruning practice you should not do is topping a tree. It is bad for the tree's health and longevity, as well as its beauty.
  - Topping is basically indiscriminately cutting branches back close to the trunk, usually to reduce the size of the tree. Contrary to some opinions, trees cannot get too large to support themselves—they're designed to be a certain size. Topping cuts leave stubs or cut back to lateral branches too small to sustain those that are left, and that is what compromises the plant's ability to support itself. If you remove more than 50 percent of the leaf-bearing crown that produces energy, the tree will take its resources and energy reserves from the roots and the trunk.

  - Severe pruning also activates latent buds that are underneath the bark and lie dormant. Once you top a tree, they break dormancy and put out growth that is fast and weak, and it's weakly attached. All the fine twigs that occur after topping are more subject to wind, ice, and other types of damage. Because they're more subject to decay, weakly attached, and fast-growing, they're also more likely to become hazards.

○ Overall, topping weakens the plant by eliminating its energy source and makes it more subject to pests. Furthermore, improper cuts close slowly, increasing the risk of disease and decay. The drastic change in the canopy from the removal of leaves that shade the trunk of the tree can also result in sunburn on the trunk, which means it's more likely to form cankers and be subject to bark splitting.

Questions to Consider

1. What should you do about codominant stems?

2. How much new growth should you remove from a 3-year-old tree?

Pruning Old and Young Trees
Lesson 8—Transcript

We've just finished developing our year-round maintenance programs to keep trees and shrubs looking their best. Now I want to add pruning to that list. It's an important part of keeping your trees and shrubs beautiful and healthy. It's also one of those tasks that many gardeners fear and some even dread, so it's often avoided and overlooked, until there is a problem, and now we're looking at fixing something rather than prevention.

So pruning is very important, but pruning paranoia is very common. So tackling those pruning tasks that you can handle and hiring a professional to do those that are maybe too big or too complicated, or maybe you're not comfortable with, is a very good way to deal with pruning paranoia. And starting the pruning process early in the life of your trees will help reduce pruning needs and cost as your trees mature. Now, we're going to focus on pruning young trees that most of us can manage, that smaller size. We'll save the bigger jobs for those of you that may have more skill or desire and the professionals with the training, equipment, and knowledge to handle those bigger jobs.

Let's start by looking at the tools that you're going to need. Safety glasses are important. They protect your eyes. And you may think, ah nothing's going to fly off the ground when I'm pruning. But when you're in there making your cuts, reaching into the plant, it's very easy to end up with a stick in the eye. The safety glasses have side shields that will protect your eyes. It's worth the investment. It's worth taking the time to find those safety glasses before you start pruning. A good pair of gloves, these are nice leather gloves, gauntlet type, that are great for pruning roses and shrubs with thorns and things, or trees that tend to have thorns like Hawthorns. A good pair of leather gloves that fit tight are excellent to protect your hands while pruning.

Hand pruners are something every gardener really needs, and you want bypass pruners. These have blades like scissors. So there are two sharp blades that cut through, a nice clean cut. Do not get anvil pruners; they crush the stems, don't make a clean cut. These are nice because they have removable blades. So if I chip or damage my blades, I don't have to replace the whole pruner, just the blades. And they are re-sharpenable, and a safety latch. A sheath for carrying your pruners out to the job is a great way to keep them handy and out of the soil. When you're selecting pruners make sure they fit your hand and the job. These are a little bit smaller, so they're great for smaller jobs and smaller hands.

Loppers extend your reach. So you could reach into shrubs to get those branches that are a little harder to take. They also handle bigger stems. Hand pruners, about a ½ inch diameter or less. If a lopper will take it, about ½ the size of the opening. And these are ratchet, so they have much more power, so you don't use as much energy when making your cut.

And a saw. Now, I typically stick to small trees and shrubs. I save the big stuff for the people with the equipment. So I like a blade that's short. It allows me to reach in there and get to those branches that are tiny and small. I also use a reciprocating saw with a pruning attachment, great for multi-stem shrubs. So you might need to make a trip to your hardware store as well. So pick out a tool that works for you and works for the type of jobs that you're doing.

Now, why prune? We mentioned when planting trees we want to wait to do our major pruning once the tree is established. We really don't want to do a lot of pruning until that tree has had a chance to root in. But we do want to do some pruning to get it off to a good start. We want to remove the major co-dominant stem issues. Now, these are stems that are competing with the main trunk. So what we like ideally is a stem that comes from the ground up, that's our main trunk, or leader, and any of the side branches should not compete with that. But, that's not always the case. So we want to prune a couple of those down so we have one main leader. Now we'll do this over a long period of time.

We also prune young trees after a couple of years to start establishing that strong framework. So initially broken, damaged branches at planting, remove any co-dominant stems, and then do major pruning after the first couple years. By establishing a good, strong framework, we'll avoid storm damage and hazards. You're also making much smaller cuts when the tree is four, five years old than once it reaches 15 or 20 years. And those smaller wounds close more quickly. We create that strong framework by pruning young trees to establish the growth in the right direction, so that's really what we're trying to do. Evenly distributed, growing where we want it, not necessarily where it occurred in nature.

Now, strong branches and their attachments are those that stand up in wind, ice, and under other stresses, and we'll talk about developing those. I mentioned a strong, central leader. For most plants we want one main trunk and all the branches coming out of that. We want branches with wide crotch angles and no included bark. Now, wide crotch angles are things you see on oak trees. Here's the trunk; here's the branch. And notice how long Oaks live, versus trees with narrow branch angles, say something like a Silver Maple, where those branches are angled like this. Those are going to grow and develop bark, and that's called included bark, between those two branches. We want the branches spiraling around the trunk of the tree. If the branches come out across from each other, or several at the same point, guess what, not strong. And that's a problem, because it's a weak point; they tend to break apart in storms. We don't want branches that cross. We don't want those that are parallel or touching, because they'll end up rubbing, and that makes open entry wounds for insects and diseases.

We're also going to need to identify the lowest branches in the permanent structure of the tree. And what that means is, as the tree grows and develops, maybe it's shading your patio. So you want to make sure the branches are above your height, above your head. So those lower branches, we're going to keep short until the time the tree is reaching maturity and we can remove those. And after about 5, 10, 15 years, we want to keep them short so when we do remove them finally, then, we're not going to have a big wound. Also, those lower branches on an ornamental tree may go closer to the ground, and that's fine too. We also want a balanced canopy, and that means we don't want all the branches on one side. It'll be more likely to be blown over by the wind.

So here's a quick overview of some of the branches that we do want to remove. So, if you take a look at this drawing, the suckers—that stem coming out of the ground next to the trunk of the tree, is called a sucker. Now some trees sucker readily, and things like the members of the *Prunus* family, plums and cherries, tend to send out lots of root suckers. Apples, trees that have been grafted, we want to remove the sucker. Not that it's sucking energy out of the tree, but that it can compete with that main trunk, end up rubbing, causing damage. We're going to cut those just below the soil surface. Do not use herbicides on there, because if you treat them with the weed killer, it can kill the parent plant.

The little stub sticking out of the trunk, stubs create great entry ways for insects and disease. And we'll talk about making correct cuts in a minute. As you move up the trunk, those two branches growing right above each other eventually will grow into each other, so one of them needs to go. And, as you look up the trunk on the left, you'll see those crossing branches. Again, one of those needs to go. And then you'll also see that that has a narrow crotch angle, so you want to remove that, leaving those branches with wide crotch angles. So those are some of the things that we want to do.

But let's start by creating a more balanced, stronger structure for our tree. We're going to create a dominant leader, managing those co-dominant stems, as I mentioned before. So, start by evaluating the existing structure. You need to identify the dominant leader, and that's typically the largest upright stem. Not always, but it should be. So you want to look from the ground level up to the top of the tree. Now, if you have several stems growing and competing to be the leader, then you need to pick the one that's closest to the center and the largest, and that will be your new leader.

Then you're going to subordinate the others over time, and that means pruning back about $1/3$ initially, so that the main leader is really leading the pack, and those others, we're reducing their size so that they won't compete and outgrow your leader. And you can see that by removing them, now we do have wide crotch angles. We have a stronger structure. You can see those branches spiral around the trunk of the tree. Here's a live example of a tree that wasn't pruned early in its life to remove those co-dominant leaders. And you can see there are large branches that are just as tall as the leader. And what happens is, not only do they compete and block sunlight, but if a storm comes through, snow or ice loads will split that tree apart. A closer look at the trunk, check out the co-dominant stems. Two main branches going straight up. When they do that, the bark on the outside of those branches comes together to form what's called included bark. The branches continue to get bigger in diameter, the bark continues to develop. They push each other away. And so what happens is it's a weak connection, and as they push against each other, cracks form and branches fail, and you end up with a split tree that maybe you've waited 15 to 20 years for it to look beautiful. And now all of a sudden you've got a crack that's formed and branches that fail.

We have this beautiful Variegated dogwood. It's a very young tree, so we want to do minimal pruning. But we do want to start training that central leader. So when we look at the trunk and follow it up, you can see that it makes sense that this should be the leader for our tree. But when you look at the top of the plant, there's a lot of branches competing to be that central leader. Now, we're not going to take them totally out, we're just going to reduce their size so that it gives that central leader a little edge, and we can then, over time, continue to reduce those lengths of those stems to keep our central leader ahead of the rest.

So I'm just going to take a few cuts here and watch the progress. And while I'm pruning, I'm also going to look for any rubbing branches or any broken branches, because we might as well take them off now before they develop into a bigger problem. And as you can see, you need to walk around the tree several times. We've got it off to a good start. Over the next few years, we'll continue to train and reduce the size of these; let the central leader take off. Now this tree tends to be a spreading tree because the branches are opposite. You'll see a lot of clustering of branches. So selective pruning over the next few years will help this develop into a good, strong structure.

As you can see, I ended up with a handful of branches, and many of you plant enthusiasts are probably going, oh, we could start some new trees from those twigs. Well, starting trees and shrubs from cuttings can be challenging, and we're going to tackle that in our last session, so stay tuned. You may also have noticed, I forgot my safety glasses. We were in a studio, and I got a little carried away. So, be sure that you keep them handy and you use them. It's really important for your safety.

Well, as we're pruning, we want to look and develop branches that go spirally around the trunk, as I mentioned. It's much stronger that way if you have a branch here, a branch there, a branch there. And, you want to look for branches with wide crotch angles. As I mentioned, think about those Oak trees or long-lived trees in your area. And this illustrates it quite nicely. The plant with the wide crotch angles, those stems, those connections are much stronger. The ones that are narrow, remember the included bark, where that bark forms around both branches, push apart and are the first to fail in the storm, or I've even seen it happen when there was no wind, but it finally gave out.

Now, when you're pruning, your side branches should be less than ½ the diameter of the trunk, that way we have a clear central leader, so keep that figure in mind. And you also want to know the form and the mature size of the tree you're pruning, because some trees tend to be spreading, some tend to be more upright, some can be weepers. And so you want to keep the mature size and form in mind as you're pruning so that you're pruning to help with that, versus interfere with the natural development.

I mentioned the lowest branches. These are temporary, so, you don't want to prune those out right away, because they have leaves that produce energy that support the growth and establishment of your tree. You just keep them shorter so they don't get too big. So, figure out where you want the lowest permanent branch eventually. Is that three feet, four feet, five feet high? Are people in vehicles going underneath, or is it an ornamental tree that can be limbed down almost all the way to the ground? Keep that in mind as you're establishing that strong framework.

Now, as I mentioned, you want to keep those temporary branches short, subordinate those. And that just keeps them smaller, so when you do finally remove them, in five or more years, they're going to be smaller cuts that will close quickly. Pruning large branches leaves larger, bigger wounds, and that means more time to close and more opportunity for insect and disease problems to develop.

We also want to balance the canopy. I mentioned earlier, an unbalanced canopy may have all the branches or most of them on one side, or one side has more branches than the other. So we need to shorten some of those branches on the heavy side of the tree, or remove a few to balance out the crown. And over time, that will help that plant develop a more balanced crown as new branches develop and the other ones start to slow down in growth.

Now, all new growth at the tips of the branch is called lion's-tailing, or over-lifting. Sometimes we get over zealous; we prune all those little stems out and leave everything at the end of the branches, or maybe you inherited a tree that was pruned that way. When you remove all that inner foliage, what happens is all the weight is at the end of the branch. And, guess what? That's structurally weak; it's more likely to break, and, it also encourages a lot of water sprouts. Now, water sprouts are those little stems that form on the branch and grow straight up, kind of like a water spout. So, when those form, then they grow into other branches and you have lots of problems.

So how do you deal with lion's tailing, if you've inherited that tree? Well, you want to allow the tree to recover. So for two to three years, you don't do any pruning. It's going to look kind of like a mess, but you're trying to get new growth to occur all along the stem. Then you're going to remove some of those water sprouts, those stems that grow straight up from the main horizontal branches, and you're going to allow those to grow into branches. So pick those you want to keep, and shorten the others, because you don't want a whole branch full of water sprouts trying to compete to be the new branching structure.

Now, ongoing pruning. So we've got our young tree planted. We've removed the broken branches. After it got started growing a couple years later, we started establishing that strong structure, picking our main branches that are going to stay, those that'll eventually be removed. So what kind of ongoing pruning do we need to do? Well first, keep in mind what are you trying to accomplish. One, we want to continue to manage that structure to keep it strong. So that should always be our guiding principle. We want to remove anything that's diseased, damaged, or dead. That happens throughout the life of the tree. So you want to make sure you keep up with that type of pruning. We want to remove any hazards. Those are branches that would fail. And if they fail, they'd harm someone—drop on your car; injure a pedestrian; or damage your property, like your house. So you may need the help of an arborist to do that, or you can tell which trees could be an issue.

Improve flowering and fruiting. Sometimes things like Apples and Crabapples, we need to remove some of the stem so more light penetrates, better flowering, and more fruiting occurs. And then we also may need to thin to allow more sun to the plantings below. That's a common request I get from gardeners trying to grow flowers and grass underneath their trees. We want to do it carefully, because the last thing you want to do is sacrifice that beautiful tree just to get some grass growing in the ground beneath it. We may need to control the size. Hopefully this isn't a common issue. Hopefully we selected carefully and we know that our tree, when it's mature, will still fit that location. But sometimes we inherit a tree that's in the wrong place, or maybe it grows bigger than the tag suggested because we gave it great care or the growing conditions were perfect. So we may need to control the size. But we do not want to top that tree. And we'll talk about that in a minute.

So what is the best time to prune? Well, there's an old saying that says any time the saw is sharp. Well, that's sort of true, but there are a few things you ought to consider. I like to prune when the plants are dormant, and you may too. I find it easier to see the structure so that I can make better cuts. Usually, if there's a lot of leaves, I can't see what branch those little branches are coming from, and I make 10 cuts when one would have done just as well. It allows you to see the overall structure much more clearly. Late winter, the wounds will close quickly as growth begins in spring. So it's a great time to do that, and you'll find that you'll get quicker healing. Plus, there's fewer disease and insects active in the garden in late winter, so you have less risk to the plants.

Now there are a couple of times you do want to avoid. Leaf expansion, as those leaves are expanding, there's a lot of sap flowing, a lot of growth occurring. It's easy to damage the trunk. And so, at that point, you can cause some damage. So, either do before they leaf out or after the leaves are fully expanded. And for those, especially those growing in cold conditions, late season, you want to avoid that time. Because pruning in late in the season could stimulate late-season growth that can be injured over winter. So keep those two times in mind to avoid whenever possible.

Now, some other considerations. Evergreens, like Pines and Spruces, are terminal growers. They grow from the tip. So if we prune behind any buds, and there's no buds and a bare stem, guess what, that branch is basically done; it's not going to sprout new buds, like say, a Maple or an Oak would do. I mentioned Pines are terminal growers. If you watch a Pine growing in the spring, you'll see the bud expands, called candles, because that's what it looks like. We can prune those off by ½ or ⅔ as that candle has expanded, and that eliminates ½ to ⅔ of the new growth. So we're not reducing the size, we're just slowing down so it doesn't get as big as quickly. Spruces you want to prune before the buds break, and prune above a healthy bud; that bud will grow into a stem or new needles. And you can do that, just look on the stem and control the size that way. We'll discuss pruning Yews, and Arborvitae, Juniper, and other similar evergreens when we talk about pruning shrubs in our next lesson.

Now, if you've pruned a Birch or a Black Walnut or a Maple in the spring, you know they tend to have a lot of sap flowing, and you'll get oozing from the cut, just like you see here. Now, the good news is it doesn't harm the trees, so feel free to prune in late winter; it's just very messy. So some gardeners feel the tree is bleeding. It isn't. It will be fine, but it does make it a little messy job for you.

And one of the things to always keep in mind is take it slow when you're pruning. If you over prune, remove too much at one time, you stimulate a lot more growth. And that means you'll have more to prune in the future. Plus pruning too much eliminates all that energy-producing growth that's needed to support the tree. Remember all those branches form leaves, and that's where photosynthesis occurs and where energy is produced.

So here are some general guidelines to consider. Remove no more than 5 to 20 percent of growth if you're growing in a cool climate, because plants tend to grow more slowly—only 5 to 20 percent of growth on mature or recently planted trees, so the really old ones or the really young ones, or, only 5 to 20 percent of growth if they're prone to decay. So you want to minimize the amount of wounds caused by pruning. Now you can do greater than this for young trees that are established, OK, once they're established. If you're growing in warm climates and have a long season, your plants are going to put on a lot of growth and you'll probably need to do a bit more pruning and if you're pruning decay-resistant trees.

Now in the first five years of a tree's life, remove no more than 35 percent at one time, so keep it simple; you want that energy going into the roots. Between 5 and 20 years of age, remove no more than 25 to 30 percent of growth. And after this, remove any remaining temporary branches, OK, those lower branches, any hazardous branches. And keep your pruning to a minimum, 10 percent or less, if possible.

Now we'll continue developing and maintaining the structure of our tree. It takes about 15, or even more, years to get that framework established. So it's an ongoing process. We're going to continue to remove crossing and parallel branches. Obviously crossing branches rub. Parallel branches, as they get bigger, actually rub and interfere. And we always want to make sure nothing's interfering with our main trunk.

I talked about water sprouts and suckers. We want to remove these over a long period of time. If you remove all your water sprouts at one time, guess what, they'll all come back and then some more. So you want to be careful with that. So with water sprouts, the reason we remove them, as they grow up, they rub the other branches, the scaffold branches coming off the trunk, and interfere. And we did some pruning on this large tree to remove those water sprouts. So you can see how that's done.

Suckers that arise from the base of the plant can either come from the root stock or the roots, and they compete with the desirable tree and rub against the trunk. And so we want to take those off right below ground level. And as I mentioned earlier, don't use a weed killer, an herbicide, a total vegetation killer, because you spray the sucker. It's translocated; it moves through that; and can kill, or at least weaken, the parent plant you're trying to keep.

So where do we make our cuts? We make them in several different places. Flush with the branch bark collar. That's the area, that swollen base of the tree, as you can see in this diagram. So where the branch meets the trunk, this tissue contains a lot of energy reserves so it will close faster, and a lot of chemicals that help prevent decay. So we want to leave that intact.

Now, if you've ever walked through the woods and you've seen a dead branch and that trunk healing over it, it's almost like a doughnut of tissue at the base. That's what we want to keep intact. And when you do cut it like that, it will be a round wound, not an oval wound, and it will close much more quickly. So take a look and watch for those good cuts and bad cuts within your community.

If we're going to do a removal cut, and that's removing a branch back to the trunk, or a parent branch, that kind of cut is good and used often for thinning, or, when we're trying to get rid of co-dominant stems. For pruning back to a shorter side branch, that's called a reduction cut. So we're trying to just take it in a bit, as opposed to remove the whole branch and thin out the crown. We can also make cuts above an outward-facing bud, and that's on finer branches. We want to make it above, on a slant, not too close to where the bud dries out, but not too far where we're leaving a stub, and that stub dries out, again, a great entryway for insects and disease.

Now, when pruning large branches, we want to do anything, say, over two to three inches. We want to remove it using the double-cut method. This prevents the weight of the branch from breaking and ripping the bark all along the trunk. Now, I used this method when I pruned off this branch on a Maple. I picked that branch because it was rubbing on a nearby branch, and it seemed like the perfect one to remove and get rid of. I made my first cut from the bottom, about a foot away from the trunk. Then, to remove the branch, I cut from above, and I cut down. And the benefit there is, if that branch were to break from the weight of the branch, it would not rip the trunk, but break off by the first cut. And then the final cut I made flush with the branch bark collar as you can see here.

Now, one pruning practice you should not do is topping a tree. You do see it a lot, and unfortunately, people think that means it's OK. But it's bad for the health and longevity, as well as the beauty of your tree. Top trees are not pretty. Now, topping is basically indiscriminately removing the branches, cutting them back close to the trunk of the tree. And this is usually done to reduce the size of the tree. And by the way, trees can't get too big to support themselves; they're designed to be a certain size. It's when we come in and compromise their roots or do damage that it's a concern. So, the cuts, because they're made back and we leave stubs, or we cut the branches back to lateral branches that aren't big enough to sustain those that are left, then, the plant can't support itself. You're removing more than 50 to 100 percent of the leaf-bearing crown, meaning, the stems that produce leaves, that produce energy to support the tree, you've gotten rid of them. So that tree is taking its resources and the energy reserves from the roots and the trunk.

Severe pruning also triggers the activation of something known as latent buds. These are buds that are underneath the bark that are somewhat suppressed and lie dormant. But once we top that tree, they break dormancy and put out growth. Now, that growth is very fast, and it's very weak, and it's weakly attached. So that means all those fine twigs that emerge after topping are more subject to wind, ice, and other types of damage. So overall, we've weakened the plant due to a lack of energy, and we've made it more subject to pests. Plus those improper cuts, those wounds close slowly, they're more subject to decay, they're weakly attached, and they're fast-growing, so they're more likely to develop into being a hazard, something that's going to damage property or people. Plus, that drastic change in the canopy, we've removed all those leaves that shade the trunk of the tree, can result in sunburn on that trunk so it's more likely to form cankers and bark splitting. And bottom line, it's ugly and expensive, so no topping please.

So what can you do to control the plant size if it's too big for the location? Remove branches back to their point of origin, as we talked about earlier. And if you're shortening a branch back to a lateral branch, make sure it's large enough to support its new job as that branch. It should be at least $\frac{1}{3}$ the diameter of the limb removing. So, if you take off a branch, that one that remains should be ⅓ the diameter of that branch you removed.

Are you feeling overwhelmed? Well, it may be time to call in a professional. And when is that the right time? Even at the beginning, to make sure that your young tree develops a good, strong structure, and also to develop a relationship with a tree-care professional. You want to call in the professionals when the trees are too large to safely and properly prune and to establish, again, a long-term relationship, because you'll be the first one that gets served when there's a storm or some damage.

Now, as you can see, pruning should start early in a tree's life. Early intervention helps establish a strong framework, avoiding the need to make lots of larger cuts on mature trees. You'll minimize pest problems, storm damage and hazards, and save money over the life of the tree. Next class we'll discuss various shrub-pruning methods to help you grow and maintain beautiful, healthy shrubs in your landscape.

Pruning Shrubs
Lesson 9

P rune shrubs to control their size; to remove diseased, dead, or damaged stems; and to remove cankers, which are sunken, discolored areas. Regular pruning can also remove borers that burrow underneath the bark and cause wilting and dieback. Besides borers, scales can attack older growth. Powdery mildew is often seen on such plants as lilac. Pruning and thinning out older stems increases air flow and light penetration, reducing the risk of powdery mildew. Regular pruning not only removes insects and diseases when they occur but also reduces the risk that they will attack your plant. In addition, it improves bark color, as well as flowering and fruiting by letting in more light.

Prune with Care

- Like trees, young shrubs need to get established before pruning. They need every leaf to put energy back into their roots. For this reason, you should prune only when it's necessary and let the plant be your guide.

- Deciduous plants, those that drop their leaves in the winter, can be pruned during the dormant season, especially for major pruning jobs; dormancy pruning is also good for summer bloomers. Because spring-flowering shrubs set their flower buds the summer before the spring when they bloom, you should wait to prune these until right after flowering. It won't hurt the plant to prune at the end of winter or in fall, but you will not have flowers; you'll have removed them by pruning.

- A rule of thumb for pruning is to remove no more than one-fourth to one-third of the overall plant. If you remove more, you'll overstimulate growth, and you'll have more pruning to do the following year.

- Do not top shrubs, just as you don't top trees. If you cut hedges straight across about 2 feet above ground, new growth will occur right beneath those cuts. The next year, then, the temptation is to cut at 2 ½ feet. Pretty soon, there are no leaves on the bottom 2 or 3 feet, and all the growth is on top. Maintain the plant size and leaves from top to bottom.

Pruning Techniques

- Thinning cuts remove a branch or a twig where it originates, at the base of the main stem, from ground level, back to an adjoining branch, or on an outward-facing bud. Prune above a bud at a slight angle, not too close or the bud will dry out and not too far or you will leave a stub. Make sure the bud is outward facing because it will turn into a branch, and you don't want it growing toward the center of the plant.

- Gradual renewal means removing a few older or dead stems right back to the ground each year, a common practice with suckering plants that are overgrown. This method helps maintain the natural form of the plant and encourages new growth from the base.
  - Look for any stems that are rubbing, broken or damaged, or have sunken or discolored areas.

  - After finishing the major cuts, go back and remove any crossing branches, those growing into the center, and anything that is sticking out of the general outline. Shorten some of the longer stems that may be wayward or crossing.

  - If you repeat this process every year for several years, you will have new growth on a much shorter, more compact plant. It's a great way to bring a large plant down to size with much less stress.

- Rejuvenation pruning cuts a whole plant down to the ground. Do this when you have an immediate need to reduce the overall size of the plant for some reason: Perhaps it died back from severe winter damage. Rejuvenation pruning stimulates new growth; thus, the next year, you would remove about three-fourths of the new stems, thinning right back to ground level. Gradually, you will reduce the overall size of the plant.

- When you're pruning evergreens grown as shrubs, such as yews, junipers, and arborvitae, use thinning and heading cuts. On arborvitae, remove only the upright branches, not the horizontal ones, because you want the plant to branch out. Upright branches are more susceptible to snow loads and damage.

Deadheading

- To deadhead roses, find a 5-leaflet leaf. Make your cut down to at least the first 5-leaflet leaf so that the new growth will be much sturdier and stiffer. You want to leave at least two 5-leaflet leaves on the stem to ensure that the plant will have enough energy to grow back.

© Ingram Publishing/Thinkstock.

After a flowering plant in a pot blooms, remove any faded flowers and transfer the plant to the ground or a larger container.

- Deadheading roses is necessary only if you need to encourage bloom. If you live in a cold climate, let the roses fade on the plant at the end of the season so the rose hips form. This helps the plant go dormant, furnishes beautiful decoration for your winter garden, and provides food for the birds, as well.

- You don't need to deadhead all flowering shrubs, but removing the faded flowers does save energy that the plant normally puts into the flowers and allows it to use it for growth. The more energy produced, the more likely the plant is to flower.

Sheared Hedges

- Shearing is a common practice for formal landscapes and hedges. When you shear and shape, no matter what tool you use, you're basically making indiscriminate cuts too close or too far from the buds and leaving entryways for insects and diseases.

- When you shear regularly, you create a veneer of green with bare stems between the trunk and the ends of the branches that prevents light from reaching the center of the plant; thus, the plant continues to grow without producing new growth toward the center. Shearing is hard on the plant, but if you like sheared hedges, here are some things to keep in mind to keep them looking good for a long time:
  - Start pruning and training before your hedge is too large. You may want to use stakes on each end and guideline strings along the sides and top to keep a straight line.

  - Make the top of the hedge narrower than the bottom. The idea is that the light can reach all parts of the hedge to ensure that you will have leaves from top to bottom. If the hedge is wider at the top, it will shade out the bottom; all the growth will be on the top, and the bottom will be bare.

  - Select a species suited to shearing, such as privet or boxwood. Typically, shrubs that tolerate shearing have small leaves that are close together. They're also able to recover quickly from severe pruning. Avoid those that are grown for flowers and fruit, because if you shear lilacs and forsythias, you eliminate all the flowers.

- ○ Maintain the hedge once it's full size by pruning in spring. If it's a fast-growing plant or you live in a very warm climate with a long season, you may need to do a second pruning.

- ○ If your hedge becomes overgrown, cut back the top and the sides to about 6 inches larger than the desired size. When the new growth forms, you can do additional pruning. Repeat this step until you eventually reach the desired size. You must stimulate new growth to ensure that you're not cutting into bare stems. Plants that tolerate rejuvenation pruning can be cut back to a foot or less above the ground and will send up new growth. Then, you can retrain them into the hedge you desire.

- Sheared evergreens won't tolerate severe pruning. You can cut yews back to bare wood, and they eventually re-sprout, but it can take several years, depending on the plant's age, health, and vigor and your climate.

- If you decide you want to unshear your hedge and your plants tolerate rejuvenation pruning, cut them back severely. Evergreens and others that won't tolerate severe pruning must be managed gradually.
  - ○ Carefully remove a couple of stems to let in light, which will encourage new growth.

  - ○ Continue to do this over time and, as new growth occurs, instead of pruning it, allow it to develop.

  - ○ Keep continually thinning out the edges of the branches. Over time, you can reclaim the plant's natural shape.

- For a more natural hedge, take advantage of the plant's natural growth habit. Select the right size and shape of plant for the purpose, use thinning cuts and heading cuts to control the size and shape, and select the right species.

After Pruning
- Take a walk around your landscape and look at your plants. Are your shrubs providing the beauty and function you desire? If not, will pruning help, or are you better off replacing?

- Note which of your plants need pruning and when is the best time to do it. Mark your calendar so you won't forget.

- Look for solutions for the places where your shrubs aren't working. Perhaps you should add a few more plants, prune some of the existing ones, or replace high-maintenance plants with something that fits in better with your landscape design.

Questions to Consider

1. How much of the overall plant should you prune to avoid overstimulating new growth?

2. Two pruning techniques are gradual renewal and rejuvenation pruning. Describe each technique and why a gardener would use it.

Pruning Shrubs
Lesson 9—Transcript

Now that you have your trees off to a good start with proper pruning, let's get busy pruning our shrubs. These plants are as an important part of the framework as the trees. They've long been used to anchor homes to the landscape, divide our property from our neighbors, screen bad views, and increase seasonal interest. We prune these plants to control their size.

Now hopefully we didn't put the wrong plant in the location, but maybe you inherited one. Or perhaps it grew a little bit better than expected. Lilacs are a great example of a plant that grows too tall and often has naked stems at the bottom and flowers two stories high. We'll talk about how you can rejuvenate that plant and bring it down to a size where you can enjoy the blooms and have a better looking plant.

We also like to prune to remove diseased, dead, or damaged stems. We'll be pruning out cankers, which are sunken discolored areas. And we'll talk more about that when we talk about disease problems. Regular pruning can also remove borers, insects that borrow underneath the bark at the plant and cause wilting and dieback of stems. Regular pruning can discourage borers and improve the health of your plants. We'll also be removing crossing, rubbing, and any inward-growing branches, because if they point to the center of the plant, eventually they'll interfere with growth of other stems. As I mentioned, regular pruning reduces the risk of insects and diseases, not only removing what occurs. Besides borer, scales can often attack older growth. So regular pruning means fresher new growth less susceptible to these pests.

Powdery mildew is a disease that we often see on plants like Lilac. Pruning and thinning out older stems increases air flow and light penetration, and that reduces the risk of powdery mildew. So regular pruning can help with that. We can also improve the bark color. Red Twig dogwoods, Yellow Twig dogwoods, are great examples. The older stems turn brown. So regular pruning removes the older brown stems and encourages new growth that's bright red or yellow that really adds color to the winter landscape. We can also improve flowering and fruiting by letting more light in with regular pruning, as long as it's at the right time.

Well, let's talk about improving the overall appearance of our plants and creating and maintaining a landscape design. Now, we'll talk a little bit towards the end of this session about formal pruning, hedges, maybe plants shaped in the shapes of round circles, and gum drops, and things like that, and also topiaries, but that we'll save for the very last lesson.

So when is the best time to prune? Just like trees, we want to wait to let those young shrubs get established before we start pruning. They need every leaf to put energy back into their roots. And we only want to prune when we need to. I often see plants that are pruned because the person is frustrated, or they think it's time to prune because everyone else is pruning, and they end up ruining their shrubs. So wait, and let the plant be your guide.

Now, deciduous plants, those that drop their leaves in the winter, can be pruned during the dormant season. It's great for major pruning jobs and great for summer bloomers. However, we want to wait until right after flowering for spring flowering shrubs. These plants set their flower buds the summer prior to the spring they bloom. So we want to prune those right after flowering. That way they'll set new blossoms, new flower buds that will bloom the following spring. That is, if you need to prune and want to maintain flowering. It won't hurt the plant to prune at the end of winter or in fall, but you will not have flowers. You'll have removed them by pruning. So, if you want the blooms, prune Lilac, Forsythia, Azaleas, Rhododendron, Quince, Pearlbush, Big Leaf Hydrangeas, Kerria, Pieris, and other spring-blooming, flowering shrubs after flowering to keep the flowers and control the growth size.

A good rule of thumb related to pruning shrubs is to remove no more than one fourth to one third of the overall plant. So when you look at the number of stems and the amount of growth, one fourth to one third. If you remove more than this, you'll over stimulate growth, and that means you'll have more pruning to do the following year. I had a great example of this happen. Somebody brought in a Forsythia. They'd cut it right back to the ground, Forsythia will tolerate that pruning, and the next year it was 12 feet tall. So obviously, they had a lot more pruning to do the following year. Did not accomplish their goal.

And, we're not going to top shrubs, just like we don't top trees. A little different reason, some people actually call this haircut pruning, and you've probably noticed this, especially when the plants are dormant, hedges, like privets, where people come by and they'll cut them straight across, about two feet above ground. New growth occurs right beneath those cuts. So then the next year, they cut it at two feet, six inches, lots of new growth, and continue the process until pretty soon there's no leaves from the bottom two or three feet, and all the growth is on top. It looks very bad, much like you see here. So we want to do some different type of pruning where we can maintain the plant size, its beauty, and leaves from top to bottom.

So, one of the things we want to do is use thinning cuts. Thinning cuts remove a branch or a twig where it originates. Either at the base of the main stem, or from ground level, or, back to an adjoining branch, or, on an outward facing bud. Those are the places we want to do our pruning. If you prune above a bud, just like we mentioned with the trees, you want to do it at a slight angle, not too close, because that bud will dry out. Not too far, you'll leave a stub. And you want to make sure it's outward facing, because that bud will turn into a branch, and you don't want that branch growing towards the center of the plant.

Now, gradual renewal is the removing of a few older or dead stems right back to the ground each year, a common practice with suckering plants that are overgrown. And that's what I did with this Red Twig dogwood. One of the reasons I love to recommend Red Twig dogwoods as a starting point for new pruners is you can actually see what to prune. It's somewhat color coded. Remember, the old stems turn brown? So those are the ones to remove. So, as I worked my way through this Red Twig dogwood, I removed those stems that lacked color; I also looked for any stems that were rubbing, one of those had to go; any stems that were broken or damaged; and then cankered stems, those that had sunken or discolored areas. And by the time I did that, I had a pretty big pile of brush, but a much better looking Red Twig dogwood.

Now, when you do this type of pruning, you may have a lot of strange-looking growth, so you can shorten some of those longer stems that may be wayward or crossing. So after I finished my major cuts, I went back through, and then I took a few more. I removed any crossing branches, or any of those growing into the center, and anything that was kind of long and sticking out of the general outline of my Red Twig dogwood.

Now, this method is much less stressful on you, and also the plant. It also helps maintain the natural form of your plant, because you're removing stems and encouraging growth as the plant normally would form. It also encourages new growth from the base. So you'll get new stems coming at the base with leaves attached, and soon you'll have leaves from ground level to the top of the plant. And because this was a Red Twig dogwood, it also encouraged colorful stem growth, because those new stems will be bright red and really help brighten up the winter landscape. And because we're only taking out about a fourth to a third of the older stems, it discourages that excess growth I talked about before. You'll get new growth, but not overly stimulated growth that needs lots of heavy pruning.

Now, if you repeat this process every year for several years, you basically have new growth—three years or younger—on a much shorter, more compact plant. So it's a great way to bring a large plant, remember that two story high Lilac I mentioned? It can bring that down to size with a lot less stress. You'll have leaves all the way up and better flowering in the case of a Lilac, and flowers at a level where you can enjoy the fragrance and the beauty.

Now, heading cuts mean you're shortening the branches back to a healthy bud or a side branch. These were those secondary cuts I made on the Dogwood to remove those wayward branches or any crossing branches. Again, slightly above a bud on an angle and making sure it points outward. Or, we make the cut back to a shorter side branch, again, an outward facing branch. Leaving no stubs—hat's where we use our hand pruners or loppers so we make those careful cuts—and we want to avoid dieback by doing just that. Also, we want to make sure that we leave that plant looking it's best by making proper cuts and selective cuts.

You can rejuvenate your shrubs as well. Now, this is much more drastic, and it might really get your pruning paranoia going in high gear, because you're taking a whole plant down to the ground. You do this when you immediately need to reduce the overall size of the plant. Maybe there's some construction going on, you're doing an overhaul for some reason, maybe the plant died back, severe winter damage, and most of it died above ground, so you need to take it back to ground level. Now certain species are treated as dieback or woody perennials in some locations, and we prune these back to the ground every year. Things like Russian sage, Crape myrtle in cooler areas, and Cockscomb tree in some areas where it's borderline hardy. Those plants tend to dieback to the ground; we prune them back: they send up new growth. And it's usually winter kill in this case, so pruning is removing the dead growth.

Now, rejuvenation pruning is basically cutting the entire plant right back to ground level, or as close to the ground level as possible. Now remember, we discussed it stimulates lots of new growth, and so we're going to have that response happen. Now, to control it, the next year we'd remove about three fourths of those new stems, thinning right back to ground level, and then gradually, over time, reducing the overall size. So it's an overgrown or misshapen plant, we take it right back to the ground, pushes up all this growth, take three-fourths of those stems back to the ground, start reducing the size and getting it back under control. A little more stressful on the plant, and usually much more stressful on the gardener.

Now, I want to talk about a modified version for Spireas, Potentillas, Hills of Snow, ?Hydrangeas, and summer-blooming Spireas. These can be pruned right back to the ground every year. In fact, if you have a lot of plants, that might be the way you need to manage them. When I was working with the city of Milwaukee Forestry, we had 121 miles of boulevard to manage. So, that's how we handled our Spireas. But, those plans tend to be floppy. Not a problem when you're talking about a boulevard, but, in your front yard, you may want something that looks a little better.

So this is what we did for some of the Spirea in the area where I was pruning, and it's a quick solution for you to do. Cut all the stems back half way, then remove half of the remaining stems right back to ground level. So what happens is the stems that you left standing will produce new growth, but it's on older stems that are a little stiffer and sturdier. The stems you cut right back to the ground stimulate new growth from the base. So you start having new stems, leafed all the way, ground to the tip, and the older stems to provide support. So you get the benefit of rejuvenation pruning, but you also get the benefit of those stems, giving it some support so it's a little less floppy growth. And so it's a great way to take care of that.

When you're pruning evergreens that are grown as shrubs, things like Yews, and Junipers, and Arborvitae, we use thinning and heading cuts that way. Now on Arborvitae, we only want to remove the upright, not the horizontal branches, because we want to have that branched out. Remember those upright branches, more prone to snow, loads, and damage.

With junipers, we're going to make thinning cuts. We're going to take long branches and cut them back to short branches, or back to the main trunk. We're going to hide our cuts so you won't even notice that that cut has been made. Pines and spruces we discussed a little bit in pruning trees. The same goes if you're growing dwarf varieties as shrubs.

Now shearing is a common practice for those of you with formal landscapes and hedges, and maybe even topiaries. Some people like geometric-shaped shrubs in their landscape, a much more formal look. I have to confess, not a huge fan. For me, it's way too much work; it eliminates some of that natural beauty of the plant; and I'm all about having plants that are much more natural in appearance, and, I don't have to do as much work.

Now, when you're shearing and shaping, you may be using electric hedgers, you may be using hand clippers, but you're basically making indiscriminate cuts. And those indiscriminate cuts mean you're cutting too close or too far from the buds and leaving lots of great entry ways for insects and diseases. Also, when you're regularly pruning, you're creating a veneer of green, just a thin layer of green with bare stems in between the trunk and the end of the branches. Now, that prevents light from reaching the center of the plant, that green veneer, and so, it continues to grow without producing new growth towards the center. It's a little harder on the plant, and that's another reason I'm not such a fan of sheared plants. But if you like them, here are some things to keep in mind to keep that plant looking good for a long period of time.

Start your pruning and training before your hedge is too big. You may want to also use a couple of stakes on either end and a couple of line strings drawn on the sides and the top to give you some guidance, because when you start shearing across the long expanse of hedge, it's hard to keep a straight line. Those strings will help guide your cutting process.

You want to make the top of the hedge narrower than the bottom. The idea there is that the light can reach all parts of that hedge so you have leaves from top to bottom. What I see more often is the hedge wider at the top, and narrower at the bottom. The problem there is it shades out the bottom, and your bottom stems are bare, and all the growth is on the top. So, select a species suited to shearing if you want to do shearing. Typically, shrubs that tolerate shearing have small leaves that are very close together. They're also plants that are able to recover quickly from severe pruning. That's why we see things like Privet hedges, and even Hedge cotoneaster, Boxwoods used as hedges, even Yews, and we'll talk about that in a minute.

But you want to avoid those that are grown for flowers and fruit, because if you're shearing your Lilacs and Forsythias, guess what? You're eliminating all the flowers. Or you have a box of yellow bloom in the spring with your Forsythia sheared into a hedge. So save those for areas where you can enjoy their natural form and their spring flowers.

Now, maintaining that hedge once you've got it in shape and formed, when it's full size, you'll want to prune in spring. And if it's a fast-growing plant, or you live in a very warm climate with a long season, you may need to do a second pruning to maintain that size and shape.

If your hedge becomes overgrown, and that's often possible, because we're doing a lot of pruning to maintain that shape, you want to cut it back, the top and the sides, so they're six inches larger than the desired size. So if you want it six feet tall, you'll cut back to six feet, six inches on the top so that you bring it down, because you're going to reduce the size over time. When the new growth forms, then you can do additional pruning. So you repeat this so you eventually get it down to the desired size. But you need to stimulate new growth so that you're not cutting into bare stems.

Now, severely overgrown hedges, with some plants that tolerate rejuvenation pruning, like Privets and Forsythia, you can cut these back to 6 to 12 inches above the ground, and they'll send up new growth, and then you can retrain them into the hedge you desire. But some plants won't tolerate this, so you need to do it gradually over a long period of time. So follow the guidelines of gradually bringing it down to size.

Now, sheared evergreens won't tolerate severe pruning. You can cut Yews back to bare wood, and they eventually re sprout, but it's pretty ugly, and it can take several years depending on the age, the health, the vigor, and your climate. I've seen hedges taken back to bare stems, and three years later just a few sprouts are starting to emerge. So before you do that severe pruning, you may decide, can you live with it, or is it time to replace it and put something better suited for that area and location?

And as I mentioned, if you're pruning back Arborvitae severely, avoid pruning those horizontal branches. You want to cut back so that you maintain that shape. And Junipers can be severely pruned, but they're very slow to recover. So you want to really think twice and try to avoid it. So if you like a hedge, it's something you need to maintain on a regular basis.

Well let's say you acquired a shared hedge and you want to unshear it, or maybe I've convinced you it's better for your plant and your landscape design. So the idea is to unshear those sheared shrubs. Now let's start with deciduous shrubs. If your plans tolerate rejuvenation pruning, cutting them back severely, you can do this; that's one good way to do it. But evergreens, and those that are not tolerant of this type of severe pruning, need to be managed gradually.

So we're going to gradually open up the veneer of leaves to let the light in. So remember we talked about how shearing causes all that fine growth at the edge. We're going to carefully, as you see in this diagram, remove a couple of those stems. So we start opening up, allowing light to the center of the plant; that will encourage new growth. We'll continue to do this over time, and as new growth occurs, instead of pruning it into submission, we will allow that new growth to develop and keep continually thinning out the edges of those branches. And guess what? Over time you can reclaim the plant's natural shape. But once again, you need to take a look at your landscape, your time, your budget. Is it easier to start over, or is it better to reclaim a sheared plant and get it back into its natural shape.

Now, after all of this discussion, you may be considering a more natural hedge. You can have screening and hedges by taking advantage of a plant's natural growth habit. You can maintain its natural growth habit and have a more informal hedge with a lot less work. The first thing you're going to want to do is select the right size and shape plant for the purpose. So you'll use thinning cuts and heading cuts to control the size and shape, versus breaking out the hedge clippers and shears.

And one of the other things you want to do select the right species. Many plants like Golden glory Dogwood, which is a Cornelian cherry Dogwood, can be used as a hedge, because it naturally grows up right. I've seen a lot of bald cypress used as hedges that have that natural shape. They'll take a little shearing, but they've got a nice shape when they're small. You can also use some of the dwarf conifers to do that. Gentsch White Hemlock, in a shady location, can make a nice, graceful hedge in a shady spot, no shearing needed. It actually prefers that you don't do it. And even Yews, the upright Yews, if allowed to grow their normal shape, will provide a nice hedge. And consider Junipers, one of the upright Junipers, or several of them, make great screening. Star Power, a new Juniper with awls that just give a nice, prickly appearance, but a very attractive blue-green appearance, make a nice hedge or a screen.

Arborvitae, left on their own, really work well. Look for one of the dwarf ones, like techny, or homestead, or technito, a dwarf variety of techny, to get that nice screening and a natural hedge between your house and the neighbors. And if your Arborvitae does grow too tall, a common question I get, can you top it? You can, but remember what happens to Arborvitae with multiple stems leading upward, more subject to snow load. So you'll need you need to retrain that for one main later.

So it's time to take another walk around your landscape. We've talked about pruning trees; we've talked about pruning shrubs now. Take a look at those plants. Are your shrubs providing the beauty and the function that you desire? If not, will pruning help? Is that a solution, pruning? Or are you better off replacing? Make a note of what some of your plants that need pruning, and when the best time to do that, mark your calendar so you won't forget. Make the note to look for solutions for the places where you're shrubs aren't working.

Is adding a few more plants the solution? Pruning some of the existing ones? Or maybe replacing the high-maintenance plants with something a little less maintenance that fits better with your landscape design? And, this will be the best way that you can have a low-maintenance, beautiful landscape, making the most of the trees and shrubs that form the framework of your landscape.

Since I'm surrounded by all these beautiful plants, I thought I'd take advantage of the opportunity to show you some more pruning tips and answer a few frequently asked questions. This time I remembered my safety glasses. And I also have my gloves, because I'll be doing a little pruning on roses. Now, minimal pruning, so I left the gauntlets off, but as you can see, I use my gloves quite often.

Now, a typical question I receive is, I want to harvest some roses to use in a vase, or, for some roses, not the knock out here, but for some roses, dead heading encourages new bloom. And where do you make the cut? And what's this five-leaflet thing that I always read about? So let's talk a little bit about exactly that. So if we're harvesting a rose to enjoy in a vase, this is a great place to pick it. It's got a small bud, it will have several days to open up. Now, if you notice, right underneath that bud is a three-leaflet leaf. Now, further down on the stem, you'll notice a five-leaflet leaf. We want to make our cut down to at least the first five-leaflet leaf. When we do this, the new growth will be much sturdier and stiffer.

Now, you want to leave at least two five-leaflet leaves on the stem so that there will be enough energy to grow back. So we've got one here and one further down, so I'm going to make my cut there. Nice for a little bud vase. I've got my five-leaflet leaves, so the new growth coming from here, with the two five-leaflet leaves remaining, will be nice, stiff, and sturdy, and will get new blooms.

Now if you're dead heading, you're going to wait for the flowers to fade. And again, that's only necessary if you need to do that to encourage bloom, and it varies from rose to rose. And if you live in a cold climate, let those roses fade on the plant at the end of the season so the rose hips form. It helps the plant go dormant, beautiful decoration for your winter garden, and food for the birds as well.

I also thought we'd take a look at pruning this Azalea. It's a young plant, so just like we discussed with our trees, we're not going to do major pruning on such a young plant, just some important things. So as I take a look at this plant, I noticed there were a few stems growing back towards the center. I'm going to pull these back so you can see it. And as you look, you can see that this stem is bending back towards the center of the plant, something we don't want. So I'm going to take that off right back at the base.

I also have a dead twig, a little stub here. We're going to get rid of that, because remember, those stubs create entry ways for insects and disease. Ah, found another stem bending back towards the center, so we're going to clip that one as well. These eventually will rub against the major part of the plant, resulting in problems. Another dead stub. Now, I picked my smaller pruners just because I'm dealing with a small shrub and it's easier for me to maneuver it in and through the plant. Taking a quick look here.

Now, you don't need to dead head all flowering shrubs, but if you do remove the faded flowers, it does save energy that the plant normally puts into the flowers, allows it to put it back into the plant, more energy produced, more likely to flower. And just something to keep in mind, when we buy a flowering plant in a pot, the roots hit the side of the pot, signals the plant it's mature, and it blooms. Now, when we put this plant in the garden, it's going to spend its energy putting down roots. That's a good thing. But, it may not flower for the first couple years. Frustrating for us, but good for the plant, because once it's well rooted, you'll have many blooms for years to come.

So let's just take a closer look here. Another one of those stems moving in. And actually, we got rid of some of our faded flowers at the same time. And really, keep it to a minimum and you'll get that plant off to a good start. Continue to look for any cross branches, any kinds of problems. Broken branches. We're going to take that one off as well. But again, keep it to a minimum, remove any faded flowers, get this plant in the ground or in a bigger container so you can enjoy it as a potted plant, and you'll have a beautiful flowering plant for years to come.

When Trees and Shrubs Fail to Thrive
Lesson 10

Y ou've selected the best trees and shrubs to create the framework in the growing conditions and available space of your landscape design. You've learned how to plant correctly and provide the proper care. But even when you do everything right, problems can occur. Whether you try to diagnose the problem yourself or work with a professional, the more information you gather, the better your diagnosis will be and the more likely you are to resolve the issue successfully.

Identify the Plant

- Problem solving starts with proper identification. Knowing the plant will help you narrow down the insects and diseases that commonly attack it. If you saved the plant tag or have a landscape plan to refer to, you're in luck. Otherwise, stop by the garden center or nursery for help.

- Leaves are a primary identifying characteristic. They are either simple or compound in type and opposite or alternate in the way they attach.
  - A *simple* leaf is one leaf blade on a petiole—a plant stem—and it occurs where the buds form at the stem.

  - *Compound* leaves are made up of many little leaflets. Bring the whole stem to the garden center for proper identification.

  - The way the leaves are arranged on the stem is also important. If the leaves are *opposite*, they occur across from each other on the stem. Leaves are *alternate* when they alternate from one side of the stem to the other.

- If you can describe your evergreens, you'll have much more success getting help with identification.
  - Pines have long needles held in bundles of two, three, or five, and you may be able to see mature or developing cones.

  - Spruces are a little pricklier than pines, and their needles are singly attached. If you pull one off, you'll see a woody stem.

  - Yew also has singly attached needles, but they're flatter, with dark green above and light green below, and much softer to the touch.

  - A juniper has a strong smell, and its greenery is called awls. On the stem are areas that look like leather pouches that cause the prickliness on the branches. Junipers also have scales and flat needles. These are conifers, or cone-bearing plants.

  - The arborvitae is much softer; because it's all scales and no awls, it's not prickly, but it's very flat, almost fan-like.

Review Your Maintenance

- Review your checklist of care. In particular, think about how often you water and by what method, and be honest with your answers. Did you run an overhead sprinkler for 5 minutes, or did you soak the plant really well? Be specific.

- Next, think about fertilization: Fertilizing too much or not enough can cause problems. Review what you used to fertilize, when, and how often. You may want to check the label to make sure you fertilized correctly.

- If the plant is mulched, note what type of mulch you used and how often you put it down. Is it piled around the trunk of the tree, or did you pull it away from the trunk or the stems of the shrubs?

- Is your yard affected by deicing or sea salt? Have other chemicals been sprayed in your yard, your neighbor's yard, or nearby public spaces?

Check the Weather
- Look at recent weather patterns: If there's been an extremely hot period, even if you watered correctly, plants may not have been able to pull up enough moisture; as a result, you may have scorch or wilting.

- Sometimes in late fall, the temperature drops quickly from 40 degrees to –4 degrees. That transition can be very difficult, as can the reverse: going out of dormancy to 80 degrees, followed by a frost. Frost damage can look like herbicide damage.

- Think about the flood or drought pattern of the past few years. Floods or droughts can have both immediate and long-term impact.

- Check the yearly growth on trees. This is a great diagnostic clue because it reflects the growing conditions and the plant's response to them.

- Keeping in mind both the care you provided and the weather patterns, compare them to the time the problem appeared. Typically, if your plants have a delayed response to significant weather patterns, it may be a long time before you see secondary pests, such as borers or diseases. If the symptoms show up immediately, the root of the problem is most likely environmental.

Look for Patterns and Examine Symptoms
- Look at the pattern of damage on the plant itself, in the landscape, and in your neighborhood, and ask yourself the following questions:
  - Is the plant of concern the only one affected?

  - Are there other plants of the same type in your yard or in the vicinity that show the same symptoms?

○ Are the growing conditions different for other plants? Soil can vary from one part of the yard to another.

○ Is the plant in an area that gets a great deal of wind?

○ Does ice or deicing salt tend to accumulate near the plant?

○ Have similar problems occurred in neighboring yards?

• Where do the symptoms appear on the plant—in old growth or new growth? The problem can often be nutrient or disease issues, depending on the part of the plant that's affected. If the damage is on just one side, the culprit likely is something environmental: pesticide, wind, deicing salt, salt spray from the ocean, or hot air from equipment.

• If your plant overall is declining, it probably has root or stem wilt. Something may be blocking the uptake of water and nutrients to the leaves and stems.

• Look at how the symptoms have spread through the plant or planting.
   ○ Did the plant die from the top down? Then, it's probably a root or stem issue, perhaps something like verticillium wilt on a maple, where you see the leaves wilting and turning brown; this disease starts at the tip and works its way down.

   ○ You may notice that individual branches are affected one at a time. Cytospora canker, a fungal disease on spruce, usually starts at the bottom. The needles start turning brown and die back, branch by branch. Usually, this disease doesn't kill the tree.

• If there's a distinct line between the dead and the living or if symptoms occur suddenly and don't get worse, the problem is probably environmental. If the symptom pattern is irregular, it's probably a disease.

- Symptoms are what we see. Consider a headache, for example. It could be caused by a number of factors, such as stress, a disease, a virus, or bacteria. The symptom's the same—the headache—but the cause is different. When you see leaf spot on a plant, it could be caused by bacteria, a virus, or an insect. Use the symptoms to help identify the cause. For example:

  - Blight is the rapid discoloration and death of twigs, foliage, and flowers.

  - Cankers are dead areas on the bark or stem. They're often sunken and discolored.

  - Chlorosis is yellowing. It can be a pH-related issue, a nutrient issue, the result of over- or under-watering, or caused by disease.

  - Decline means that the plant is progressively slowing down in growth. It can be caused by root rot, stem rot, environmental damage, or poor drainage.

  - Dieback describes a condition that starts at the tip and causes the shoot, branch, or root to die back.

  - Galls are abnormal growths that, in most cases, are not harmful to the plant.

  - Gummosis is the exudation of a sap that usually has a smell and is discolored. This disease builds up in the sap of the tree and actually pushes sap out through wounds or cracks. It can't be treated; the plant will have to be replaced with one that's not susceptible.

  - Distorted leaves could be twisted, cupped, or rolled. They can be caused by insects, disease, or environmental stress.

- Leaf scorch occurs in hot, dry weather, when plants can't get the moisture they need, and the edges of the leaves turn brown. When you see scorching, look at watering or fertilization issues, but there could be other causes.

- Leaf spots are typically a disease problem.

- Necrosis means dead tissue, and it could be secondary to chlorosis. It could also be dieback from a moisture issue or rot occurring in the root system.

- Witch's brooming occurs in salty conditions; it affects buds and causes proliferation of twig formation, which can lead to dwarfing.

- Holes in leaves usually mean that chewing insects are present, such as caterpillars, sawflies, beetles and weevils, earwigs, or bees and wasps.

- Holes in the stem indicate a bore or some insect feeding inside the trunk or stem. Speckling can be from an insect with needle-like mouth parts, such as aphids, mites, or thrips.

The activity of chewing insects is usually not harmful to plants.

Look for Signs Above and Below

- In contrast to *symptom*, the term *sign* refers to the actual disease or insect that is causing damage. Seeing the beetle that's eating the leaf makes the problem much easier to identify. The cause of the symptom may be an insect or disease that's attacking the aboveground portion of the plant, but keep in mind, half the plant is underground. That makes it challenging for you and the professionals to diagnose root rot and wilt. Are these problems the result of poor drainage or fungal disease?

- Once you dig up the plant, root rot is easy to identify. You'll see black, slimy root systems. The cause may be a girdling root growing around the trunk. As the trunk expands, the root expands, chokes the tree, and stops the flow of water and nutrients.

- The black vine weevil is an insect that does its damage underground. The grubs of this insect chew on roots. You will see small half-moon areas, where they feed aboveground on the leaves. The aboveground feeding doesn't hurt the plant. It's the eggs the weevils lay, the grubs that hatch from them, and the feeding damage the grubs do on the roots that cause problems.

- When you're looking at a large tree, many things could be going wrong inside. You may want to consult an arborist, who may take small samples from the tree to diagnose the problem.

Questions to Consider

1. Identifying the plant will help you narrow down the pests or disease that may be causing problems. What are the identifying characteristics of evergreens?

2. If symptoms appear suddenly and don't get worse, what is the likely cause?

When Trees and Shrubs Fail to Thrive
Lesson 10—Transcript

So far, you considered selecting the best trees and shrubs to create the framework of your landscape design. And of course, you considered selecting the best plant suited to the growing conditions and the available space. You've learned how to plant it correctly and provide the proper care. But even when you do everything right, problems can occur. And then there are those times when you inherit a plant or a landscape, and some or all of the plants develop abnormal growth, spotted leaves, or are invaded by insects. And when your plants are looking bad or declining, you may decide to intervene.

So whether you're trying to diagnose the problem yourself, or searching on the internet, or work with a professional, the more information you gather, the better your diagnosis, and the more likely your success at resolving this issue.

Now, problem solving starts with proper identification of the plant. Knowing the plant will help you narrow down the potential insects and diseases that commonly attack that plant in your area. Now, hopefully, you saved the plant tag or have a landscape plan to refer to. Or maybe you're planning to stop by the garden center or nursery for help with identification. Now, I brought along a few samples into the studio to help you with some terms and ID skills that will help you get a better identification, no matter where you look.

The first thing we want to discuss are leaves. There are different kinds of leaves. Now, you may recognize this Mulberry leaf. It's a simple leaf, and that means there's one leaf blade, this big portion here is a leaf blade, on a petiole, a plant stem. And that occurs where the buds form at the stem. So this is a simple leaf.

Now, there are also things called compound leaves. Here we have a Honeylocust. And, it's a pinnately compound leaf. Here's one leaf. I'm going to pull that off the stem. That's where the bud would be. There's your stem. And then, this leaf, this whole thing is considered a leaf, is made up of lots of little leaflets. It's a pinnately compound, pinnately, because it looks like a feather, compound, because it's made of many different leaflets.

Now, you can guess if you brought just one leaflet into the garden center, they'd have a hard time correctly identifying this plant. Best bet is bring the whole stem, a piece maybe something like this size, into the garden center or nursery. That will make it much easier for them to help you identify your plant.

Now, the way the leaves are arranged on the stem are also important. So if you take a look, this is a Maple; you may have recognized the leaves. And these leaves are opposite. And if the leaves are opposite, the stems are opposite, and you can see that here. Now, when you look at a tree, you may see some alternate, some opposite, meaning some branches that occur singly on the stem. That means a squirrel or somebody pruned that off. Opposite, the leaves and the branches occur across from each other on the stem. We'll go back to the Mulberry. This one is alternate. Take a look here. We've got the leaves marching up the stem, and they're alternate, alternating from one side of the stem to the other. So simple, compound, types of leaves. Alternate or opposite, how they're attached. That will help you greatly in identification.

Now, let's talk about evergreens. I always have to chuckle, because when people tell me they're having a problem with their pine, the more discussion we have, I find out it could be a Spruce, a Juniper, an Arborvitae. It seems like whatever evergreen they learn first is what every evergreen is now called. Well, this is actually a pine that you see here. And you can see, this one happens to have needles that are very long. We've got a young pinecone starting to develop and a mature cone here. But what I wanted to show you is that, on pines, the needles are held in bundles of two, three, or five. And so then you know it's a pine, and the number of needles will help you narrow it down, so, pines, needles in bundles.

Spruces are a little bit more prickly than pines, and their needles are singly attached. So let's take a look at this Spruce. Can you see that individual needles are attached to the stem? If we pull them off, there's a little bit of a woody stem on there, and so that's a Spruce. There's some others that are singly attached, but this one kind of bites back, so, a Spruce.

When you get to some of the shrubs around your house, probably one of the most common is a Yew, y-e-w, or *Taxus*. And these needles are also singly attached, but they're flatter, dark green above, light green below, and much softer to the touch, often used around the foundation of your house.

Now, if you stick your hand in this plant, you'll probably take it out quickly. This is a Juniper, very strong smell. It has awls, and if you look at the stem, you can see these little areas that look like leather punches, and that's what causes the little prickliness on the branches. And they also have scales, and those are flattened, flat needles that are pressed. These are all conifers, or cone-bearing plants. And the last one I want to talk about is the Arborvitae, and look at how flat this is. Much softer, all scales, no awls, so it's not prickly, but it's very flat, almost fan like. So if you can identify or describe these, you'll have much better success getting help identifying your plant, and narrowing down the choices of insects and disease.

Now, if you take a look at this, I've had a lot of these brought into my office, when I'm doing plant diagnostics. And people go, what's wrong with my plant? These are woody strobiles from an Alder. It's normal. The female cone-like structures, those round things, release the seeds. The long things are catkins that pollinate them. Those are normal, and persist on the plant. You may see this plant turning fall color, and at first look you go, that's an evergreen. The needles are turning brown. It must be sick. It's actually a deciduous conifer, a cone-bearing plant that loses its needles in fall. This is normal. No need to be worried.

Now unfortunately, I've heard stories of grounds maintenance people thinking it was dying and remove the tree, and it was healthy. It was just turning fall color. So know what's normal for your plant, and if it's something that you need to worry about, or something you need to enjoy, because it's part of that ornamental appeal.

Now, the next step is to review your checklist of care that we provided, that you've prepared. You know, we have our maintenance plan. We're looking at watering and fertilization. So, the professional you work with, or the website you visit may say, how often are you watering? Now, the answer I usually get is, "often enough. You know." No, I really don't, and we all think we're doing it right, but often, the more I ask questions, the more I find, well, I was on vacation for a couple of weeks, or I didn't know I had to water it. And so review and be honest with your answers. That's the way you can get help. How did you water? Overhead sprinkler for five minutes, or did you soak it really well? Kind of look over some that detail. You may find you can answer the question yourself, but be specific.

Fertilization, as we talked about, fertilizing too much and not enough can cause problems. So, what did you used to fertilize, and when did you fertilize, and how often did you apply it? You may want to check the label as well to make sure you can give that professional you're discussing it with, or when you're searching on the Internet, the information needed. Is the plant mulched? What type did you use? How often? Is it piled around the trunk of the tree, or did you pull it away from the trunk or the stems of the shrubs?

And how about deicing or sea salt? Remember we talked about that spraying onto the plant and desiccating the leaves or stems and causing problems. Are there any other chemicals that may have been sprayed in your yard, or your neighbor's yard, or public spaces? We'll talk about how you help narrow that down. But look around for clues of other chemicals that may have been applied.

Now let's look at recent weather patterns. You know, immediate past. Was there a frost recently? I've seen frost damage that looks like herbicide damage. Have we had an extremely hot period? Even if you water right, remember we talked about plants not being able to pull up enough moisture, and maybe you have scorch or wilting. Was it cold? Sometimes fall can come quickly, where we go from 40 degrees to 4 below. That transition can be very difficult. And in the reverse, going right out of dormancy to 80 degrees and then a frost. Keeping track of those weather patterns is very helpful.

And then, think about over the past few years. Have there been floods and drought? Remember, we talked about how that could impact immediately and long term. I like to visit with my local weather folks. They often provide a calendar, or your local university or extension service may have a weather calendar that tracks significant weather events in your area. I find it easy to trust them to do the data collection. I buy the calendar or subscribe to the information, and then I can review, in case I've forgotten something significant.

And then, we're going to check the yearly growth on trees. And this is a great diagnostic clue, because it helps reflect the growing conditions and the plant's response to that. And here's an example of what you may be looking at. As you look at that top branch, you can see that the recent growth is six inches. That means probably adequate moisture and proper care was applied. Prior to that, four inches. Not bad, but not the best growth. And then, prior to that, two inches. So that could have been the year the tree was transplanted. It could've been a drought year. It could have been a place where there were high insect problems that really stunted the growth.

And then you look at the bottom one. Again, it looks like great growth three years ago, and recently, it's declining. So when you see a steady decline in the yearly growth, and that's from the bud scale scar, you see those ridges where the arrows are pointing? That's the bud scale scar that identifies yearly growth. That can give you a clue. Is your tree responding to just a quirk in the weather, you know, a dry summer? Or if it's declining over time, there might be something more significant going on.

Now, keep in mind both the care you provided and the weather patterns, and you want to look at those and compare them to the time the problem appeared, because the time of year can be a good clue. Obviously, if the damage occurred right after a frost, that would be the first place I'd look. If the damage occurred right after you applied a broadleaf weed killer to your lawn, or your neighbor did, that would be something to examine. Was there an ozone alert in your area? Pollution can also damage trees and shrubs. So keep an eye on what's happening and the immediate past when that occurred. As I mentioned before, significant weather patters, floods and droughts, it may be a long time before you see secondary pests, like bores, like diseases. But if the symptoms show up immediately, it's most likely environmental. If it's like overnight, something happened that caused that dieback. Gradual, it's usually an insect or disease problem.

Now sometimes, I have people say, it happened overnight. But as we looked back, we discovered, well, maybe it was yellowing a little bit last year.

Maybe the growth has declined. So monitor your landscape as you walk through, and just kind of check things out and enjoy your landscape. Keep an eye on things, how they're growing, and make sure they're healthy. Catching problems early makes your job a lot easier.

Now, again, we need to keep all this in mind as we look at the patterns of damage on the plant itself, in the landscape, and in your neighborhood. Is the plant of concern the only one affected? Is it just one tree or one shrub on your landscape? And are the growing conditions there different for the others, especially those of the same type in your landscape? Soil can vary from one part of the yard to the other. Has this been exposed to some different conditions than your other plants? Is that in an area that gets a lot of wind? Does the ice tend to accumulate there? The deicing salt? Anything like that.

And then look around your yard and neighboring yards to see if there's any similar problems occurring. Are there other plants of the same type in your yard, or in the vicinity, showing the same symptoms? So if you have a Crabapple showing problems, are any other Crabapples in the area? Because that could mean there's a disease or insect problem if the same type of plants are being affected. And also related plants. So Crabapples are related to Roses, are related to Mountain ash, are related to pears, and they're susceptible to many of the same insect and disease problems.

Or, if there's a variety of unrelated plants, say you've got a Maple, you've got a Crabapple, you've got a Kerria shrub, and a Hydrangea all affected, my guess would be it's a chemical issue, something nonliving, because that indiscriminately can kill plants. So it's likely something in the environment. Then, think about where those symptoms appear on the plant. Is it on old or new growth? That can often be nutrients or disease issues, depending on the part of the plant that's affected. If it's just one side, likely pesticide, wind, deicing salt, salt spray from the ocean, hot air from equipment, something, again, that's environmental, that just that one side of the plant was exposed to.

Now, if your plant overall is declining or showing symptoms, it's probably root or stem wilt. Something's blocking the uptake of water and nutrients, and they're not getting to the leaves and stems. And then you start seeing decline in general.

Now, look at how those symptoms have spread through the plant or planting. Did it die from the top down? Then, it's probably a root or stem issue, maybe something like verticillium wilt on a Maple, where you see a little bit of flagging, wilting of the leaves. They turn brown, and it starts at the tip and works its way down.

Maybe it's individual branches, one at a time. Cytospora canker, a fungal disease on Spruce, usually starts at the bottom, one branch of the time. The needles start turning brown, purply brown, and die back, branch by branch. Usually it doesn't kill the tree; that's the good news. The bad news is, it looks pretty ugly after a couple of years. So watch at how those disease, insect, or symptoms that spread throughout the plant. That will help you with diagnosis.

Now, are all the needles or leaf tips dying? And if there's a clear, distinct line between the dead and the living, and it's uniform, it's probably a chemical problem, whether it's an herbicide, a deicing salt, or a pollutant. If there's a clear line, it's probably environmental. More irregular, probably a disease problem.

Symptoms also can occur suddenly, but if they occur suddenly and don't get worse, again, it's probably environmental. These are tatters. And what happens is, many times Oaks and Maples and another leaves, as they start to leaf out in the spring, the bud scales peel back, and the frost hits those exposed tissues. The leaf opens up. There's holes, because of the frost damage. Nothing you can do, no need to treat, it's environmental, and the new growth will be fine. So tracking weather, watching the progression, you know. If you suspect an insect, you'll see more and more damage. And if you don't, it's either environmental, or that insect is done eating, and has moved on, and no need to treat.

I mentioned frost and herbicide damage. This is a Spruce. The person thought their neighbor sprayed something that killed it. What they forgot to do is look at the weather, and there was a frost right before the damage occurred.

Those newly expanding Spruce buds, very tender. Buds, as they open, are very tender to cold temperatures, and we saw frost damage.

Now we want to take a look at symptoms. And symptoms are what we see. You know, we have symptoms like a headache, and that headache could be caused by a lot of things. Stress. It could be from a disease, like a virus or a bacteria. The symptom is the same, the headache, the cause, is different. So when we see a leaf spot on a plant, it could be caused by a bacteria, a virus, or an insect. So, we need to use the symptoms to help us identify the cause. And sometimes that's easy, and sometimes it's a little more challenging. So let's look at a few that you may find on your trees and shrubs.

Blight. Now blight is the rapid discoloration and death of twigs, foliage, and flowers. This happens to be fire blight, very common problem on Apples and Pears and some Crabapples. It looks like somebody burned that tip. It's black and curled.

Cankers, on the other hand, are dead areas on the bark or stem. They're often sunken, discolored. This is golden canker on a Pagoda Dogwood. They're very sensitive to dry conditions, and so when they go through a drought, they're more susceptible to this fungal disease.

Chlorosis is the yellowing of plants. And you look at this Red maple. It likes acidic soil, so when we grow it with a high-pH, alkaline soil, it can't pull up the iron and manganese it needs. So notice the leaf blade on this Maple is kind of a pale green to yellow. The veins are dark green. Now, if we don't fix the problem, some of that tissue ends up dying. But this is chlorosis. Chlorosis can be a pH-related issue, a nutrient issue, overwatering, under watering, and also could be a disease problem. Again, the symptom, first step to finding.

Now, when we say a plant is in decline, it just means it's progressively slowing down in growth, declining in vigor, like that one branch we saw, where it was six inches, four inches, two inches. We saw that it wasn't growing as vigorously each year. It's declining. Could be a lot of reasons, root rot, stem rot, things like that, or environmental, poor drainage.

Dieback is when we actually have things die, that it starts at the tip, and that shoot dies back, or the branch dies back. Or we have a root that starts to die back. Can't see it, but that's what's happening if we dig it up.

Now, galls, or gall-like growths are abnormal growths. And in most cases, they're not harmful to the plant. This little mite fed on the leaves of the Maple as the leaf was developing. The tree actually put on that reddish growth. The mite is inside. So, no need to treat. It won't hurt the plant, but, it does cause that abnormal growth. And even if you did decide to treat, the tree is protecting it. So it's one of those things that may disturb us, but not bother the plant. Crown gall is another one, and we'll talk more about that later.

Gummosis. That's the exudation of a sap, very common in cherries, and plums, and things like that. And look at that sap. It usually has a smell. It's usually discolored. This disease builds up in the sap of the tree and actually pushes out through any wounds, any cracks, and that's gummosis. Nothing you can really do to treat it, other than replace it with something not susceptible.

Now often we find leaves that are distorted. They could be twisted, cupped, rolled like you see here. These are caused by mites on this Honeysuckle. The insects suck the plant juices, cause the leaves to fold over top. Could be insects, could be disease, again, it could be environmental stress. We're looking at the symptoms.

I talked a lot about leaf scorch when we talked about watering. This is a great example. Horse chestnuts are very susceptible to leaf scorch. Any hot, dry weather, they can't get the moisture they need, and the edges of the leaf turn brown. So when we see scorching, we typically look at watering over and under, or fertilization issues, but there could be other causes, scorch.

Leaf spots, that's probably the easiest one. You'll go, I know this one. Spots on the leaves, typically a disease problem. This happens to be black spot on Roses. Hopefully, you don't recognize it from something in your yard, but those black spots develop on the leaves.

Necrosis just means dead tissue, and that could be secondary to chlorosis, as I mentioned before, could be dieback from a moisture issue, could be some rot occurring on the root system. But necrosis means dead tissue. If you know some of these terms, including wilt, and you can probably figure that out, the leaves just droop, that's going to help you with diagnosis.

Here's one that especially those folks that live near salty conditions might recognize. This is witch's brooming. Salt, an insect, something affects the buds. You get this proliferation of twigs forming. They call it brooming, and that can often lead to dwarfing. In fact, some dwarf conifers are collected from brooms, like the bird's nests spruce was collected from a broom, you can see here, of a Norway Spruce, so sometimes it can be a good thing.

Holes in leaves usually mean chewing insects are present. Think about who chews, caterpillars, sawflies that look like caterpillars, knowing the difference is important. Beetles and weevils, they're crunchy when you step on them. Earwigs, they're the ones with those little pinchers. Even bees and wasps can chew leaves, but usually not harmful. Tent caterpillars form those webby tents. Diseased leaves, however, those spots can die, drop out, and then you have a hole. So you want to be careful to look at the whole plant, not just the hole.

Now, if we have holes in the stem, it's a bore, some insect feeding inside the trunk or stem. If we have speckling, like you see here on the Redbud, that can be from an insect with needle-like mouth parts. Those are things like aphids, mites; thrips have file-like tongues that just rub against the plant leaf, make a little scratch, and they lap up the sap. So when you see something like this, suspect aphids, mites, things like that.

Now signs, when we talk about signs, are the actual disease organism, or the insect causing the damage. When we can see the beetle that's eating the leaf, makes it a lot easier to identify. Here, we see the mushroom. Now that's only the fruiting body of the fungus that's inside that tree causing decay, but it tells us there's decay going on. It might be secondary, but at least it's visible and a good clue.

Here we have a caterpillar, a tussock moth, feeding on the leaves. We know they are the ones that cause the problem. The bores are inside, under the bark. This is the immature stage of a butterfly, and this caterpillar is boring through the stem. So if we peel off the bark, or if we remove the tree, we can find that.

Now, the cause of the symptom may be an insect or disease that's attacking above ground portion of the plant, but keep in mind, half the plant is underground. When I did a lot of plant diagnostics, I'd always say, my patients are half-buried already, and they can't talk. So that makes it challenging for you and the professionals to diagnose root rot and wilt. Are they due to poor drainage or fungal disease?

Now once you dig up the plant, you can see that root rot is easy to identify—black, slimy, poor root systems. Maybe it's a girdling root, like you see here, where the root is growing around the trunk of the tree. As the truck expands, the root expands. We choke the tree and stop the flow of water and nutrients. We'll show you how to discover those when they're underground.

The black vine weevil is one of those that does its damage underground. You can see that the grubs are chewing on the roots. The clue is those little half-moon areas they feed on aboveground on the leaf. The above ground feeding by the weevil doesn't hurt the plant. It's the eggs they lay, the grubs that hatch from that egg, and the feeding damage the grubs do on the roots that cause the problem. So often we see a decline in the plant. See those little half-moon areas eaten by the black vine weevil, we know to look underground for our answer.

Now, professionals have some tools we don't have as a home gardener, to see what's going on below ground. Now, here's an example from Wachtel Tree Science and Service, where they're using some tools to see what's happening underground. First, they walked up to this Norway Maple, and they saw it had a flattened crown. They looked at the trunk and noticed it was growing straight into the ground like a telephone pole. Remember our surface roots, the root flare? We want that to be right at the soil surface? Well, those were buried. That's a clue there's a problem.

And they also know that Norway Maples are very susceptible to girdling roots. So, they started blowing away the air from the root system using an air excavation tool. So they carefully blew the soil away without damaging the plant to see what was going on underground. And you can see, as they went through the process, they did uncover several girdling roots, not just near the soil surface, but also further down.

Now, they've had some experience removing those, so they decided to remove the roots. Sometimes this is a decision that has to be made on a judgment call by the professional arborist, based on their experience, having removed girdling roots before, the health and vigor of the tree, the future of that landscape, the importance of that tree, as well. So they're looking underground to make some decisions on how they're going to take care of it. They decided to remove the problem, and they backfilled with soil, the existing soil, watered in, and mulched. And the key thing is for that homeowner or that condominium association to provide the proper care to keep that tree looking good for years to come.

Now, arborists also can take a look at what's happening inside the tree. You know, when you're looking at a big tree, a lot of things can be going wrong inside. Those bores under the bark, is there decline from rot? Before we see the mushrooms, do we need to be concerned? So they start looking at the tree by, has there been construction damage? Any ideas that there might be some internal decay, mushroom, soft spots, rotten areas on the trunk. Has the grade around the plant changed?

So professionals, some use an electronic high-resolution needle drill. It's a resistance measurement device that they can put into the trees, so they don't have to damage the tree much; they just make a slight pull, and they measure the resistance to see if there's rot. Now this can help them decide, is the tree safe to leave, or is it a potential hazard? Because if there's more rot than sound tissue, it's probably going to be safer to remove the tree. But they don't want to do that unless it's necessary.

So here you can see they're using the high-resolution needle drill resistance measurement device—what a name—to measure that resistance on the stem. And, there's also a printout that goes along with that resistance measurement.

So, what they can do is look at that and see how much rot and how much sound tissue. Now, we drilled through a sample of a tree that was already removed, so you could see how that readout corresponds to the healthy and decayed portion of the tree, and look at how that tells you what's going on inside.

Now this is a high-tech tool, and they use it, along with the visible symptoms, such as leaf size, decline, overall vigor of the tree. And that allows them to make an informed decision about the future of the tree. Can it be saved, or should it be removed? Because if it's declining, and it's in a place where if that tree falls down and harms a person, property, that makes it a hazard, it might be safer to remove it. But nobody wants to take down a tree if it's sound and has a good chance to survive and live for many years.

Well, now that you have a better idea of what to look for, take a closer look at the individual members of your framework, the trees and shrubs, or portions of your landscape that may be suffering. Make notes on any signs and symptoms you uncover, then review your maintenance practices and any recent weather extremes. In our next session, we'll take a look at the next steps for bringing your framework back to health.

Restoring a Landscape to Health
Lesson 11

In the last lesson, we looked for patterns of symptoms and signs of insect and disease problems. Once you've diagnosed the cause of a problem, you must decide if it's really worth treating. Perhaps what you originally thought was a problem is just a normal process, which means that no treatment is needed. Or you may need to decide whether it's practical to treat certain problems. Knowing what is and isn't normal for a plant can help with this decision. In many cases, you can adjust the environment or your care practices or replace the plant with one that's more resistant to reduce maintenance and improve the health and beauty of your landscape.

Define the Problem

- Knowing what is normal for your plants and what isn't will help you decide whether to treat. For example, a female alder will have cone-like structures that release seeds and catkins that pollinate them. These cones are called *woody strobiles*, and they are normal.

- Slime mold fungus grows on mulch, sometimes climbing up the side of a tree or shrub. It feeds off the organic matter in the mulch, and you see it during wet, gray periods. Lightly rake your mulch to dry it out. Or wait—it eventually dries out on its own.

- Another good example of a non-problem is seasonal needle drop. The needles of evergreens turn bright yellow, then brown from the ground to the tip on the inner side of the branches. We know it's seasonal needle drop because of this pattern. Some years, all the older needles fall off, and if there's been a drought or insect problem, more needles will drop. Proper care will help reduce the issue, but this is a normal process.

- Some galls are caused by insects feeding on stems, which forms a growth on the stem with the gall inside. A healthy tree can tolerate this damage. But the euonymus crown gall is caused by a bacterium and can kill the plant. Eventually, it girdles out the stem. Cut off the stem beneath the gall as far as possible, and disinfect your tools between cuts. Keep an eye on the plant to make sure no other galls show up.

Is Treatment Practical?

- Needle blight on spruce can cause dieback of branches and thinning of the plant. Chemicals can control it, and you could spray the tree when the needles are half expanded, then again when they're fully expanded. The problem is that spraying at the right time and getting full coverage are difficult. Further, as you spray, you will probably cover yourself with pesticide. You may want to hire a professional, or you may decide that the value of the tree doesn't justify the cost of treating it.

- Anthracnose causes spots on the leaves of maples, sycamores, ashes, and walnuts. In sycamores, it can cause twig dieback. Anthracnose on maples usually is related to weather. But by the time you see the spots, it's too late to treat. Do the best you can with sanitation. Healthy trees in the right place can usually tolerate anthracnose.

- With any of these cases, decide whether this is a key plant in the landscape—a focal point or the plant that your whole landscape is planned around. If it is, then it may be worth treating, if treatment is practical and you can afford it.

Control Disease and Pests

- Options for disease and pest control include sanitation, that is, raking and destroying diseased leaves to prevent them from reinfesting other plants. In many cases, simply destroying diseased leaves is a good way to control problems. It may not provide 100 percent protection, but it can help reduce infection the following year.

- Pruning is another option. Let's say you have *Phomopsis blight* on junipers caused by a fungal disease. You'll find sunken and discolored areas—cankers—on the branches. Prune 9 to 12 inches below the canker, back to the trunk, or back to a healthy branch. This same approach can be used with *Phimopsis* (fire blight), as well. Disinfect your tools with 1 part bleach to 9 parts water between each cut; if you accidentally cut into a canker, then cut into healthy tissue, you can spread disease.

- Pruning is also useful for eliminating pests, as is trapping.
  - One type of a trap is a simple bag infused with pheromones, with a sticky substance to trap insects. You can use these traps when you see insects present, as opposed to applying chemicals based on the calendar.

  - You can also use burlap and twine to effectively trap and control gypsy moths. Wrap the burlap around the trunk of the tree; use the twine to tie halfway through and make a flap. Gypsy moths travel up and down the tree during the day and get trapped in the flap. Knock them into a can of soapy water, and you can greatly reduce their population without the need to climb the tree or use a spray.

  - Japanese beetle traps have the opposite effect from what you want: They bring in the insects you're trying to keep out. Instead, try treating preventively with an organic product called Neem that acts as a repellent.

- Some soil systemics, that is, insecticides that are put in the soil, are absorbed by the plant and concentrate in the leaves. Restrict your use of these products. If you use too many pesticides and treat every plant, insects develop resistance; it's best to save pesticide use for those plants that are struggling.

- To control aphids, a yellow container filled with soapy water may not be the most attractive solution, but it works. Some research shows that reflective mulch helps to trap aphids, too. Nature is a good option, as well. Lady beetles eat aphids. Immature and adult lady beetles can eat hundreds of aphids in one day.

Prevent Disease and Infestation

- Diseases occur when three factors converge: a susceptible plant, favorable weather, and the presence of a disease. Eliminate one of these, and disease cannot occur. Thus, you can avoid disease problems by making sure your plants are not susceptible hosts. Provide proper growing conditions: full sun, plenty of room, and proper pruning for good air flow and light penetration.

- Some diseases, such as cedar apple rust, need two hosts: the juniper we sometimes call cedar and an apple, quince, or Hawthorn tree. After a warm spring rain, a gelatinous growth forms and releases spores that infect the nearby apple, quince, or Hawthorn. The nearby tree then develops orange spots. Once those mature, they release spores back on the juniper to perpetuate the cycle. Get rid of one of the hosts and you take care of the disease.

- Apple scab is caused by a fungus and is most common when the weather is cool and wet. You obviously can't control the weather, but you can do some preventive pruning to open up the canopy and speed up drying of the leaves, offering less opportunity for the disease to infect. Sanitation—removing and destroying diseased material—will help reduce the source of infection for the following year, but neighboring yards and nearby green spaces must be sanitized, as well.

- One of the key issues with treatment is to time it based on plant growth, temperatures, and weather, rather than the calendar.
  - With disease problems, treatment is usually preventive.

  - With insects, time treatment for when plants flower. The temperatures needed for certain plants to flower are often the same for certain insects to develop.

- One of the most effective steps you can take to reduce the threat of invasive pests is not to move firewood, wood chip mulch, and debris from infected areas to non-infected areas. When you do that, you often take the pest along.

Buy wood for backyard fires locally to avoid introducing pests into your landscape.

- In thinking about disease and pest prevention, consider your maintenance and pruning schedule. Do you need to do more extensive cleanup in the fall or throughout the year to get rid of infected material? If you plan to use pesticides to eliminate insects, make sure you read the label and follow the directions carefully. You don't want to damage your plant or kill the "good bugs" that help keep the "bad bugs" under control.

Questions to Consider

1. What are some problems that are impractical to treat?

2. What are some options for dealing with pests?

3. How can you stop a disease from occurring?

Restoring a Landscape to Health
Lesson 11—Transcript

Last time we looked for patterns of symptoms and signs of insect and disease problems. Once we've diagnosed the cause, we must decide if the problem is really worth treating. Perhaps it's not even a problem, just a normal process, so no treatment is needed. A good example is seasonal needle drop. This is a time when the needles of an evergreen turn bright yellow, then brown from the ground level to the tip, but just on the inner side of the branches. And we know it's seasonal needle drop because of the pattern. Now, some years may be worse. All the older needles will eventually fall off, but if we've had a drought or insect problem, you'll see more needle dropping. So, proper care will help reduce that, but this is a normal process, so no need to break out the spray or do anything.

This is dog vomit fungus, a slime mold, and you often see this growing on mulch, sometimes sliming up the side of a tree or shrub. It's not harmful. It feeds off the organic matter in the mulch. We often see it during wet, gray periods and when your mulch is staying moist. Lightly rake your mulch to dry it out. That's all you need to do. Or wait; it eventually dries out on its own, looks disgusting, annoys you, but really nothing you need to worry about or treat.

Now last time we talked a lot about galls. And we talked about the galls that are caused by insects. Here we have an oak stem gall. And again, it was this one's caused by an insect feeding on the stem of the oak; it forms this growth; the gall is inside. No need to treat, the plant will be fine. A healthy tree can tolerate this damage. Even if we decided to treat, it's too late at this point, and we'd have to treat preventatively. And it may or may not be a problem in subsequent years, so, why waste the chemical and your time treating?

This is a mossy rose gall. They come in all kinds of different sizes and shapes, quite intriguing, so I wanted to share a few with you. Now, this gall is one of concern. This is the euonymus crown gall. And you often see this, it's kind of the size of a golf ball, at the base of the plant. Now this is caused by a bacteria, and it can kill the plant. Eventually it girdles out the step. So when you're buying this plant, make sure there are no galls present. You don't want to buy a problem. If you find it, remove that gall; disinfect your tools between cuts. So you'd cut off the stem beneath the gall as far as possible, and then disinfect your tools between cuts. And then keep an eye on the plant to make sure no other ones show up.

You also may need to decide, is it practical to treat? You know, it may be necessary, but is it practical? Let's take tar spot on Maple, for example. You know, basically, the leaves look like somebody dripped tar on the leaf. Now, it does look unsightly. It won't kill your tree if it's healthy and mature. And by the time you see the spots, there's really no effective treatment. Now spraying a large tree is costly, not always practical, and timing is very difficult.

Now, given the amount of the disease in your area, that may make this control less effective. So sanitation is an option, rake and destroy the leaves. But guess what? If your neighbors have tar spot and don't rake and destroy their leaves, or the public green space across the way has tar spot, it's not really going to solve the problem. I choose to recycle my leaves. And often diseases run their course, and eventually take care of themselves.

Needle blight on Spruce is another good example. This disease can cause dieback of branches and thinning of the plant. And there are chemicals that control it. We could spray it when the needles are half expanded and then fully expanded. The problem, timing is difficult, so getting someone out there, or yourself out there, with equipment to do that job at exactly the right time can be challenging. Getting good coverage, all those tiny little needles, can be difficult. So that can limit your success. And if you're going to spray, I recommend you take the garden hose, spray the tree with water, and see how wet you get. Do you really want to have that kind of pesticide coverage on yourself? That's where hiring a professional comes in handy. So you may decide that, you know what, the cost versus the value of the tree just isn't worth it. I hate to ever sentence a tree to death, but you may decide it's a little too costly to treat.

And timing for such things, like anthracnose. Anthracnose causes the spots you see on the leaves of maples, and sycamores, and ashes, and walnuts.

Now in sycamores, it can cause twig dieback. Healthy trees in the right place usually can tolerate it. And anthracnose on Maples, and oaks, and those trees, usually isn't a yearly occurrence. It's related to weather. So rake and get rid of those leaves. But by the time you see the spots, it's too late to treat. So do the best with sanitation. Keep the plant in good health. That's the best you can do.

And with any of these cases, you want to decide, is this a key plant in the landscape? Does it serve a focal point? Is this the plant that your whole landscape is planned around? Then it may be worth treating, if treatment is practical and you can afford it. Is it critical to energy savings? Again, this is my former house in the city, and you can just see that street tree peeking over that provided that air conditioning that was so critical. And I added a few other trees, my Candymint Crabapple, and a Serviceberry, to shade more of those west-facing windows to help keep my house cool. If any of those disappeared, my energy costs and discomfort would rise.

Maybe there's a reason for sentimental purposes. You planted a tree in honor of the birth of a child, or in memory of someone important in your life. If so, you may decide that treating it is worth it, even if it's costly. Because it's so important to your memory, your design, or your comfort. So let's talk about a few control options. I mentioned sanitation earlier, raking and destroying diseased leaves. Now typically, we destroy those diseased leaves and don't keep them on our property so that they can re-infest other plants. I mentioned with tar spot, I just rake my leaves up, shred them, and use them, mainly because it's so ever present. But many cases, getting rid of those leaves is a good way to control the problem. Now, as I mentioned with leaf spots, it may not provide 100 percent control, but in some cases you can greatly reduce the infection for next year.

Now, perhaps it's pruning that you're going to do. Here's an example, Phomopsis blight on Junipers. Now, this is caused by a fungal disease, and you'll find cankered areas on the branches, sunken and discolored areas. You want to prune 9 to 12 inches below that canker, or back to the trunk, or back to a healthy branch. And this goes for fireblight as well, that also produces cankers.

Disinfect your tools between each cut, because if you accidentally cut into a canker and cut into healthy tissue, you can spread that disease. Now, disinfect your tools with a one part bleach to nine parts water. It's tough on the tools, so be sure to clean them up when you're done pruning, or, rubbing alcohol. Either way, it works quite well. I like to have two pruners when I'm pruning something that's diseased. So cut, dip, grab the next one, so that I can have a clean pair of pruners with every cut. Makes the job quicker and easier.

And here's an example of pruning out some of the cankered dogwood. We did some renewal pruning on this plant, and you can see, I focused on those stems that had cankers. So, I not only made the plant look better, but I took care of some disease problems at the same time.

You may also want to do some hand picking or pruning off insect infested branches. If you've seen European pine sawfly that you see here, you won't forget them. They usually feed in colonies, like you see here. And if you put your hand up close, they kind of do a little dance. So they're quite entertaining. Until, that is, they eat all the needles off the branch. Now, they leave the new growth, and they go from branch to branch to branch. So that colony will eat the needles back, go to the next branch, eat the needles. They won't kill the tree. But you'll have tufts of growth at the end of branches, not quite the look you're going for for your evergreens.

So, a couple things you can do. You can take a leather clad glove and just smash those insects, disgusting but effective. If that's a little too much for you, try pruning out the infected branch. As I mentioned, they usually go from branch to branch to branch. So prune out that branch and destroy it. That is, unless they've infected all of your branches. Then you might want to think twice.

Now, trapping is another option that you might want to try. And there are two ways to look at traps. One is to monitor the pest. So we trap. OK, these pests are present. And if we need to control, we're only applying a product when it's needed, not based on the calendar. Now, I want to show you a few traps. You can buy commercial traps. They are usually something simple like this. They come with a sticky substance that will trap the insect. But what attracts them to the trap is a pheromone; it's a chemical that insects give off to attract other insects. Females give it off to bring in the males. So this will bring the insects in. We can monitor. And if needed, do treatment. Usually done for monitoring, not for control.

You can also make your own. This is just a wooden apple that somebody made for me. And red looks nice, but research showed that gray was very attractive. Cover it with the sticky substance, and there are some commercial varieties, or make your own. And one of the cool things is the insects will stick. So let's say apple maggots are your problem. And, what will happen is you can go, oh, the apple maggots are out. It's time to treat. Because in the olden days, we used to treat by the calendar. And you know, year to year, the weather is very different, and that means the insect population will vary. So we were spraying way more than necessary.

I also brought along some burlap and twine. It's a great way to effectively trap and control gypsy moths. As you can see in the picture, we wrapped the burlap around the trunk of the tree, used the twine to tie halfway through, and make a flap. Gypsy moths travel up and down the tree during the day, and so we trap them under here, knock them into a can of soapy water, and greatly reduce their populations without the need to climb the tree or use a spray.

Now, some traps also can cause problems in the garden. Now, Japanese beetle traps bring in the insects, and we're trying to keep them out of the garden. So if you've used a Japanese beetle trap, you know they're very effective. You'll get thousands of them and bring them to your garden. But we really don't want to bring them to the garden, but rather, keep them out. I had one gentleman say to me, so, if I give all my neighbors Japanese beetle traps and I don't put one in my yard, will that work? Yes, it would. So be aware of any friends and relatives that live nearby giving you a Japanese beetle trap.

This is what a Japanese beetle looks like, so there's no doubt. You can't miss them. They eat and mate in broad daylight, and feed on several hundred different varieties of plants. Usually don't kill healthy plants, but we're gardening for beauty, and you can see that's quite disturbing. So you may want to take a can of soapy water, go out early in the morning, they tend to congregate, and knock them into the soapy water.

You could treat preventatively with an organic product called neem, N as in Nancy, E-E, M as in Mary. Neem is an organic product that acts as repellent. So treat at least 30 days in advance. I know you'll cheat, so you've got a few to play with. And, that will help keep them away. But once they arrive, you'll need to use something that will kill them as a fully applied insecticide.

There also are some soil systemics, insecticides we put in the soil that are absorbed by the plant and concentrate in the leaves. Now, I would restrict your use of this, and here's why. If we use too many pesticides and we treat every plant, insects develop resistance. So we want to save those for those special trees, say birches who maybe have struggled through drought and have had problems with bore. This will reduce the stress, so save that for those plants that are struggling.

Milky spore is an organic control for Japanese beetles, but it controls the grubs. So it's often applied to our lawn, so that grubs don't eat the roots of the grass. Now that sounds like a great idea. If I kill the grubs, the immature, I'll take care of the beetles. The problem is you'll kill the grubs, but the adults can fly up to two miles. So treating your lawn after three years usually will build up enough of this disease organism to kill the grubs. You can still get adults coming in from outside. So you'll help keep the population down, but it's not a solution to the above-ground feeding. So just be aware of that.

Hopefully you don't recognize this, but I bet you do. Aphids, a common insect pest on annuals, perennials, trees, and shrubs. They feed together by the hundreds. And as I mentioned earlier, they have piercing, sucking mouth parts, like little needles. And so they prick into the leaf and suck the juices out. Now, they cause speckling. They cause distortion. And again, usually a healthy plant can tolerate it. But, you may want to do some control.

Those are the cast bodies of the aphid. Aphids come in green, and orange, and peach color, and black. That black stuff is called sooty mold. Because aphids, mites, white fly, scale suck plant juices, secrete the clear, sticky stuff called honeydew—that's often how you notice the pest. And this mold, this fungus, sooty mold, forms on the honeydew. It's not hurting the plant directly. But if you get enough of that sooty mold on the leaf's surface, the sunlight can't get through. The leaves can't photosynthesize. They turn yellow and drop off.

Now, there are traps that will work with aphids. A yellow container filled with soapy water may not be the most attractive, but it does work. Reflective mulch, there's been some research that shows that reflective mulch helps to trap the insects. The aphids orient, apparently, by seeing the sky. They see the sky above, the sky reflected in the mulch below. They get confused, crash, and die. I did try it. It worked, but not the most aesthetically pleasing way to manage aphids. Good news, a strong blast of water or heavy rain often takes care of them.

Nature is a good option as well. Notice the lady beetles eating the aphids. The immature and adult lady beetles can eat hundreds of aphids in one day. So if you do nothing and wait, often the ladybugs will come in and take care of the problem for you. And there's lots of good eco-friendly products on the market, like insecticidal soap also, that are more eco-friendly and will help take care of the problem.

Now, you can sometimes adjust the environment, your care practices, or replace the plant with something that's more resistant to really reduce your maintenance and improve the health and beauty of your plant and your landscape. Now, diseases are a great example of this. Diseases occur when we have a susceptible plants, favorable weather, and a disease present. And you can see that in this disease triangle. Take one of these away, and disease cannot occur.

So, powdery mildew is a great example. If you've grown lilacs, you've probably seen powdery mildew, even on maple trees at times. It's a fungus disease. And it usually occurs when we have fluctuating humidity and the environment is right for the disease to develop. So, what you can do is avoid the problem. Look for disease-resistant varieties. Lilacs, for example, Palibin, and a lot of the Asian Lilacs, are resistant to the powdery mildew.

So, eliminate the problem by getting rid of one of the factors, a susceptible host. Provide proper growing conditions, full sun, plenty of room, proper pruning so you get good air flow and light penetration. That reduces the risk of the disease. And then treatment is a possibility, but you need to spray weekly, whether using an organic or a synthetic, fungicide labeled for treatment of powdery mildew on the plant you're treating. Weekly sprays, that's a lot of work and a lot of chemical going into our environment. So, if you're like me, not too practical.

Keep in mind, your plants will probably tolerate the disease. They probably had it for years and keep coming back. They just look bad. Mask the problem. Put something in front of it that masks the leaves but not the blooms. That's a great way to have both. And then fall cleanup will reduce, not eliminate, the source of disease for next year. So do a combination of those things and you can reduce the problem.

We mentioned Phomopsis blight earlier. And basically, we pruned out the problem. You can get resistant varieties as well. Now some diseases, like cedar apple rust, need two hosts—the Juniper, we sometimes call Cedar, and a Crabapple, Quince, or Hawthorn tree. The gelatinous growth you see is what happens on the Red Cedar or Juniper. And after a warm spring rain, that gelatinous thing forms, releases spores that infect the nearby Crabapple, Quince, or Hawthorn. Then they develop the orange spots that you see. Once those mature, they release spores back on the Juniper. It's a cycle that goes on and on. Get rid of one of the hosts, you take care of the disease. Unfortunately, it's usually your neighbor that has one of the hosts that's not willing to get rid of their plant. So again, avoiding problems—look for resistant varieties or don't plant the two plants that are needed for this disease to complete its life cycle.

I mentioned apple scab earlier. And apple scab is common on Apples, and Crabapples, and Pears, Mountain ash. And it's caused by a fungus. And it's most common when the weather conditions are cool and wet. So if we have a cool, wet spring, we're likely to see problems with that. Now remember that disease triangle? Remove one factor, you eliminate the problem. Now we obviously can't control the weather, but we can do some pruning preventatively to open up the canopy and speed up drying so the leaves dry out faster, less opportunity for the disease to infect.

Sanitation, we can rake and destroy the leaves, so that's a great way to reduce the source of infection for next year. But we need to get our neighbors and the nearby green spaces to do the same. There's a scab pretty much out there all over, but do the best you can. And then look for varieties. A lot of the new Crabapples have been introduced for disease resistance, for fire blight, and apple scab, as well as persistent fruit.

And if you do decide to spray, timing is critical for successful control. You want to start spraying at the pink stage, just as those buds are starting to open, and repeat. You'll need at least four to five applications, 7 to 10 days apart. Follow label directions. You may be rethinking this idea. Maybe it's time to replace that Crabapple with something that's more resistant. Or, landscape so you enjoy the flowers, but don't look at the tree once all the scab infested leaves drop off.

And one of the key things when we are looking at timing is we want to time treatment based on plant growth, and temperatures, and weather, versus the calendar. And with disease problems, it's usually done preventatively. With insects, we can time it for when they're present, not by the calendar. But some insects are easier to see than others. When I used to do some work back in the extension service about 25 or 30 years ago, when we were recommending treatment for bore, it was spray once a month for four months, hoping the timing would be right. Now we have some better clues for you.

So we time insect development based on the time when plants flower. The temperatures needed for certain plants to flower is often the same for certain insects to develop. Pine needle scale is a great example of this. Pine needle scale looks like somebody spilled white paint on your Mugo pine, flecks of white. And if you spray them, that hard covering protects the insect below. Now you can use a dormant spray labeled for controlling that pest on the plant you're spraying. But you want to be sure to read and follow label directions so that you don't cause any damage.

Otherwise, you can use an eco-friendly product like insecticidal soap and treat when the little eggs underneath that white fleck hatch, the little nymphs are crawling all around, you can't see them, but they're out and about at the same time that Vanhoutte Spirea, you may know as Bridalwreath Spirea, and Annabelle Hydrangeas are blooming. So we know to treat at that time with insecticidal soap or a lightweight horticulture oil. So we're timing the spray based on a plant that's blooming, something we can see, so that we can use less pesticide, maybe more eco-friendly products, and get better control.

Some insects, like the emerald ash bore, Asian longhorned beetle, have really been destroying a lot of our urban and natural forest. The emerald ash bore, as you can see here, is a very tiny insect. And one of the problems is it can be feeding under the bark of the tree for several years. And as you can see, you won't even notice it's small exit holes. The tree can look fine for the first couple years. But the tree is infected. By the time we notice the damage of wilting and browning, this tree is really gone. And probably the emerald ash bore has infected nearby trees.

So some concerns, we're looking at maybe calling it a professional that has some chemicals that they can inject into the tree to take care of it. There are some products that have been quite effective for you. And the good news, there's a lot of new research out for more eco-friendly products that will take care of it. So sanitation, removing dead, infected trees, very important, and reading and following label directions if you do decide to treat yourself.

But one of the best things we can do to reduce the threat of invasive pests, like the emerald ash bore, or thousand cankers disease of black walnut, is not to move firewood, wood chip, mulch, and debris from infected areas to non-infected areas. Because when we take that firewood, we often take the pest with us. So buy your firewood locally at the campground where you're camping, in your community if you're having bonfires in your backyard. Don't bring pests in or take them into uninfected areas.

Now we've mentioned a lot of problems that can happen from disease and insect, and a few of the nonliving problems when we talked about a year in the life. But I want to talk about one that's really a big issue beyond frost, salts, and sea salt. One that I get hundreds of inquires about each year, and that's plants failing to thrive, even declining, under a Black walnut tree. One of the things that you may or may not know is Black walnuts contain a substance called juglone, and it's in their leaves, the nuts, the husks of the fruit, the roots. And when susceptible plants come in contact with that, say the roots of the Black walnut or leaves in the soil, they absorb that juglone, and it causes them to wilt and die. So it's really an allelopathic response. So many plants have this so they keep the competition at bay by stunting or inhibiting growth, so they have the opportunity to take over the space, fine in the woods, not so good in your landscape.

So keep in mind that all parts contain this juglone. And they're in the soil. But the concentration of the roots, as in that diagram, show that it's the greatest closest to the trunk of a tree, within 50 feet. Now, trying to keep your plantings away from that will increase success. And I'll talk in a minute about other strategies you can use. Now, maybe you want to remove the tree. It won't be an immediate solution, because you have to wait for all those roots and debris in the soil to decompose, maybe five, as much as 10 years. And sometimes, that Black walnut is an important tree in your landscape, or worse yet, your neighbor's. So removal is not an option.

Now we can tolerant plants. Unfortunately, there's no complete list. Check online, check the internet, ask at your local university outreach office, check with garden centers. But I found it's not a good, complete list. So you may want to do your own testing. You may want to take a plant that you haven't found on a list as being susceptible or resistant, plant one or two near your Black walnut. If successful, you can always add more. If it's starting to decline, move it to an area further from that black walnut tree.

Now, as I mentioned, you want to keep your plants that are susceptible at least 50 feet away, though I have seen damage several hundred feet away, following the major routes from that black walnut. The other thing you can do is try a raised bed. And here's what I recommend. Make your raised bed. Line it with weed barrier, that fabric we showed that you could use under rock mulch. And that will help keep those Black walnut roots from going underneath the raised bed and into that wonderful soil. And so that's one option you could do.

So, now that we've taken a look at what can go wrong and how you can manage your problems, you may want to start looking at, do I need to improve my maintenance, make some adjustments? Maybe I need to adjust my pruning schedule, better clean up in the fall or throughout the year, getting rid of disease-infected material, and finding a way to keep them out of the yard, but don't give them to someone else.

Maybe you do want to do some pest management. And if you opt for treatment, whether it's organic or natural, always read and follow label directions carefully. Make sure the plant you're treating is included on the label and the pest you're treating is also listed. Read any warnings, because these products are made to kill things. And you don't want to damage your plant or kill the good guys that help keep the bad guys under control. And, it may even involve removal of plants in their prime to avoid long-term treatment and use of chemicals.

So now I want you to go take a look at the list you created after our last discussion. Are there problems and are there damages you need to deal with? And then I want you start your recovery plan to help revive your framework. In the next session, we'll take a look at some fun and perhaps a bit more challenging ways of including trees and shrubs in the landscape, and ways you can expand your tree and shrub collection.

Expanding Your Landscape's Framework
Lesson 12

Pruning normally is used to control size, improve flowering, and manage pests. But pruning can also enhance the beauty and interest of your garden or landscape. A number of pruning strategies enhance the ornamental appeal and space efficiency of large-scale landscape plants, including espalier, topiary, and propagation.

Espalier

- Espalier is a pruning method used to train trees and shrubs to grow flat against a wall, a fence, or other structure. Because espaliering requires a fair amount of work, before you begin, evaluate how much time and energy you're willing to devote to pruning. Start small, with one or two plants.

- First, select the right space. You'll need a sturdy structure, the right growing conditions, and perhaps an east- or south-facing wall to avoid the hot afternoon sun. Because the plants will be heavily pruned, you need to protect them from exposure to sunlight, cold, and other, more trying conditions. Keep in mind that plants growing against a brick wall will also have some heat gain.

- Select a 1-gallon potted plant or a bare-root plant. Place it at least 6 to 10 inches away from the wall, and prune sparingly the first year.
  - Anchor support wires to the wall or, if you use posts, set them next to the fence or wall, and leave enough room to get behind them to do maintenance work.

  - Use I-bolts and screws, U-bolts, or plastic masonry plugs to secure the system, with 12- or 15-gauge wire strung between. Your nursery staff or hardware store can help in terms of building supplies and guidance.

  - You may also want to build a trellis.

- The next step is to decide on a pruning strategy, choosing from the many different ways you can train plants to grow.
  - Belgian fence is a great way to provide a divider between different spaces. You can see through but still have some privacy. This method involves planting young whips, small trees, or shrubs next to each other, then training them into a basket weave.

  - The cordon system is a straight up and tiered method but much more densely planted for greater screening.

  - The palmette system is a variation on the cordon system, where branches go out and up. It requires a little more skill.

  - For a serpentine system, the support is in the shape of an S curve, and individual stems are trained to follow it.

- Your initial pruning will be somewhat light, depending on your plants. Most subsequent pruning will be done in late winter to stimulate new growth.

- If you start with a bare-root plant, you want to encourage growth to enable training. Keep in mind that flowering trees or shrubs or fruit trees set their flower buds the year before; thus, you should do your pruning right after flowering.

- Pruning in midsummer encourages dwarfing, which is great once your plants are close to mature size. Avoid late-summer pruning, especially in cold climates, because that can stimulate late-season growth that may be killed in winter.

- Once you choose the training method, select branches that help you develop that framework. Tie those branches to the support system with a string, cloth, or twist tie; loosen the ties as the stems grow in diameter, or they will choke and eventually kill the branch. Prune any branches that are not part of the design, including healthy branches that just don't belong.

- Don't tip-prune the key branches until they're full size; you want them to continue to grow straight, not branch out too heavily. Allow side shoots to reach about 12 inches before you shorten them. Do touch-up pruning as needed to maintain your design.

Pleaching and Topiary

- Pleaching is a way of creating tunnels or arbors in very narrow spaces and of training trees for a very small space. Start with young, flexible stems planted fairly close together and interweave them either with each other or onto a support to create the shape.

- Topiary takes the sheared hedge concept a step further by pruning the plants into animals, spirals, or other interesting shapes. Be sure to select the right plants, such as small-leafed boxwoods, yews, hollies, and junipers. Young plants with evenly spaced branches are easier to train than more mature plants.

- Creating shapes from individual shrubs requires a pruner, a few guidelines, and a yardstick. Start small and give yourself some guidance with some string and a ruler. For more complex topiaries, use a wire form as a guide to get the desired shape, and do regular pruning to maintain the form.

Containers

- Growing trees and shrubs in containers allows you to expand your planting space and gives you a great deal of control and flexibility.
  - For example, what if you want to plant blueberries, but you know they need moist, well-drained, slightly acid soil? You can create the perfect soil in a pot.

  - You can also grow lime and lemon trees even if you don't live in Florida or California. Move the trees outside in the summer and back in for the winter.

- To grow trees and shrubs in pots, select a pot with drainage holes that's made from material that can tolerate year-round weather conditions. If you don't want to use plastic, concrete and fiberglass are long-lasting. Wood takes the cold and the heat and works quite well year round.

- The larger the container, the better the root insulation, which is critical in cold climates for the winter and in hot climates for the summer. Plus, you'll be watering less often with a bigger pot.

- If you have a beautiful ceramic pot and don't want to leave it out during the winter, double potting is an option. When the soil freezes, it expands and can crack the pot. Plant your shrub in an old nursery pot and set it inside the ceramic pot. When fall comes, remove the plant in its nursery pot, bury it in a vacant part of the garden or put it in an unheated garage, and store the decorative pot for the next season.

- For container planting, you also need a good potting mix that has good drainage and will hold moisture. Incorporate a slow-release fertilizer in the potting mix to keep feeding the plant over time. Water thoroughly and check daily. Watering needs will vary with the size of the pot, the type of potting mix, the size of the plant, and your weather conditions. Fertilize at least once a year, but avoid fertilizing in late summer in areas where plants go dormant for the winter. You don't want to encourage growth right before the dormant period.

Microclimates

- Microclimates are small areas within your landscape that have slightly different growing conditions. For example, if one side of your house is sheltered from the winter wind, it may be a little milder during the winter.

- Avoid planting in low spots that are subject to cold and frost. Instead, consider slopes facing the south or west that tend to be warmer if late-spring frosts are a concern.

- In areas with hot summers, add some shade structures: a pergola, an arbor, or perhaps some small-scale trees to shade some of your shrubs. Grouping your plants together will increase humidity and reduce care, as well.

Propagation

- Keep in mind that many new plants are patented. Nurseries develop these plants and patent them to recoup their investment in breeding. For that reason, some people believe that no patented plant should be propagated.

It can be great fun to experiment with planting seeds from fruit you had for breakfast or lunch, such as apples, oranges, lemons, or limes.

- Propagating takes patience and some research. Trees and shrubs are more difficult to root than houseplants and flowers. Gather your supplies or do an inventory before you get started propagating cuttings.

  o A good, sharp knife and hand pruners are essential.

  o Containers should be deep to encourage plants to root well, and trees and shrubs need plenty of room for root development.

  o Rooting hormone encourages root development, and some fungicides discourage rot.

- You'll need a starting mix, as well. Vermiculite is an inert material that holds moisture but also has good drainage. Seed-starting mix is also good for starting cuttings. Plastic will help with humidity.

- Hardwood cuttings are from such plants as forsythia, privet, olive, wisteria, spirea, hemlock, and many other woody plants. During the dormant season, make 4- to 8-inch cuttings with at least two nodes, and store them in a cool, moist area.

- Semi-hardwood cuttings are from dogwoods, pittosporum, holly, azaleas, citrus, and many other broadleaf, evergreen, and deciduous plants. Take those cuttings in summer, when the new growth has matured. Take about 3- to 6-inch-long cuttings in the morning when the leaves and stems are firm and full of moisture.

- Softwood cuttings are the new growth of spring: lilacs, magnolia, weigela, spirea, and many fruits. Make those cuttings about 3 to 5 inches long from that tender, new growth in spring. Be sure to remove any flowers, flower buds, or seeds because you want the plant's energy going into developing roots, not flowers and seeds.

- If you take cuttings from a plant with the stem attached, cut above a good healthy bud or where a branch joins another branch. For the most part, cuttings should be short. Longer cuttings have more leaves, creating more moisture loss and more stress on the plant.

- Using vermiculite, place your cutting in potting mix and water to keep the rooting medium moist and encourage root growth. Loosely cover with plastic to hold the humidity in; this will ensure that you water less, lose less moisture from the leaves, and increase your chances of success. Put the cutting in a bright area but not in direct sunlight; you don't want moisture loss or energy used for photosynthesis. Keep the cutting in a warm spot and, hopefully, in several weeks, you'll have some roots.

- Starting trees and shrubs from seeds can be fun, but you need to be patient to grow a large tree from a small seed. Plant seeds at a depth twice the diameter of the seed in a seed-starting mix and water. Cover loosely with plastic and put the seeds in the refrigerator for 3 months or longer to give them the chill they need. Bring them out in spring and get them growing in a sunny window in a warm spot; transplant them outside after the last spring frost.

1. What are some of the systems you can use for espalier?

2. What is a microclimate?

3. What tools do you need for propagation?

Expanding Your Landscape's Framework
Lesson 12—Transcript

We have discussed pruning to control size, improve flowering, and manage pests. Now it's time to look at pruning strategies that enhance the ornamental appeal and space efficiency of these large-scale landscape plants. Let's start with espalier. This is not for the pruning paranoid or those with extremely busy schedules.

Espaliering is a pruning method used on trees and shrubs to grow them flat against a wall, a fence, or other structure, or free standing, very space efficient and very artistic. I consider them a form of living art. As you can see here, this Apple has been espaliered against a decorative fence, a nice open screening, great for small spaces, or even large areas where you want to have a little privacy, save some space, or add some decoration.

Now, espaliering does require a fair amount of work. So before you decide to jump on board, evaluate your time and energy. You may want to start small, maybe with one or two plants. Now keep in mind if you're growing fruit trees, you may need two plants for pollination and fertilization. Many fruit trees, like most Apples, need two different cultivars or varieties to pollinate to ensure that you get fruit. So do a little homework first.

First you want to select the right space. You'll need a sturdy structure, whether it's a wall or a fence or a trellis system. The right growing conditions, of course, and perhaps an east-facing wall. That way, you avoid injury, because you'll have the morning light, but protected from the hot afternoon sun. Perhaps a south face will work as well. Remember, these are heavily pruned plants, so you want to protect them from any exposure of sunlight and cold and other more trying conditions.

Now keep in mind that plants growing against a brick wall will also have some extra heat gain. So especially if you're in a hot climate, you may want to be careful where you place those. Now the good news? Some nurseries will have plants already started for you. They started the training process, so you just need to keep the plant in shape and continue pruning to get it to its ultimate mature size.

But you may also want to start from scratch. That's part of the fun of this. Select a one-gallon potted plant or a bare-root plant, much easier to manage and to get it started young. Place it at least 6 to 10 inches away from the wall. You're going to plant and prune sparingly that first year. Now, you are going to need to anchor the support wires to the wall, or if you use posts, set next to the fence or wall. Now I like putting posts next to a wall to make sure I have enough room to get back there if I have to paint the house or do any kind of maintenance. So leave enough room that you can get behind there to do any maintenance work. You'll use eye bolts and eye screws, U bolts, plastic masonry plugs to secure the system, 12- or 15-gauge wire strung between those eye bolts or between the posts, and turn buckles for tightening. Your nursery staff, or maybe, better yet, your hardware store can help with this, in terms of building supplies and some guidance.

You may also want to build a trellis. Again, it's a nice way to have it stand alone as you see here. This tree is really the fence in itself, nothing more than posts and wire and the fence. You could have it near the house or standing alone to maybe segregate different living spaces, outdoor living spaces, in your larger backyard or some privacy next to your deck.

Now you need to decide on the pruning strategy. There's many different ways that you can train these plants to grow. This is a Belgian fence. And this is a great way to provide a divider between different spaces in your outdoor area, or maybe a bit of separation from you and your neighbor, a friendly fence. You can see through but still have some privacy. And basically, it's planting young whips, small trees or shrubs, next to each other and then training them into a basket weave-type mix. Those are loosely tied together where they cross and then cross back to form this nice weave.

I love this because if you had a flower garden behind, you'd have the benefit of the hedge, a little bit of break, a little backdrop, almost like a wattle fence, only living, and your flower garden beyond. The cordon system is a basic system that you often see. And you can see here they've trained some apple trees, bit of a slight angle and spreading up on a trellis system. A little bit more intense, straight up and tiered method, but much more densely planted, so if you really want more screening.

Against a brick wall, this is the palmette system. Notice how those branches go out and up, kind of a variation on the cordon system, little bit more intense, requires a little more skill, so you may want to start with something easy. This is a serpentine system. And they basically bought the support in the shape of a serpentine, or an S curve, and trained the individual stems that way.

Now I mentioned your initial pruning needs to be somewhat light, depending on the plants you purchased. If you bought a bare-root plant, it may already been pruned to an extent that it's ready to go in the ground. You may also need to prune that first time back just above the first set of tier, where you're going to have those branches going out. Or, you may want to line it up so that your lowest tier is in line with the first set of branches, if it's at the right height.

Now, most of your pruning after that will be done in late winter, and that stimulates new growth as you're trying to get this system established. You're going to start with a bare root, kind of a small plant. And so you're going to want to encourage growth so you can train it. Now, in spring, if you've got blooming plants, like flowering trees or shrubs or fruit trees, they set their flower buds the year before, as we discussed during pruning. So, you're going to want to keep that in mind, because you're probably going to want the flowers to enjoy, as well as training. So you may do your pruning right after flowering so you get the best of both.

If you prune in mid summer, that kind of encourages more dwarfing. You don't get as much growth. That's great once your plants are pretty close to mature size. Now, as usual, we want to avoid late summer pruning, especially those of you in cold climates, because that can stimulate late-season growth they can be winter killed. And remember, these plants are pretty exposed because we're doing heavy duty pruning, so we want to make sure we give them every opportunity to survive, especially cold winters and hot summers.

Once you select those key branches that you're going to train on your wire system, whether it's a tiered method, where the branches grow horizontal, or it's a palmette method, where they go up kind of in a fan shape, or like a candelabra, keep that in mind and select branches that help you develop that framework. And then you're going to prune to do that.

Now, you're going to tie those branches to a support system with a string or cloth or a twist tie. But you want to keep after it, because you need to loosen those as the stems get larger in diameter. Otherwise, that can choke or girdle and eventually kill the branch. You're going to prune out any branches that are not part of the design. That's where all this extra pruning comes in. And maybe your pruning paranoia comes to the surface, because you're going to be taking out a lot of healthy branches that just don't belong there.

Don't tip prune your key branches, those that form the framework, until they're full size, because you want these to continue to grow straight, not branch out too heavily. Allow side shoots to reach about 12 inches before you shorten those. And then touch-up prune is needed to maintain your design. Now there's a lot of good, more detailed information on the Internet that you may want to check out. It's really all about giving it a shot and not being afraid to use your pruners to train the trees to the right structure, and of course, a good, sturdy support to keep that plant in place.

Now pleaching is a little bit different than espaliering. It's basically creating tunnels or arbors, like you see here, or walls in very narrow spaces—pleaching. And, it's a way of training your trees for a very small space. We start with young, flexible stems, so young trees, planted fairly close together. And then we either interweave them with each other or onto the support when they're young to create that nice, dense shape.

This is just for a little bit of fun. These are willow trees planted in smart pots. They're just cloth pots filled with potting mix. And this is in Quebec, Canada, so these plants can take the cold of Canada. And then they trained those young willow trees to form this dome. I also saw some as arbors and other decorative features. What a fun way to have a living gazebo in your backyard or over your deck or on your balcony.

Now, topiary is another form of pruning, and it takes that sheared hedge concept just one step further. The plants are sheared, sometimes into animals, spirals, or other interesting shapes. And here you see a quite intricate animal, kind of the cloud garden, which is very Japanese-garden style; a parterre, which has geometric shapes intertwining; a knot garden; and a mix of formal shearing with some plantings. And it could be as extensive or simple as you choose.

Now obviously, this is going to be a little bit of work. Now I'm seeing more and more of these spirals and geometric shapes at the garden center, so you could start with a topiary that's already been trained. But you have to keep up. Otherwise, it's going to grow just like the other junipers or boxwoods that you see out there. So, couple things to keep in mind. If you're doing a topiary, select the right plant. Small-leafed plants, like Boxwoods, Yews, Hollies, Junipers, are commonly used for topiaries. So that would be a good place to start. Young plants with evenly spaced branches are much easier to train than more mature plants. And you may want to start with something simple, as I mentioned. The juniper cloud is basically just removing all the branches on the lower ends of the stems and then just creating mini clouds on the tips of the juniper plant. Or the spiral, as I showed, a great way that you could probably buy it already started and just keep after it.

Geometric shapes from individual shrubs, or the spirals, or even animals are going to require a pruner, a few guidelines, and a yardstick for most people. Because I'll tell you, I've tried doing a topiary with no guidelines, and it did not look pretty. I was lucky enough to go to a nursery where they do a lot of topiary. And the workers have done so many that we watched them in five minutes take a juniper and make it into a spiral, no rulers, no guidelines, just a pair of hand pruners and a lot of expertise working it. It was amazing. But that's years of practice and hundreds of topiaries formed. So give yourself a break and maybe start small. And give yourself maybe some guidance with some string and a ruler.

Now the more complex topiaries, animals, people, things like that, you may want to have a wire form as a guide. Often people will develop a wire form and then prune around, and that's one way to get the desired shape. They do need regular pruning to maintain that desired form. So just like espalier, maybe even more so, you need to make sure that you have the time and energy to do it. You'd hate to invest in a topiary initially and then lose it as you go. But, then again, the fun of gardening is trying something new. You want good, steady, even growth and a healthy plant. And if it is a healthy plant, you're going to be pruning several times a year.

Now, I like to push the limits, and I know most of you do, too. And so one way to push the limits with growing trees and shrubs is put them in containers. It allows you to expand your planting space. So if you only have a balcony or deck, guess what? You can grow trees and shrubs. They can do the same job in a pot that they do in the ground. And, in a little bit, we'll talk a little bit about microclimates and how to push the limits some more.

But consider containers. You can to control the soil. So guess what? Containers also allow you to plant things like blueberries that need moist, well-drained, slightly acid soil. And if you don't have perfect soil for the plant you choose, you can create that in the pot. So again, expanding not only planting space, but the type of plants you can grow.

And, you can also grow plants like Limes, Citrus, Lemon, even if you don't live in Florida and California. This tree goes out for the summer and in for the winter. So you're expanding, again, the number of plants you can grow because you're taking your climate with you—outside when it's nice and warm and back indoors. And as you can see, we even had some Limes.

Now here are some tips for growing trees and shrubs in pots. First of all, select a pot with drainage holes. And one that's made out of a material that's able to tolerate year-round weather conditions. Now, I garden in a very cold climate for winter, and I have used plastic pots. Now, they'll last me a couple years, as long as I don't hit them with the shovel when I'm shoveling the snow in winter. But I have to replace them every few years. And that's usually about the time my tree or shrub needs repotting.

If you don't want to use plastic, concrete, fiberglass, work great. They're long-lasting. Wood. Those are things that take the cold and the heat and work quite well year round. We don't want to use glazed pots because they'll crack in the winter if you have a cold winter. Now the larger the container, the better the root insulation. And that's critical in cold climates for the winter and hot climates for the summer. Plus, you'll be watering less often with a bigger pot.

Now, double potting is an option if you have that beautiful ceramic pot but you don't want to leave it out during the winter, because, when the soil freezes, it expands, and crack goes your pot. So, if you don't have a weatherproof pot, but you want to use it and have it beautiful, double pot. Basically, we have our shrub and an old nursery pot; we set it inside our beautiful pot. So when fall comes and I need to protect this plant from the cold winter, my decorative pot is safely stored. And, all I have to do with this is bury it in a vacant part of the garden or put it in an unheated garage or insulate the roots in another way. But it's an old nursery pot. It doesn't matter if it really suffers or is buried or gets dirty. And my nice pot is ready for next season. So double potting is a way to do that.

Now, besides a container with drainage holes, you want a good potting mix and one that has good drainage, one that will hold moisture. I like to incorporate fertilizer in my potting mix, because, if I use a slow release fertilizer at planting, it feeds that tree and shrub the whole time through. Now, if you have a big pot, you may want to get some help moving it, a pot lifter, maybe a plant stand on caster wheels. Any of those things will help you move the pot, and a good, strong friend never hurts.

So we've got our pot with drainage; we've got a good potting mix; we've incorporated a slow release fertilizer. Now we need to make sure we water. Water thoroughly, check daily. The watering needs will vary with the size of the pot, the type of potting mix, the size of the plant, and your weather conditions. So keep that in mind, but check frequently. And I mentioned fertilizing with a slow-release fertilizer at planting. And you'll need to do that at least once a year. But avoid fertilizing in late summer in areas where your plants go dormant for winter. You don't want to encourage growth when we're going into that dormant period. Instead, spring and early summer.

Those in cold climates will need to provide extra protection, as I mentioned. Bury your pot in a vacant area of the garden, the double potting method. Move to an unheated garage. Or put it with other plants in a sheltered location. And cover those roots with wood chips, snow, or other material to insulate. If you're interested in doing more with containers, see our "How to Grow Anything" containers course. We've got lots of tips on growing trees, shrubs, and other plants in containers.

Now, another way to expand your planting options is to create a microclimate or take advantage of an existing one to expand your choice of plants. Microclimates are just small areas within your landscape that have slightly different growing conditions. And you've probably experienced that yourself. Maybe it's a side of the house sheltered from the winter wind, so it tends to be a little milder during the winter, maybe shaded from the winter sun or the summer heat, good place for those plants that just can't take that intense sunlight.

The east side of your house usually gets morning sun, but not the hot afternoon sun. A southern exposure or one near reflective surfaces will give you additional heat, could be good, could be bad for some plants. Avoid low spots that are subject to cold and frost. Instead, consider slopes facing the south or west that tend to be warmer, if late spring frosts are a concern. And remember those wind breaks we talked about? Planting near those will create a nice wind-free zone, great for many of your plants. Now, areas with hot summers, you may want to add some shade structures, either existing or put some in. A pergola or an arbor, or maybe some small-scale trees to shade some of your shrubs. Grouping your plants together will increase humidity and reduce care as well.

Now, we can also expand our plant collection by propagating. Trees and shrubs are more difficult, though, than houseplants and flowers to root. I remember my first attempt was a Lilac, and I thought I did everything right. Then I did my research and found I took my cutting at the wrong time. So, it can be done. Takes a little patience and maybe a little bit of research in mind. I do want to remind you that many of the new plants are patented. And, you need to handle this whole thing carefully. Nurseries develop these plants, patent them to help get their money back on their investment of breeding.

Now some people believe that you shouldn't propagate any patented plant, because the grower should have the fees that are required. Others believe, as long as you're not planning to sell those new plants that you're propagating and just use them in your own yard that there's not a problem. But in any case, we want to support those growers who are developing new plants that we all love to have in our gardens.

But let's talk about starting trees and shrubs from cuttings, and let's get started planting. You want to gather your supplies or do an inventory before you get started propagating cuttings. Well, you're going to need plant material, and we'll talk about the different types of cuttings you can take in just a moment. But here are some of the supplies you'll need: a good, sharp knife; hand pruners, one or the other or you might like both; containers, they should be nice and deep, because you're hoping that they'll root well, and trees and shrubs need plenty of room for their root development; rooting hormone, and this basically contains hormones to encourage root development and some fungicides to discourage rot, so that will help improve your success rate.

We'll need a starting mix as well. Now, I've got two different kinds. Vermiculite, and I'm going to use it in this purple pot where I've lined it with a paper towel, because the holes are kind of big, and the vermiculite's kind of small. This is basically an inert material that holds the moisture but also has good drainage, so we're filling that up. We're also using a seed starting mix, which is also good for starting cuttings. So we'll put that in place. And I've got the plastic ready here, so that will help with humidity.

So let's talk about the type of cuttings that you can take. Hardwood cuttings, those are plants like Forsythia and Privet and Olive, Wisteria, Spirea, Hemlock, and many of the other woody plants, do well with hardwood cuttings. These are made during the dormant season, because you're taking the previous season's growth. So the leaves have dropped off these plants. These are a little bit longer, 4- to 8-inch cuttings, with at least two nodes. Now that's the point where the buds and leaves occur. Remember when we did our ID lesson? Those are called nodes.

And then we're going to store those cuttings in a cool, moist area. It's got to be above freezing for the winter. So a spare refrigerator would work well, or if you're in a milder climate, a cool spot out in the garden. In spring, we're going to stick the cuttings in our rooting hormone for woody plants and start them. And we'll show you that in a minute.

Semi-hardwood cuttings, those you can use on Dogwoods, Pittosporum, Holly, Azaleas, Citrus, Olive, and many other broadleaf, evergreen, and deciduous plants. Now, those cuttings we take in summer, when the new growth has matured. So they put out new growth, and it's starting to get hard, not as flexible. Those are semi-hardwood cuttings. Those, we're going to take about 3- to 6-inch long cuttings in the morning when the leaves and stems are firm, full of moisture.

Softwood cuttings, on the other hand, are the new growth of spring. Those are the Lilacs. Now my mistake is I took a hardwood cutting of Lilac. I should have waited until after flowering and that new growth appeared. So Lilac, Forsythia also work as software cuttings. Magnolia, Weigela, Spirea, many of your fruits, and then there are other trees and shrubs that also work well as softwood cuttings. Make those cuttings about 3- to 5-inches long from that tender, new growth in spring. But be sure to remove any flowers, flower buds, or seeds, because we want the energy going into developing roots, not developing flowers and seeds.

So we're going to use some of those prunings from our Dogwoods from the trimmings we made earlier. So, I've got this stem that we already took. But if I was taking cuttings from a plant and the stem was attached, here's where I'd make that cutting, just like a good pruning cut. I would cut above a good healthy bud, or here, where a branch joins another branch. So that leaves me this cutting. Notice I've got growth coming here and a node. Remember the node is that area where leaves or stems come out when we're doing our plant ID? That's where the point of new growth will be.

Now cuttings need to be short, for the most part, as you saw. The dormant one is a little bit longer. But if we use longer cuttings, the problem is more leaves, more moisture loss, more stress on the plant. We'll increase our chance of success with shorter cuttings. Now, I'm going to dip it in water. That's just to moisten the bottom of the stem so that the rooting hormone sticks. Then, we're using vermiculite in this case, and we'll just stick our cutting. Then, I also have one prepared already. Do the same thing. And we'll stick it in potting mix. We'll water, because you want to keep that rooting medium moist to encourage root growth.

Notice I have these set in baggies, because the other thing we can do is loosely cover them with plastic to hold the humidity in. So we water less, lose less moisture from the leaves, and increase our chance of success. We'll put these in a bright area but not in direct sunlight, because we don't want a lot of energy used at photosynthesizing and moisture loss in bright sunlight. Keep it in a warm spot, and hopefully, in several weeks you'll have some roots.

Now some of you may be saying, I always root my things in water. Well, I'm a big fan of using a well-drained potting mix or vermiculite or perlite. The roots that form in water are slightly different. So you really force your plant to root twice. But if it works for you, my theory on gardening, if it works, it's safe, and it's good for you and the environment, just keep doing it.

Now, we had some cuttings started a few weeks ago of these boxwoods. Let's just see if we've got any roots forming. Kind of hate to do this. Well, I think we've got a couple of things just starting to shoot out. Now, evergreens are a little tricky, because they make you think that they're still holding their own, and they are. But they tend to hold their leaves longer than deciduous plants. But they still feel nice and firm, so they're doing well. I think they just need a bit more time. And that's one of the keys to success; keep the rooting medium moist, in a warm spot, the humidity high. Always plant your cuttings as soon as possible. Or, like we did, wrap them in moisture, plastic bag, and in the fridge until you have time to start them.

Starting trees and shrubs from seeds can be lots of fun, great experiment. But you do need to be patient to grow a big tree from a small seed. If you start wandering around your yard looking for opportunities, you'll probably find the seeds of trees and shrubs in interesting fruit, like Crabapples, or maybe even pods, like this jacaranda. You'll need to get the seeds out of the fruit before you plant them.

Now, some fruit we're familiar with, like Apples, Oranges, Lemons, and Limes. And it's fun to start trees from things that maybe we ate for lunch or dinner. But keep in mind that if you collect seeds from these plants, that Apple you get that you grow and produces fruit will probably be different than the one you had for dinner. But that's part of the fun, isn't it? So Apple seeds, like we have here, are plants that grow in more temperate areas with cold winters. So that's a clue to you. If you're starting seeds from a plant and you don't know exactly how to treat it, if it's native to an area that has cold winters, it's a good idea to give it a cold treatment.

So we're going to take these Apple seeds, and we're going to plant a couple in each pot just to make sure. Typically, we put our seeds a depth twice the diameter of the seed's deep, and we've got a seed-starting mix, nice and light, holds moisture, sterile. And we're going to water it in. And this will help it germinate. But, we're not going to count on it starting yet, because these seeds need a cold period. So we're going to cover them with plastic, loosely, and we're going to put them in the refrigerator for three months to give them the chill they needed, or longer. Then you can bring them out in spring, get them growing in your window, a sunny window in a warm spot. Get them started indoors, then transplant them outside, if you live in a cold area, after the last spring frost. So that's how we'd start plants like pears and apples, maybe crabapples, things that we've seen outdoors.

Now how about those lemons, limes, and oranges? Those are native to areas that typically don't get cold temperature. So once we collect the seeds—we collected some from our lime tree here—once we collect the seeds, we want to get all the material off of it, the fleshy part of the fruit. And then we're going to start those indoors. Basically, again, plant them a depth twice the diameter of the seed. Cover them with a potting mix. Now these we can put in a sunny window or a warm spot right away. Warmth is the most important thing when starting seeds. Once they sprout, we need to make sure they get plenty of light. Loosely cover with the plastic. We don't want to tie it tight. We just want to loosely cover it to keep the humidity up so that they'll have a good chance to sprout and grow. It's a lot of fun. And you don't have a lot to lose but a little bit of time and a little bit of soil. And as you can see, I recycled some containers.

Now, seeds with hard seed coats, like this avocado or maybe a honey locust, need to either be pierced or use a file—scarified is what we call that—so that that seed can take in the water, roots form, and the seeds sprout. So we scarify or scratch hard seeds. We stratify or chill seeds that need a cold temperature to germinate. And the rest we can start just like we do our annuals.

It's a lot of fun and something you may want to give a try. Well now that we've explored the beauty and function of trees and shrubs and how they really fit into your landscape design and goals, I hope you'll feel more comfortable adding them to your landscape. You have seen how to create quick results while ensuring long-term benefits. Plus, with proper selection, planting, and care, you can increase beauty, decrease your workload, and increase your success. So go out and green your landscaping community with a few new trees and shrubs.

Plant List

Common Name	Botanical Name	USDA Hardiness
Lesson 1		
American elm	*Ulmus americana*	Zones 3 to 9
Larch	*Larix*	Zones 2 to 7, varies with species
Dwarf Alberta spruce	*Picea glauca* Conica	Zones 2 to 6
Dwarf blue spruces Montgomery: 6–8′ × 3–4′ at 10 years old Fat Albert: 15′ tall Glauca Globosa: 3′ tall × wider	*Picea pungens*	Zones 3 to 7, 8 to 9 on U.S. West Coast
Golden arborvitae (white cedar) Yellow Ribbons: 10′ × 3′ at maturity Sunkist: 10–15′ × 4–5′	*Thuja occidentalis*	Zones 3 to 7
Dwarf mugo pine Var. mughus: 8′ × 16′ Sherwood compact: 2′ tall and wide Slavinii: 3′ × 5′	*Pinus mugo*	Zones 3 to 7
Dwarf white pines Compacta and Nana: variable Minima: grows 1″ per year, bluish-green needles	*Pinus strobus*	Zones 3 to 7
Dwarf Scotch pine Watereri: 10′ tall, steel blue needles	*Pinus sylvestris*	Zones 3 to 7

Common Name	Botanical Name	USDA Hardiness
Snow Sprite deodar cedar	*Cedrus deodar* Snow Sprite	Zones 7 to 8
Bur oak	*Quercus macrocarpa*	Zones 3 to 8
Flowering dogwood	*Cornus florida*	Zones 5 to 9
Butterfly magnolia	*Magnolia* Butterflies	Zones 5 to 9
Red-leafed Japanese maple	*Acer palmatum* Atropurpureum	Zones 5 or 6 to 8
American cranberry bush viburnum	*Viburnum trilobum*	Zones 2 to 7
Korean mountain ash	*Sorbus alnifolia*	Zones 4 to 7
Crape myrtle	*Lagerstroemis indica*	Zones 7 to 9
Scotch pine	*Pinus sylvestris*	Zones 3 to 7
Red twig dogwood	*Cornus sericea*	Zones 2 to 7
Paperbark maple	*Acer griseum*	Zones 5 to 7

Weeping beech
 	
    Purple Fountain: narrow with pendulous branches
 	
    Pendula: large weeping form
	Fagus sylvatica	Zones 4 to 7

European mountain ash	*Sorbus aucuparia*	Zones 3 to 6
Carol Maackie Daphne	*Daphne x burkwoodii*	Zones 4 to 7
Lilac	*Syringa*	Zones 3 to 7, varies with species and cultivar
Bloomerang® lilac	*Syringa* Bloomerang®	Zones 4 to 7
Kentucky coffeetree	*Gymnocladus dioicus*	Zones 3 to 8

Common Name	Botanical Name	USDA Hardiness
Ninebark	*Physocarpus opulifolius*	Zones 2 to 7
Diabolo®: purple foliage, 8–10' tall and wide		
Summer Wine: purple foliage, 5–6' tall		
Little Devil™: smaller purple leaves, 3–4' tall		
Dart's Gold: new growth is bright yellow, turning green; 4–5' tall		
Center Glow™: new growth is red-wine with yellowish center, 8–10' tall		
Coppertina: coppery new growth turns bronze, 6–8' tall		
Arborvitae (white cedar)	*Thuja occidentalis*	Zones 3 to 7
Tiger eyes sumac	*Rhus typhina* Tiger Eyes®	Zones 4 to 8
Willow amsonia	*Amsonia hubrichtii*	Zones 4 to 9
Allium (flowering onion)	*Allium*	Zones 3 to 9, varies with species
Juneberry, Serviceberry	*Amelanchier*	Zones 2 to 9, varies with species
Beech	*Fagus sylvatica*	Zones 4 to 7
Purpurea: purple-leaf beech		
Rohan Trompenburg: upright reddish-purple leaves		
Catalpa	*Catalpa speciosa*	Zones 4 to 8
Knock Out® rose	*Rosa* Knock Out® Series	Zones 5 to 11
Black lace elderberry	*Sambucus nigra* Eva Black Lace®	Zones 4 to 7

Plant List

Common Name	Botanical Name	USDA Hardiness
Lesson 2		
Camellia	*Camellia*	Zones 6 to 9, varies with species
Paper birch	*Betula papyrifera*	Zones 2 to 6
Norway maple	*Acer platanoides*	Zones 4 to 7
Honeylocust	*Gleditisia triacanthos inermis*	Zones 4 to 9
Redbud	*Cercis*	Zones 4 to 9, varies with species
Arborvitae (white cedar)	*Thuja occidentalis*	Zones 3 to 7
Boxwood	*Buxus*	Zones 4 to 9, varies with species
Black lace elderberry	*Sambucus nigra* Eva Black Lace®	Zones 4 to 7
Shenandoah switchgrass	*Panicum virgatum* Shenandoah	Zones 3 to 9
Star magnolia	*Magnolia stellate*	Zones 4 to 8
Black chokeberry	*Aronia melanocarpa*	Zones 3 to 8
Red chokeberry	*Aronia arbutifolia*	Zones 4 to 9
Bald cypress hedge	*Taxodium distichum* Shawnee Brave®	Zones 4 to 11
Musclewood	*Carpinus caroliniana*	Zones 3 to 9
Snow Sprite deodar cedar	*Cedrus deodar* Snow Sprite	Zones 7 to 8

Beech
 	
  Purpurea: purple-leaf beech
 	
  Rohan Trompenburg: upright reddish-purple leaves
	Fagus sylvatica	Zones 4 to 7

Tricolor beech	*Fagus sylvatica* Roseomarginata or Tricolor	Zones 4 to 7
Red-leafed Japanese maple	*Acer palmatum* Atropurpureum	Zones 5 or 6 to 8

Common Name	Botanical Name	USDA Hardiness
Blueberry	*Vaccinium*	Zones 3 to 9, varies with species
Raspberry	*Rubus*	Zones 2 to 7, varies with cultivar
Raspberry Shortcake™	*Rubus* Raspberry Shortcake™	Zones 5 to 9
Threadleaf/Cutleaf Japanese maple	*Acer palmatum* var. *dissectum*	Zones 5 to 8
Black lace elderberry	*Sambucus nigra* Eva Black Lace®	Zones 4 to 7
Crabapple	*Malus*	Zones 3 to 8, varies with cultivar
Pleached apple (trained over arch)	*Malus*	Zones 2 to 8, varies with cultivar
Cornelian cherry dogwood	*Cornus mas*	Zones 4 to 7

Lesson 3

Common Name	Botanical Name	USDA Hardiness
Blue spruces	*Picea pungens*	Zones 3 to 7, 8 to 9 on U.S. West Coast
American cranberry bush viburnum	*Viburnum trilobum*	Zones 2 to 7
Pagoda dogwood	*Cornus alternifolia*	Zones 3 to 7
Ironwood	*Ostrya virginiana*	Zones 3 to 9
Gentsch white hemlock	*Tsuga canadensis* Gentsch White	Zones 3 to 7
Boxwood	*Buxus*	Zones 4 to 9, varies with species
Yews	*Taxus*	Zones 2 to 7, varies with species
Arborvitae (white cedar)	*Thuja occidentalis*	Zones 3 to 7
Oakleaf hydrangea	*Hydrangea quercifolia*	Zones 5 to 9
Fothergilla	*Fothergilla gardenia*	Zones 5 to 8

Plant List

Common Name	Botanical Name	USDA Hardiness
Garden Glow dogwood	*Cornus hessei* Garden Glow	Zones 4 to 7
Red cedar/Juniper	*Juniperus virginiana*	Zones 3 to 9
Crabapple	*Malus*	Zones 3 to 8, varies with cultivar
Hawthorn	*Crataegus*	Zones 3 to 8, varies with species
Rugosa rose	*Rosa rugosa*	Zones 2 to 7
Blue mist spirea/Bluebeard	*Caryopteris x clandonensis*	Zones 5 to 9
Clematis	*Clematis*	Hardiness varies with species
River birch	*Betula nigra*	Zones 3 to 9
Larches	*Larix*	Zones 2 to 7, varies with species
Bald cypress	*Taxodium distichum* Shawnee Brave®	Zones 4 to 11
Red maple	*Acer rubrum*	Zones 3 to 9
Alder	*Alnus*	Zones 2 to 9, varies with species
Black chokeberry	*Aronia melanocarpa*	Zones 3 to 8
Red chokeberry	*Aronia arbutifolia*	Zones 4 to 9
Elderberry	*Sambucus*	Zones 3 to 9, varies with species

Lesson 4

Common Name	Botanical Name	USDA Hardiness
Buckthorn	*Rhamnus cathartica*	Zones 3 to 7
Tree of heaven	*Ailanthus altissima*	Zones 4 to 8
Honeysuckle	*Lonicera*	Zones 3 to 9, varies with species

Common Name	Botanical Name	USDA Hardiness
Butterfly bush	*Buddleia*	Zones 4 to 9, varies with species
Lo & Behold butterfly bush	*Buddleia* Lo & Behold®	Zones 5 to 9
Nandina	*Nandina*	Zones 6 to 9
Broom	*Cytisus*	Zones 5 to 8
Multiflora rose	*Rosa multiflora*	Zones 4 to 9
Lesson 5		
Homestead Ohio Buckeye	*Aesculus* x Homestead	Zones 4 to 8
Lesson 6		
Sugar 'n Spice™ viburnum	*Viburnum carlesii* J. N. Select	Zones 4 to 7
Endless Summer® hydrangea	*Hydrangea macrophylla* Endless Summer®	Zones 4 to 8
Hosta	*Hosta*	Zones 3 to 8, varies with species
Coralbells	*Heuchera*	Zones 3 to 9, varies with species
Lesson 7		
Knock Out® rose	*Rosa* Knock Out® Series	Zones 5 to 11
William Baffin	*Rosa* William Baffin	Zones 3 to 8
Parkland roses	*Rosa* Parkland Series	Zones 2 to 7, varies with cultivar
Explorer roses	*Rosa* Explorer Series	Zones 2 to 9, varies with cultivar
Buck roses	*Rosa* Buck Series	Zones 4 to 10, varies with cultivar
Wax myrtle	*Myrica*	Zones 1 to 9, varies with species
Oleander	*Nerium oleander*	Zones 8 to 11

Common Name	Botanical Name	USDA Hardiness
Sweet gum	*Liquidambar styraciflua*	Zones 5 to 9
Japanese tree lilac	*Syringa reticulata*	Zones 3 to 7

Lesson 8

Common Name	Botanical Name	USDA Hardiness
Variegated flowering dogwood	*Cornus florida* Variegata	Zones 5 to 9
Yew	*Taxus*	Zones 2 to 7, varies with species
Arborvitae (white cedar)	*Thuja occidentalis*	Zones 3 to 7
Juniper	*Juniperus*	Zones 2 to 9, varies with species
Paper birch	*Betula papyrifera*	Zones 2 to 6
Black walnut	*Juglans nigra*	Zones 4 to 9
Maple	*Acer*	Zones 3 to 9, varies with species

Lesson 9

Common Name	Botanical Name	USDA Hardiness
Lilac	*Syringa*	Zones 3 to 7
Forsythia	*Forsythia*	Zones 4 to 8
Red twig dogwood	*Cornus sericea*	Zones 2 to 7
Spirea	*Spiraea*	Zones 3 to 8, varies with species
Pearlbush	*Exochorda*	Zones 5 to 8, varies with species
Kerria	*Kerria japonica*	Zones 5 to 9
Quince	*Chaenomeles*	Zones 4 to 9, varies with species
Big-leaf or Mophead hydrangeas	*Hydrangea macrophylla*	Zones 6 to 9
	Hydrangea macrophylla Endless Summer®	Zones 4 to 8
Smooth hydrangea	*Hydrangea arborescens*	Zones 4 to 9

Common Name	Botanical Name	USDA Hardiness
Oakleaf hydrangea	*Hydrangea quercifolia*	Zones 5 to 9
Panicle hydrangea	*Hydrangea paniculata*	Zones 3 to 8, 9 and 10 on U.S. West Coast
Azalea	*Rhododendron*	Zones 4 to 9, varies with species and cultivar
Rhododendron	*Rhododendron*	Zones 4 to 9, varies with species and cultivar
Pieris	*Pieris*	Zones 4 to 9, varies with species
Russian sage	*Perovskia atriplicifolia*	Zones 4 to 8
Butterfly bush	*Buddleia*	Zones 4 to 9, varies with species
Crape myrtle	*Lagerstroemis indica*	Zones 7 to 9
Cockscomb tree	*Erythrina crista-galli*	Zones 7 to 11
Potentilla	*Potentilla fruticosa*	Zones 2 to 6
Privet	*Ligustrum*	Zones 4 to 10, varies with species
Boxwood	*Buxus*	Zones 4 to 9, varies with species
Hedge cotoneaster	*Cotoneaster lucidus*	Zones 4 to 7
Golden Glory dogwood	*Cornus mas* Golden Glory	Zones 4 to 8

Lesson 10

Mulberry	*Morus*	Zones 4 to 9
Maple	*Acer*	Zones 3 to 9, varies with species
Honeylocust	*Gleditisia triacanthos inermis*	Zones 4 to 9
Pine	*Pinus*	Zones 2 to 9, varies with species

Common Name	Botanical Name	USDA Hardiness
Spruce	*Picea*	Zones 2 to 7, 8 and 9 on U.S. West Coast
Arborvitae (white cedar)	*Thuja occidentalis*	Zones 3 to 7
Yew	*Taxus*	Zones 2 to 7, varies with species
Juniper	*Juniperus*	Zones 2 to 9, varies with species
Alder	*Alnus*	Zones 2 to 9, varies with species
Larches	*Larix*	Zones 2 to 7, varies with species
White oak	*Quercus alba*	Zones 3 to 9
Red oak	*Quercus rubra*	Zones 3 to 7
Red maple	*Acer rubrum*	Zones 3 to 9
Sugar maple	*Acer saccharum*	Zones 4 to 8
Horsechestnut	*Aesculus hippocastanum*	Zones 4 to 7
Redbud	*Cercis*	Zones 4 to 9, varies with species
Honeysuckle	*Lonicera*	Zones 3 to 9, varies with species
Rose	*Rosa*	Zones 2 to 9, varies with species
Crabapple	*Malus*	Zones 3 to 8, varies with cultivar

Lesson 11

Linden	*Tilia*	Zones 3 to 9, varies with species
Paper birch	*Betula papyrifera*	Zones 2 to 6
Maple	*Acer*	Zones 3 to 9, varies with species

Common Name	Botanical Name	USDA Hardiness
Lesson 12		
Holly	*Ilex*	Zones 3 to 9, varies with species
Privet	*Ligustrum*	Zones 4 to 10, varies with species
Olive	*Olea europaea*	Zones 8 to 10
Forsythia	*Forsythla*	Zones 4 to 8
Wisteria	*Wistera*	Zones 4 to 9, varies with species
Hemlock	*Tsuga*	Zones 3 to 7, varies with species
Spirea	*Spiraea*	Zones 3 to 8, varies with species
Pittosporum	*Pittosporum tobira*	Zones 8 to 10
Magnolia	*Magnolia*	Zones vary with species
Weigela	*Weigela*	Zones 5 to 8
Lime	*Citrus*	Zones 8 to 11
Lemon	*Citrus*	Zones 8 to 10
Orange	*Citrus*	Zones 9 to 11
Pear	*Pyrus communis*	Zones 4 to 8, varies with cultivar
Apple	*Malus*	Zones 2 to 8, varies with cultivar
Crabapple	*Malus*	Zones 3 to 8, varies with cultivar
Podocarpus	*Podocarpus macrophyllus*	Zones 8 to 10
Nandina	*Nandina*	Zones 6 to 9

Plant List

Bibliography

General

Brickell, Christopher. *The American Horticultural Society A–Z Encyclopedia of Garden Plants*. New York: DK Publishing, 1997.

Brickell, Christopher, David Joyce, and American Horticultural Society. *Pruning and Training: The Definitive Guide to Pruning Trees, Shrubs and Climbers*. London; New York: Dorling Kindersley, 2011.

Dirr, Michael A. *Manual of Woody Landscape Plants: Their Identification, Characteristics, Culture, Propagation and Uses*. 6th ed. Champaign, IL: Stipes Publishing, 1998.

Gilman, Edward F. *An Illustrated Guide to Pruning*. 3rd ed. Albany, NY: Delmar Cengage Learning, 2002.

Myers, Melinda. *Can't Miss Small Space Gardening*. Nashville, TN: Cool Springs Press, 2006.

Lesson 1

Arbor Day Foundation. http://www.arborday.org/.

Colorado Master Gardener Program. "Water Wise Landscaping: Principles of Landscape Design." http://www.ext.colostate.edu/mg/gardennotes/413.html.

Project EverGreen. http://projectevergreen.org/.

Lesson 2

McIntyre, Linda. "Treeconomics." http://ccuh.ucdavis.edu/industry/files/Treeconomics.pdf.

McPherson, E. Gregory. "Energy-Saving Potential of Trees in Chicago." http://www.fs.fed.us/psw/programs/uesd/uep/products/cufr_189_gtr186b.pdf.

One Green World. https://www.onegreenworld.com. Edible ornamentals source.

Lesson 3
Streich, Anne, Donald E. Janssen, Roch E. Gaussoin, and Steven Rodie. "Landscapes for Shade." http://digitalcommons.unl.edu/cgi/viewcontent.cgi?article=2714&context=extensionhist.

Lesson 4
Science Horticulture. "Physical Properties of Soils." http://www.tekura.school.nz/departments/horticulture/ht106_p6.html.

Watson, W. Todd. "Influence of Tree Size on Transplant Establishment and Growth." http://horttech.ashspublications.org/content/15/1/118.full.pdf.

Wisconsin Department of Natural Resources and University of Wisconsin—Extension. "Rain Gardens: A How-To Manual for Homeowners." http://learningstore.uwex.edu/assets/pdfs/GWQ037.pdf.

Lesson 5
Colorado Master Gardener Program. "The Science of Planting Trees." http://www.ext.colostate.edu/mg/gardennotes/633.html.

Lesson 6
Clemson Cooperative Extension. "Transplanting Established Trees and Shrubs." http://www.clemson.edu/extension/hgic/plants/landscape/shrubs/hgic1055.html.

Colorado State University/Denver County Extension. "Caring for Trees in a Dry Climate." http://www.colostate.edu/Depts/CoopExt/4DMG/Trees/caring.htm.

Perry, Thomas. "Tree Roots: Facts and Fallacies." http://arborcaresolutions.com.au/treerootfacts.pdf.

Lesson 7
Barrett, Juliana. "Connecticut Coastal Planting Guide." http://web2.uconn.edu/seagrant/publications/coastalres/CTCoastal_planting.pdf.

Purdue University Cooperative Extension Service. "Salt Damage in Landscape Plants." http://www.extension.purdue.edu/extmedia/id/id-412-w.pdf.

Virginia Cooperative Extension. "Trees and Shrubs That Tolerate Saline Soils and Salt Spray Drift." http://pubs.ext.vt.edu/430/430-031/430-031_pdf.pdf.

Lesson 8
Gilman, Edward F., and Amanda Bisson. "Developing A Preventive Pruning Program: Young Trees." http://hort.ufl.edu/woody/documents/ch_12_mw04.pdf.

International Society of Arboriculture. "Tree Owner Information." http://www.treesaregood.com/treecare/.

Lesson 9
Purdue University Cooperative Extension Service. "Pruning Ornamental Trees and Shrubs." http://www.hort.purdue.edu/ext/ho-4.pdf.

University of New Hampshire Cooperative Extension. "Pruning Evergreens in the Landscape." http://extension.unh.edu/resources/files/Resource000594_Rep616.pdf.

Lesson 10
American Phytopathological Society. http://www.apsnet.org/Pages/default.aspx.

Niemiera, Alex X. "Diagnosing Plant Problems." http://pubs.ext.vt.edu/426/426-714/426-714.html.

University of Kentucky Cooperative Extension Service. "Diagnosing Plant Problems." http://www2.ca.uky.edu/agc/pubs/id/id194/id194.pdf.

Lesson 11

Johnson, Warren T., and Howard H. Lyon. *Insects That Feed on Trees and Shrubs*. 2nd ed. Ithaca, NY: Comstock Publishing Associates, 1991.

Sinclair, Wayne A., Howard H. Lyon, and Warren T. Johnson. *Disease of Trees and Shrubs*. 2nd ed. Ithaca, NY: Comstock Publishing Associates, 1987.

Lesson 12

Cornell University. "Shrub Topiaries." http://www.hort.cornell.edu/livingsculpture/pdf/shrub_topiaries.pdf.

Evans, Erv, and Frank A. Blazich. "Overcoming Seed Dormancy: Trees and Shrubs." http://www.ces.ncsu.edu/hil/hil-8704.html.

Hartmann, Hudson, Dale E. Kester, Fred T. Davies, Jr., and Robert Geneve. *Hartmann and Kester's Plant Propagation: Principles and Practices*. 8th ed. Upper Saddle River, NJ: Prentice Hall/Pearson, 2011.

Moore-Gough, Cheryl. "Growing Trees and Shrubs from Seed." http://msuextension.org/publications/YardandGarden/MT199604AG.pdf.

University of Florida. "Espaliers." http://edis.ifas.ufl.edu/mg273.

Notes

Notes

Notes

Notes